Adapting Configuration Management for Agile Teams

Adapting Configuration Management for Agile Teams

Balancing Sustainability and Speed

Mario E. Moreira

A John Wiley and Sons, Ltd., Publication

A catalogue record for this book is available from the British Library.

ISBN: 9780470746639

Typeset in 11/13 Palatino by Laserwords Private Ltd, Chennai, India

Printed in Great Britain by Bell & Bain, Glasgow

Dedication

I dedicate this book to the following people who keep me motivated in life and keep me young:

Seeme, Aliya, and Iman

Contents

Publisher's Acknowledgements

Some of the people who helped bring this book to market include the following:

Editorial and Production

VP Consumer and Technology Publishing Director: Michelle Leete
Associate Director - Book Content Management: Martin Tribe
Associate Publisher: Chris Webb
Executive Commissioning Editor: Birgit Gruber
Assistant Editor: Colleen Goldring
Content Editor: Claire Spinks
Copy Editor: David Price

Marketing

Senior Marketing Manager: Louise Breinholt
Marketing Executive: Kate Batchelor

Composition Services

Compositor: Laserwords Private Limited
Proof Reader: David Stone
Indexer: Robert Swanson

Preface

For some Configuration Management (CM) professionals, notions of agility have been around and applied into CM practices for years. When I hear people talk about continuous integration and builds in an Agile context, it only reminds me that I and many other CM professionals established build processes that support frequent builds or on-demand builds much like continuous integration, but that was in the early 1990s. After all, CM is an enabler for change and can be adapted to the context and method it works in. CM professionals may have been working in more traditional methods, but it never stopped us from streamlining and automating build processes or introducing ways to make change easier. The primary reason is that, like me, many CM professionals understand that the more you automate and streamline, the more work can be done and the more time we have to focus on new value-added work. From the perspective of the CM professional, bringing value to our customer is important. In all cases, CM professionals should engage with their customer, which in most cases is the engineering team, to understand their needs, understand the technologies they use and the methods and practices they follow. I have found this an effective way to gain CM adoption and build a strong relationship with the engineering team.

As I gained experience in Agile methods back in the late 1990s, I found that many Agile teams struggled with their infrastructure. Since I happened to manage both the CM team that focused on tools and practices and the Unix System Administration teams that provided server and workstation support at a time when Agile was being introduced, I saw the impact when the focus of the Agile team was building functionality while their CM and infrastructure needs were being ignored. Not surprisingly, soon after they cobbled together a package and released it, they could not effectively put together a baseline of code for the next release and quickly realized that pieces were missing because of the ad hoc manner in which change, code, build, package, and release processes were handled. A short period of chaos and regression to the product ensued. In addition, there was no branching and merging process to support the next release and apply bug fixes to the existing release, and there was a very limited problem- management process to effectively manage the defects coming in. This initiated a CM project to establish right-sized CM functionality for the Agile team.

During a recent fact-finding mission on Agile implementations, I networked with companies who had implemented Agile (primarily smaller ones) and asked them what some of their Agile challenges were. Interestingly enough, I heard that getting their infrastructure set up was a challenge when trying to get Agile going, since Agile had instant demands on the infrastructure. I then had a flashback of the late 90s and realized that similar problems still exist with getting infrastructure and technology established.

The advent of Agile into the mainstream has raised awareness of the challenges in getting CM functionality established that suits the working processes of Agile methods. While not necessarily new to some CM professionals, the primary challenge is how to adapt CM practices in a tangible way that supports Agile values while not discarding the CM values that ensure integrity of the product under development. Using my experience of implementing CM on over 100 product lines that applied various methods (including Agile) and my experience of implementing and working on teams applying Agile, I embarked on writing this book.

As I was writing the book, I realized the combination of CM and Agile can form a very powerful partnership. Agile is a facilitator of change ensuring the customer gets more closely to what they want, while CM is an enabler of change ensuring the integrity and control of change. In order to run rapidly in a consistent and lean manner, some level of process and tool structure must be in place. This helps us maintain a velocity to get us to the finish line ahead of the competition while not dropping pieces along the way. In other words, an Agile team must be able to maintain a rapid pace without losing control. This is particularly true as we deliver one release after another.

This unique and innovative book provides very tangible options for implementing CM practices, from build management for continuous integration and build, to iterative CM planning, to support for refactoring, test-driven development, and pair programming (and so much more). It is intended to help the reader bridge the gap in a tangible way to ensure we have rigorous, yet lean, CM practices and infrastructure to support the Agile capability of moving fast and constantly delivering business value.

Acknowledgements

I want to thank Birgit Gruber, Colleen Goldring, Claire Spinks, Ellie Scott and Chris Webb from John Wiley & Sons, Ltd for their patience and support in helping me complete this book.

A special thank-you to Damon Poole and Bob Aiello for each contributing a chapter within this book and reviewing the rest of the book.

Thank you to Steve Berczuk for reviewing my book and providing great feedback.

Thank you to Brad Appleton, Robert Cowham, Curtis Yanko, Bill Langston, Joe Townsend, Alex Elentukh, and Chris Brookins for contributing to good discussions that helped me hone my thoughts as I worked on this book.

Thank you to the many folks who contributed to my surveys and provided feedback to my Configuration Management and Agile articles.

About the Author

Mario Moreira

Mario is both an Agile and a Configuration Management (CM) professional who has worked in the CM field since 1986 and in the Agile field since 1998. He is an IT professional who has been working in the communications, networking, product, open source, and financial industries for over 23 years. Mario brings additional experience in Architecture, Project Management, Software Quality Assurance, Requirement Engineering, and IT Governance, as well as Enterprise-Level Program Management, Coaching, and Team-Building expertise.

Mario has spoken in numerous conferences, including the International SCM Conference, the Swedish Configuration Management Summit, SD West, and SD East. In addition he has been the primary speaker for numerous seminars and webinars discussing Configuration Management, Agile, Build Management, Release Management, and Requirements Engineering, and has spoken on behalf of various product vendors.

Mario is a published author, who in addition to this book, *Adapting Configuration Management for Agile Teams*, also authored the CM book entitled, *Software Configuration Management Implementation Roadmap* in 2004, a Wiley publication. The latter book is unique in that it provides tailorable step-by-step guidance for implementing CM.

Mario is also a columnist for the CM Journal (www.cmcrossroads.com) and a writer for the Agile Journal (www.agilejournal.com). He has experience with several Agile methods, including Scrum and XP, and he is a certified ScrumMaster (CSM). He also has experience with numerous CM technologies and processes and has implemented CM on over 100 products, which include establishing global CM infrastructures. Mario holds an MA in Mass Communication from Bowling Green University (Ohio) with an emphasis on advanced communication technologies. His blog can be viewed at http://cmforagile.blogspot.com.

Contributor Biography

Bob Aiello

Bob is the editor-in-chief for CM Crossroads and a software engineer specializing in Software Process Improvement, including Software Configuration and Release Management. He has over 25 years experience as a technical manager in several top NYC Financial Services firms where he was responsible for company-wide Configuration Management (CM), often providing hands-on technical support for enterprise Source Code Management tools, build engineering, continuous integration and automated application deployment. He has developed a number of effective process improvement methodologies by combining the disciplines of Industrial Psychology with modern Software Engineering, including both Agile and more traditional processes. Bob demonstrates a passion for spreading CM best practices and good corporate citizenship through the successful implementation of IT Controls. He has practical experience in large scale SOX compliance by establishing Configuration and Change Management controls using the Cobit framework. Bob has also served as a Subject Matter Expert (SME) on Standards (e.g. IEEE, ISO) and frameworks (e.g. CMMI, ITIL) to government agencies, defense contractors and financial services firms.

Bob is the vice chair of the IEEE 828 CM planning Standards working group and serves on the IEEE Software and Systems Engineering Standards Committee (S2ESC) Management Board. He is a long-standing member of the Steering Committee of the SEI-sponsored NYC Software Process Improvement Network (CitySPIN), where he has served as the chair of the CM SIG. Bob holds a Masters in Industrial Psychology from NYU and a B.S. in Computer Science and Mathematics from Hofstra University. You may contact him at raiello@acm.org or link with him at http://www.linkedin.com/in/bobaiello.

Damon Poole

Damon Poole is founder and CTO of AccuRev, a leading provider of Agile Development tools specializing in Configuration Management (CM). Damon has eighteen years of software development methodology, CM, and process improvement experience spanning the gamut from small co-located teams all the way up to 10,000-person shops doing global development. Damon is president of the Agile Bazaar (http://agilebazaar.org) in Boston and is a certified ScrumMaster. He writes frequently on the topic of Agile development and as one of AccuRev's product owners works closely with AccuRev's customers pioneering state-of-the-art Agile techniques, such as Multi-Stage Continuous Integration, that scale smoothly to large distributed teams. Damon has spoken at numerous software development and Agile-related conferences, including SD Best Practices, Software Test & Performance, Q-Con, Deep Lean, Agile 2008, and Agile Development Practices.

Damon is also the founder of CM Today, the first daily CM news site, which was acquired by CM Crossroads in 2003. Damon is the author of four pending CM patents, and is also the author of *The TimeSafe Property – A Formal Statement of Immutability in CM*. He earned his B.S. in Computer Science at the University of Vermont in 1987. His Agile Development Thoughts blog is at http://damonpoole.blogspot.com.

Introduction: Racing with Confidence

Effective Agile allows a team to move fast with confidence. In order to move with such speed and confidence, you need to have a very smooth, well-built, and maintained roadway. This ensures speed and the ability to stay on track. If you look at the road surface of automobile race tracks for the very fast racing cars (e.g. Formula 1, Indy car, stock car, and dragsters) you will find that the road surfaces are built with precision incorporating high-quality race construction and surface materials. All of this is to ensure

Figure 1-1 CM raceway for Agile teams.

the race-cars are allowed their maximum speed and maneuverability with a balance of minimal friction and maximum control.

Configuration Management (CM) provides many of the same elements as a high-speed raceway. While a gravel road may allow for speeds of up to 40 or 50 mph without you getting thrown off course or crashing, and a standard paved roadway may allow for speeds of 120 mph, a smoothly paved and well-constructed raceway for high-speed race cars allows for speeds of 250 to 300 mph and beyond. Similarly, the values of CM and Agile can be a very powerful combination.

Agile methods, along with well-trained and seasoned Agile professionals, are the engine and the driver, while CM is the road surface. CM brings order and control to the world of Agile – an order that can be counted on and repeated with integrity, so that the Agile professionals can focus on the high-value tasks of building and delivering functionality to the customer for the checkered flag and the win!

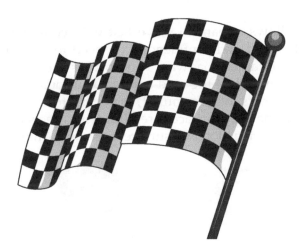

Figure 1-2   Checkered flag for the Agile win!

On the one hand, CM professionals have seen Agile "pretenders" and "cowboys" claim that Agile is without process, tools, and discipline. This misrepresents Agile and damages its reputation. On the other hand, some Agile professionals have felt "heavy" CM adds too much process that burdens their velocity. The key is finding the balance that allows you to stay on the track while maintaining a high velocity.

Agile relies more on the strength of the team and their interactions than on processes and tools. However, Agile does not discard processes and tools, it just aims to use them in a lean way to strengthen the ability to interact more effectively and deliver value. This implies that the effort to define the need for processes and tools should be driven by the people and their interactions.

Pit Stop

Agile encourages change while CM is an enabler for change. This powerful combination ensures change can be frequent while under control.

CM should adapt to the needs of the lifecycle method (in this case Agile), which means it should be adjusted and honed for the changing needs of the method and the project without sacrificing the values of CM. Anyone who has ever established a CM infrastructure (environment, tools, and processes) knows that CM can be implemented in a number of different ways. I have implemented CM in over 100 different product lines and have adapted to the product, project, standards, framework, and method on numerous occasions. So why should implementing CM on a project using Agile be any different? Both Agile professionals and CM professionals should learn enough about each other's values and principles in order to understand each other's perspective to comprehend what it means to adapt CM to align with the values of Agile. Just like a racetrack, the goal is to establish CM so that it reduces friction between the Agile race-car and the road surface. But just like a well-constructed racetrack, the goal of CM is to ensure the car stays on track while allowing it to maintain a high velocity.

While both speed (for Agile) and control (for CM) are important, it is ultimately driven by the ability to quickly get value to the customer while maintaining the integrity of the deliverable, so that the customer can have confidence in what they are receiving.

Pit Stop

The goal with adapting CM for Agile teams is not to discard any of the values of each. Instead it is to determine how best to integrate the values through a leaner CM implementation that still provides those projects that follow Agile with the sticky surface needed to keep it on track and with the integrity the customer expects.

1.1   Focus of this Book

This book focuses on how Configuration Management (CM) with its practices and infrastructure can be adapted and managed in order to directly benefit Agile teams. It is intended to be a pragmatic guide but neither exhaustive nor prescriptive. It can be applied when a team is embarking on new product development following Agile methods or when being applied to legacy products that are introducing Agile methods. While this book focuses on those with an Agile mindset, please note that many of these adaptations can be done for traditional methods as well, and gain similar benefits.

1.2   Who should Use this Book

This book is intended for the following:

- The **primary group** who will benefit from this book includes:
  - Agile professionals such as: Agile coaches, Agile project managers, Agile team members, and product managers. An Agile team member can be anyone with a background in programming, analysis, testing, architecture, design, quality assurance, (anyone who plays a full-time and active role on the project using Agile methods). This book will help Agile professionals broaden their perspective of CM and infrastructure and become familiar with CM values, and gain knowledge of CM, while considering leaner ways of implementing CM in the work context.
  - CM professionals such as: CM managers, CM tool engineers, CM coordinators, and build & release engineers (i.e., anyone who plays a CM-related role). This book will help CM professionals broaden their perspective of Agile methods, become familiar with Agile values, and gain primer level knowledge of Agile methods, while learning about leaner approaches to implementing CM in an Agile context.
- The **secondary group** who will benefit from using this book includes:
  - Product managers and product owners who are considering Agile methods for their product line. This book will provide them with a primer level understanding of Agile and Configuration Management and the implications of Agile to CM and infrastructure, focusing on leaner ways to approach them.
  - VP of Engineering and Senior Management who are considering Agile methods for their organizations. This book will provide them with a primer level understanding of Agile and Configuration

Management and the implications of Agile to CM and infrastructure, focusing on leaner ways to approach them.

○ Quality Assurance professionals who want to learn more about both Agile and CM and recognize how each help improve quality across the lifecycle of both the product and projects therein.

○ Operations and Infrastructure professionals who want to understand both Agile and CM better and recognize the implication of Agile to their field with more incremental and optional ways of establishing infrastructure on a project.

○ Development, test, analyst, project management, and architect professionals who want to learn more about both Agile and CM and understand the implication of Agile and CM to their field.

○ Project stakeholders and customers who want a primer level understanding of Agile and CM and want to recognize the benefits and implications of Agile and CM to their roles.

1.3 Navigation through this Book

You can read this book in a number of ways. Of course you are welcome to read the full book from front to back. However, you can also navigate the book according to the level of knowledge you have in Agile and/or CM, the profession you are in, and/or what challenges you are trying to solve. Below is a view of the sections within this book with navigation from top to bottom or to selected sections per your current need.

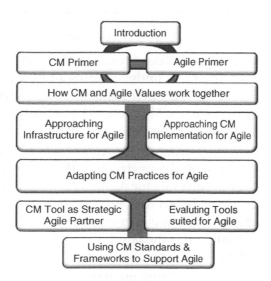

Figure 1-3   Navigation thru the chapters of this book.

First identify the column that is aligned with your profession and read the navigational details.

Agile Professional	CM Professional	Other Professional
If you are an Agile professional, first read the "CM Primer" section of the book. This will ensure you have a solid understanding of CM values and practices which will help you understand what CM areas and adaptations may help you in your work.	If you are a CM professional (you have experience as a CM engineer, build engineer, release engineer, CM coordinator, etc.), consider first reading the "Agile Primer" section of the book. This will ensure you have a solid understanding of Agile values, methods, and practices leading to an understanding of the Agile mindset.	Other professionals, (product manager/owner, VP of engineering, senior management, QA, project management, development, test, analyst, and architect, operations and infrastructure, and project stakeholders, etc.) should read the "Agile Primer" and the "CM Primer". This will give you a background in both fields so that you can understand each perspective.

Then review the following sections per your interest or current challenge.

- The "How CM and Agile Values Work together" chapter provides a merging of the minds and an understanding of how each are committed to change. This chapter includes recent survey results that highlight the importance of CM practices by Agile professionals while also providing an Agile perspective on the various CM practices.

- The "Approaching Infrastructure for Agile" chapter provides an understanding of the underlying structure that all products need and possible ways to approach this for Agile. Within this section, consider if you are introducing a brand new product line or are modifying an existing product line. If it is the former, visit the "Infrastructure Envisioning" section, or it is the latter, visit the "Infrastructure Refactoring" section.

- The "Approaching the CM Implementation for Agile" chapter provides guidance on implementing CM for Agile. Consider if you are implementing CM for a brand new product line that is following Agile methods or if you may need to adapt CM for an existing product line moving to Agile methods. If it is the former, visit the "CM Envisioning" section. If it is the latter (adapting CM for an existing product line), visit the "CM Refactoring" section. However, if you have CM standards within the organization that are expected to be applied to a new product line and you have not yet experienced implementing CM for a product line following Agile, then you may want to read both the "CM Envisioning" and "CM Refactoring" sections.

- Most importantly, read "Adapting CM Practices for Agile". This will provide you with specific insight, guidance, and considerations for adapting CM for the various Agile practices and adapting CM practices in a leaner way.

- The "CM Tool as Strategic Agile Partner" chapter provides an understanding of the more modern CM features that can help with implementing Agile in an effective manner. Continued reading of "Evaluating Tools Suited for Agile" may help if you are considering an effective approach to evaluating tools that better align with your Agile needs.

- The "Using CM Standards and Frameworks to Support Agile" chapter helps if you are implementing Agile and must also implement an industry standard and/or framework. This will provide guidance in understanding the value of these standards and frameworks and how best to apply them in an Agile context.

Sprinkled throughout the book are "Pit Stops". Pit Stops provide insightful information in bite-size chunks that highlight aspects of the section they are in. They should be part of the reading within each chapter. They may also be used as a means to browse through the book in order to get a sense of what each chapter and section therein is about.

1.4   Value of this Book

This book provides a number of valuable insights, details, guidance, and considerations when applying CM to Agile. Specifically, the value and benefits of this book include:

- It provides a unique perspective on how to adapt Configuration Management for teams that are using Agile methods. This book includes specific guidance, details, and considerations for adapting CM practices to support Agile values while still maintaining the values of CM. It also provides a unique approach to implementing CM for new Agile teams in a more iterative manner.

- It gives you enough information on Agile to understand its many facets from the various Agile methods, Agile practices, Agile roles, and the Agile mindset. It forms the basis of a stepping stone to seek more knowledge of Agile methods and practices.

- It provides specific details on CM, allowing readers to understand CM values, CM practices, CM roles, and the CM mindset.

- It provides a unique view in the area of implementing infrastructure for Agile. This is particularly beneficial when you are establishing a new product line following Agile methods. It helps you consider how you can more quickly establish infrastructure to ensure it is ready for the first iteration of development.

- It gives the reader an insight into both the Agile and CM mindset to better understand each perspective. It highlights Agile roles and Agile types (from Agile Champions to Agile Pretenders) along with the CM roles and how to integrate CM responsibilities into an Agile team.

CM Primer

Configuration Management (CM) is an engineering and management discipline that focuses on the management of change. CM enables change with its core attributes of identifying configuration items, controlling changes to items, auditing on the baseline of items, and reporting on the items. The basis for a CM process includes a set of functions that improve the integrity and quality of code, tools, documents, designs, and virtually any item that an organization desires to manage. Simply put, CM enables a person or group to manage changes to a project, a product, and even an organization. Since software development is not predictable, by identifying the pieces of the effort, a product or organization is better able to control changes to the individual pieces, the culmination of their software product, and the environment in which it is being built.

There has been a lot written in books and articles about CM and its capabilities. The objective of this section is not to recreate volumes of definitions and descriptions of what CM is. Instead, it aims to provide a concise summary and context for those involved with Agile specifically and for anyone in the software engineering field in general: to understand what CM is, in order to better support Agile and thus ensure we have speed with sustainability as we move into the future.

CM not only helps you manage the change, it attempts to provide a proactive model for change. Traditionally, changes should be considered and made after determining the impact of the change and the correct course of action instead of having to figure out what was changed after the fact. The CM model asks you to: understand what you want changed and why; make a decision to change or not; control the change; verify that the change was made; and communicate the change. In effect, CM provides a lifecycle for a change. In Agile, there are also many proactive decisions made that address what should be changed moving forward, beginning with iteration planning.

Pit Stop

As an enabler of change, CM instills the notion of proactively managing change for the right reasons.

A key benefit of CM is helping management and engineering manage changes. This ensures we can protect our assets, understand the changes to them, and reproduce the product as needed. Essentially CM provides the ability to ensure consistency, reliability, reproducibility, sustainability, and integrity of our assets.

Another key aspect of CM which is not often discussed is that CM provides a basis for communication and collaboration. It does this by providing the ability to identify and control so that we have a sense of how the product is evolving and discussions can therefore be based on known progress.

Interestingly enough, Agile also provides mechanisms to ensure we discuss proposed changes in a collaborative manner and then introduces daily stand-ups and end-of-iteration reviews to ensure we are aware of known progress. CM then provides the infrastructure where the team can work together using CM tools, branching strategies, and build processes.

Finally, CM enables the possibility for reuse that allows a team to avoid recreating something that may already exist and reducing the waste of the time spend on this activity. A side effect of reuse is that it facilitates communications amongst the project team so that everyone is aware of the functionality of the reusable items.

2.1   Brief History of CM

Configuration Management has been around since the 1950s, primarily used by the United States Department of Defense to manage changes to hardware and then to their software engineering work as software development became more prevalent. Early CM was mostly manual but as the volume of items that needed control grew, CM tools sprouted. CM tools provided a more automated way to manage changes while maintaining a historical record of the changes.

The first CM tool was called Source Code Control System (SCCS), developed by Bell Labs in the early 1970s, which primarily provided version control functionality. Subsequent early tools included Revisions Control System (RCS), Panvalet, Change and Configuration Control (CCC), and Concurrent Version System (CVS). While some of these older tools are still around, there was a significant increase in vendors getting into the business as development became more complex and companies were looking for more features and support. The CM tool market has become so large that it is now a multi-billion dollar business.

While CM tools expanded, CM practices that went much beyond tools were key to organizational and product delivery success. Over time, many other companies began using CM practices because of the control they realized and the ability it provided to protect their assets and ensure integrity of their products. Today, CM is pervasive in most software development organizations, with varying levels of discipline being followed.

CM has since been recognized and adopted by many organizations as well as frameworks and standards such as the Capability Maturity Model Integration (CMMI), the International Organization of Standardization (ISO), the Information Technology Infrastructure Library (ITIL), and others. It should be noted that each standard and framework model has its own definition of CM but the notion of identifying and controlling changes is consistent across all.

2.2   CM Values

Traditional CM comprises four fundamental values or components. They include Identification, Control, Audit, and Report (a.k.a., Status Accounting). It is important to communicate the definitions and interpretation of these components to those in the workplace to establish a common understanding.

Figure 2-1   Four fundamental values of configuration management.

Below are overviews of the four CM components that may help in communicating the definitions in more general terms. This can help facilitate a quicker understanding of CM throughout the organization.

2.2.1 Identification

The first value that CM provides is the ability to *identify* all configuration items (CIs) related to the product and the changes therein.

Figure 2-2   First value of CM – identification.

By identifying CIs, you establish a baseline of software-related items where you can then control, audit, and report the changes occurring to this baseline. CIs may include the product deliverables and the corresponding plans, requirements, specifications, designs, source code, executables, tools, system information (i.e., software & hardware platforms, etc.), and test cases, etc. Further consideration is given to the exact version of the tools you are using. Are you using release 4.1 of a tool or release 5.0? A different release of a tool may output different results.

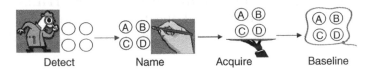

Figure 2-3   CM identification sub-process.

The component of identification may be divided into four sub-processes: *Detect, Name, Acquire,* and *Baseline. Detect* refers to defining and identifying the CIs that make up your product. This is more than just source code. This may be web pages, documents, or even requirements. *Name* refers to developing a nomenclature that is unique, unambiguous, and traceable to easily identify and locate the CIs. This typically evolves into naming conventions. *Acquire* is the process of collecting the CIs under CM control. *Baseline* is the process of establishing a cohesive and meaningful set of CIs. Within the context of Agile, the identification sub-processes should be adapted to support Agile projects. More specifics on this can be found in chapter 7 – "Adapting CM Practices for Agile".

2.2.2 Control

The second value that CM provides is the ability to *control* changes to all configuration items (CIs) in your product. While the first value (identification) provides us with a means of identifying when changes have occurred, control allows us to take a proactive approach to change so that we can decide when change will occur.

With the proactive nature of control comes the ability to request changes and track requested changes to closure, including the change control process of approving or disapproving the changes.

Figure 2-4   Second value of CM – control.

The sub-processes of Control are *version control, change control, build management, and release engineering.*

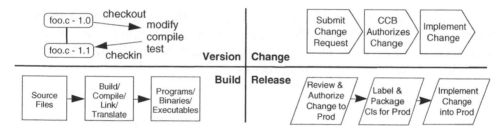

Figure 2-5   CM control sub-process.

Version control refers to the versioning of configuration items. Changes are typically controlled by a ''version control'' process and all changes are versioned incrementally. Modern version control processes typically are integrated with tools with version control capabilities. *Change* refers to an effective means of proactively controlling changes to a product. An effective way of facilitating control over changes to a product is to implement a Change Control Board (CCB). The CCB represents interests of the project manager and all groups who may be affected by the change to the software baseline. The CCB authorizes the establishment of a software baseline, reviews and authorizes changes to a baseline, and approves the creation of products (via releases) from a software baseline. *Build* refers to a standard repeatable and measurable build and release packaging process. *Release* refers to a controlled way of acquiring approval for release deliverables, installing and configuring the product into production thereby establishing the production baseline, and making the product generally available to the customer. Within the context of Agile, the control sub-processes should be adapted to support Agile projects. More specifics on this can be found in chapter 7 – ''Adapting CM Practices for Agile''.

2.2.3 Audit

The third value that CM provides is the ability to ensure correctness, completeness, and consistency of baselines. This helps us ensure the integrity of the product under development so that it can be determined if the actual configuration of the product and changes therein are aligned with the physical and functional specification that were agreed upon. In other words, is what we said we would change actually what *was* changed and were there any unauthorized changes?

Figure 2-6 Third value of CM – audit.

The sub-processes of Audit include two activities. The first is to analyze the baselines and processes. The second is to assign action items for issues and non-compliance so that improvements can be made. In effect, this provides CM with a continuous process improvement loop.

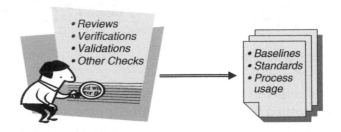

Figure 2-7 CM audit sub-process.

CM auditing may be implemented by selecting members from the project who work with CM personnel to periodically audit different CM areas. By carrying out the CM auditing function, a more systematic improvement of the quality of the software assets may begin.

It is important to note that the term "audit" can bring about considerable resistance in an organization. You may consider changing the word "audit" to "analysis" or "assessment" to make this task appear less threatening and start by performing limited analysis or assessments when the organization is very young or less mature and using the results for improvement and not punishment. Within the context of Agile, auditing needs to be lean and adapted for an Agile process based on how value-added the activities are perceived to be. More specifics on this can be found in chapter 7 – "Adapting CM Practices for Agile".

2.2.4 Report

The fourth value that CM provides is the ability to record and report the status of components surrounding projects. This is a form of communication that helps us understand what has changed, the evolution of changes, and the status of CM in general.

Figure 2-8 Fourth value of CM – report.

More traditionally, reporting is referred to as *Status Accounting*. The primary benefit of reporting is that it affords an opportunity to systematically collect the data needed, record the data in a measurable, meaningful, and repeatable way, and then report on the data to the appropriate personnel for improvement opportunities.

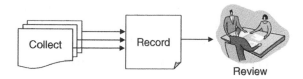

Figure 2-9 CM report sub-process.

The sub-process includes documenting and reporting on changes, providing quality and productivity metrics, providing results of software baseline audits, version history of configuration items, and meeting minutes. If the generated CM reports are important for tracking the efforts of a project, then these reports should be kept in a repository. This provides a traceable way of reviewing past reports and comparing them with current information. Within the context of Agile, CM reporting should be kept lean and focused on the status and metrics that are perceived to be of high value to the Agile team. More specifics on this can be found in chapter 7 – "Adapting CM Practices for Agile".

2.3 CM Practices

Within the world of CM, there are a number of practices that are implemented on a product and projects therein. CM practices are an extension of the CM values and provide an approach for conveying those values in a workplace. CM professionals define practices for their organization, product, or project in order to improve the way CM work is done.

A practice is typically a collection of processes, approaches, techniques, strategies, and tools that work together to achieve a repeatable goal. A "best" practice is tailored in a specific way to help a unique team achieve superior performance. In most cases a best practice for one team or organization is not necessarily a best practice for another.

Pit Stop

A "best" practice is tailored to help a unique team achieve superior performance. In most cases a best practice for one team is not necessarily a best practice for another.

For example, a general CM practice is "version control". Since there are so many different ways version control processes and tools can be applied, what is best can vary from team to team. As mentioned, practices are defined in different ways depending on the need of the workplace. Below is an attempt to loosely define the common CM practices.

2.3.1 CM Planning Practice

Configuration Management (CM) planning focuses on establishing a common approach for how CM will be implemented consistently and effectively on a product line and projects therein. A CM Plan (CMP) has traditionally been established as a document that specifies the way configuration items and their attributes will be:

- Identified uniquely and as a configuration set
- Controlled via version control, change control, build management, or release engineering of the configuration set (the size of the set will vary based on the focus of the control) and specifically control and who authorizes changes.
- Audited per the configuration baselines and the configuration items therein at any given point in time.
- Reported where the results are accurately recorded on any of the identification, control, and audit activities to verify integrity and consistency of the configuration set and changes therein.

While the name "CM Plan" seems to imply that there is an actual project plan for Configuration Management, the "plan" is really a strategy to ensure you have considered the CM elements for the product and effort therein. Also, the CM Plan effectively becomes the hub for all CM-related components and activities. A typical CM Plan includes the following sections:

- Introduction – this is where you document the CM scope and objectives for the product.
- CM roles and responsibilities – this is where you list the roles and the corresponding responsibilities of those who perform CM tasks. In more traditional methods, many of the CM responsibilities will have separate CM personnel allocated to them. In an Agile world, CM responsibilities may be shared.
- Overall CM structure – this illustrates how CM fits into the product team and/or organization.
- CM terminology – this includes the common CM terms and acronyms used on the product and/or organization.
- CM documents – this includes descriptions and links to CM documents, such as policy, processes, tools, templates, and any other artifacts that may have an impact on CM and the product.
- CM activities – this provides the list of work necessary to implement and maintain effective CM, revolving around the CM values of identification, control, audit, and report.

A key benefit of CM planning is that it allows the team to consider the CM values, processes, tasks, roles and responsibilities, and structure needed for the product. Because it provides an overall perspective of what is needed for CM, the team can consider implementation strategies for CM based on the methodology. In general, it makes you reflect on your CM needs and consider the options moving forward. For example, a more traditional lifecycle methodology may apply a big effort, up-front approach, while a more Agile lifecycle methodology may apply a more iterative approach to the implementation of CM. In having a perspective of the CM picture provided by a CM Plan, the team may also decide to only implement the areas they see of immediate value and consider others down the road.

Another reason why a team may need to implement CM planning is if the organization in which the product team lives is following an industry framework or standard (see below). These frameworks or standards include a CM component because they recognize the importance of CM to organizations. It is important to review any framework or standard so that you understand the impact and details when implementing CM.

- Institute of Electrical and Electronics Engineers (IEEE).
- Information Technology Infrastructure Library (ITIL) CM.

- International Organization for Standardization (ISO).
- Capability Maturity Model Integration (CMMI) CM (process area in level 2).

It is also important to understand that CM planning approaches and plan templates vary across the industry. If your organization follows a specific industry standard, then identifying the specific CMP template for that industry standard is appropriate. However, if you are not following any industry standard, it is worth identifying the various CMP approaches and templates available on the Internet and within other industry standard organizations. In the case of Agile, the details in chapter 7 – "Adapting CM practices for Agile" will provide insight into approaching CM planning for Agile teams.

2.3.2 Version Control Practice

Version control is a CM practice that combines a sequential numbering scheme for artifacts within the same lineage as they are changed and a repository and tool which automates the management of archiving the artifacts and their changes using a check-out/check-in process. Version control is the most widely used CM practice and the one found most valuable by Agile teams.

Version control systems, referred to more commonly as CM tools, have basic version control functions. However, the more modern CM tools include more functionality from branching and merging, to change sets, to workspace management, to build features, and more. Because version control is so important, its functionality is built into word-processing programs, document management tools, and databases.

The most important benefit of version control is that it is one of the key mechanisms that protect your software assets (code, documents, etc.) via a secured code repository. These days a quality version control system should version control not only source code, but also executables (a.k.a., deliverables), document, data files, and a variety of other elements that require version and change tracking. In addition, modern systems provide version control of the directory and align and track the contents within the directory to the directory container.

CM version control technology is perceived to be core and critical to the job function of a CM professional's work and they believe it is critical to maintain the source code of the product. Version control is typically the first technology that a product team wants and it is the first tool implemented. Some of the CM professional's work revolves around installing, improving, and maintaining the version control technology. By having a control mechanism of change, this helps avoid one engineer overwriting changes made by another.

The documented version control procedure is valuable when there are company standards like Capability Maturity Model Integration (CMMI). Otherwise, the value of a documented procedure diminishes over time, depending on the use. Keep in mind that CM professionals, like Agile professionals, do not want to write a document if it will not be used. However, in the case of the check-out/check-in procedure, when they must continually show people this process when engineers are new, then the value of the procedure or training is seen as high.

Agile teams perceive version control to be of high value. Consider reading chapter 7 "Adapting CM practices for Agile", chapter 8 "CM Tool as a Strategic Agile Partner" and chapter 9 "Evaluating Tools suited for Agile" to get a better understanding of your version control needs for Agile.

2.3.3   Change Control Practice

Change control is a practice that is used to proactively manage changes to a baseline or environment. This typically includes defining the baselines for control, establishing a Change Control Board (CCB) who authorize the establishment of and changes to a baseline, defining CCB conduct guidelines, and defining repeatable change control processes to manage changes to the baseline(s).

The change control practice is initiated once the baseline is formally approved. An example is a requirements baseline. After several weeks of discovering, collecting, prioritizing, documenting, and reviewing requirements, a set of requirements is approved and baselined. Once this occurs, the change control practice is initiated to manage changes to the requirements baseline. Within this practice, changes are initiated via the stakeholder who submits a change request that highlights the requested change. The change is analysed to understand the details and estimated effort of the change. Then the CCB meets on a periodic basis to review and rule on the change. If it is accepted, then the requirements baseline is updated with the change and the work is assigned to a change agent, typically a programmer.

The benefit of initiating a change control practice is in ensuring that there is a way to manage changes to the product. The goal is to be open to change but a traditional method tends to constrain change, since stability in the baseline tends to be the goal. Interestingly enough, a type of change control does occur in Agile in relation to the iteration planning sessions. More details on this topic can be found in chapter 7 – "Adapting CM Practices for Agile".

2.3.4   Build Management Practice

Build management is a common and highly valued practice in CM and in software development that includes a tool and process component. Build management (a.k.a., build) is the process of identifying source code (preferably in a CM version control system), and through some means of compilation or generation (via a compiler, linker, IDE, etc.) produces a set of executables and other files which can be used to perform a run-time function that represents a deployable product in part or in whole. These executables and deliverables form the basis for the product release and are the income-producing assets for software companies. Often, the build process is combined with the package, migrate, and release processes, since there is a strong affinity amongst them with a focus on getting a product from development into production.

Traditionally, build processes are a combination of manual and automated steps with a simple set of scripts, often hard-coded to specific systems, and developed by CM professionals and/or development staff on an ad hoc basis. With the advent of a growing need to support a number of platforms and languages, the move into geographically distributed development, and new methodologies like Agile, there is an increasing need for more sophisticated and advanced build tools. Also, in many cases the build engineer attempts to automate at least some part of the process, if not all of it.

The build process incorporates the use of a build tool. The build tool should support your process. It should also have the ability to establish end-to-end automation of the process, from identifying and preparing the code and build space, to building the code, to migrating deliverable into the smoke test area. The tool should provide the ability to build on various platforms without having to initiate a build per platform. It should be able to build in a distributed nature on various platforms. It should provide the ability to automatically gather and send build errors on any platform. It should integrate easily with test tools and problem management tools. It should be easy to administer the tool and provide the ability to utilize naming conventions (labeling), the standard build process, and stages therein. When approaching the build process, a key consideration should be given to the method that is being followed and how much build feedback the team is able to handle.

Build management is considered very important by CM and Agile professionals alike. A build process informs a team of the health of a product when their code is compiled and linking successfully, and when it is not. Product teams that use build management effectively find that more frequent builds help them identify integration and build issues earlier in the lifecycle, providing the opportunity to resolve issues more readily and allowing the team to have more stable and unified software. Effectively the more frequently you build, the more you reduce the risk of having unstable software.

Introducing Agile methods that focus on engineering practices raises the bar in this area by introducing continuous integration and build. This provides continuous awareness on the product health and its ability to integrate and compile together. Consider reading chapter 7 – "Adapting CM Practices for Agile" to get a better understanding of adapting build management for Agile teams.

2.3.5 Release Practice

Release is a common and highly valued practice in CM and Agile that focuses on managing changes into production. This typically includes defining a release migration infrastructure and a repeatable release process, which may include identifying baselines, attaining approvals from the CCB or customer, and installing deliverables into production (e.g., on servers or onto media).

The key deliverable of a release practice is the product release package and release notes that include the list of features in the release (typically based on the requirements or stories), defects corrected, installation instructions, and other information that is pertinent to the installation and maintenance of a release. The role most commonly assigned to execute this practice is the release engineer.

The benefit of a release practice is that it provides the product team with a repeatable way to get a release into production. It also ensures that the stakeholders are the ones who make the decision whether to accept or reject a release. A way to ensure repeatability and integrity of the release package is to automate the process as much as possible and ensure the release deliverables come from the CM version control repository.

2.3.6 Problem Management Practice

Problem management is a common and highly valued practice in CM and Agile that focuses on managing and resolving problems in a project, product, or organizational lifecycle. A "problem" may be divided into (but not limited to) types such an issue, a defect, and noncompliance. This practice typically includes establishing a problem management infrastructure and a repeatable problem management process to track problems to closure.

Problem management is initiated at the beginning of all project lifecycle methods, including traditional and Agile methods, since problems can arise at any time. Problems are managed much like changes to formal baselines: where a problem is identified, it is analysed and prioritized, a decision is made about when it will be corrected (release, patch, etc), and it is assigned to a programmer to fix.

Pit Stop

I had heard of an Agile project that was using their defect tracking tool as the system of record for work. They entered their stories as change requests into the system. This essentially became a master backlog of work which they managed to.

The benefit of having a problem management practice is that it provides a repeatable and closed-loop way of ensuring problems are identified, considered, and corrected and so problems that have been uncovered do not get lost. When a number of problems are identified and require tracking, it is beneficial to have an automated problem management tool (a.k.a., defect tracking) to reduce the effort of tracking problems manually and to enable problem management metrics (e.g., defects open, time to closure, defect severity counts, etc.). Consider reading chapter 7 – "Adapting CM Practices for Agile" to get a better understanding of adapting problem management for Agile teams.

2.3.7 Audit Practice

CM Audit is used to determine the integrity of baselines and to assess compliance to CM policy, processes, and technology usage. This typically includes defining a repeatable audit process to assess compliance, recommend improvements, and report audit results. The CM Audit practice is more often used in mature organizations, organizations that build mission-critical or health-related products, and organizations that align with industry standards and frameworks. This is because there must be an assurance that what was requested to be built can be clearly identified in downstream baselines.

The CM Audit practice may include an audit checklist. Audit checklists include areas of focus that help determine if the users of the CM system are following the CM processes (and their corresponding roles), if the deliverables being developed can be identified in the development (and production) baseline and traced to the requirements to verify their traceability and integrity of the release deliverables.

Since CM focuses primarily on the development or code baseline, this tends to be the place where the CM Audit occurs. From an Agile perspective, this helps identify if what was supposed to be worked on is actually being worked on, and to identify any over-production where programmers are working on changes that have not been allocated or approved. The CM Audit process can be somewhat automated, particularly if there is an interest in comparing the source code baseline with the production baseline.

The benefit of the CM Audit is that it provides a way to evaluate and compare downstream baselines with upstream baselines to ensure the right work is occurring. However, it is often seen as a heavy practice, so thinking of creative ways to keep it lean and streamlined are important. Consider reading chapter 7 – "Adapting CM Practices for Agile" to get an understanding of adapting CM Audit for Agile teams.

2.3.8 Report Practice

The CM report practice focuses on communicating the status of CM tasks to the team and management. This typically includes establishing necessary CM reports from a repeatable report process that will collect the CM status on progress, measures, training, resources, achievements, audits, and outstanding issues.

As you approach CM reporting, consider automating all or part of the data collection, report generation, and distribution of the CM report. If the report is too difficult to collect and generate, then the report process will not be sustainable over time. If this is the case, consider another approach or do not collect and generate that particular data. Consider the value of the status on each report and ensure it is useful (e.g., can it be used to validate that processes are running well or to make improvement decisions?). Otherwise, it may not be cost-effective to produce the report.

In addition, the report practice focuses on establishing CM metrics to determine the health of CM-related practices and product development in general. This may include lines of code, change rate, build times, and a myriad variety of metrics. However, it is important to assess the value of each metric to ensure you are applying metrics that provide the biggest benefit for a reasonable amount of effort. The benefit of applying this practice is that it stresses communication of CM activities in order to continuously improve the support CM provides to the team. Consider reading chapter 7 "Adapting CM practices for Agile" to examine lean approaches to CM reporting and metrics.

2.3.9 Other Practices

It is important to understand that there are other practices in the CM space. This may include identification, naming conventions, branching and merging, global distributed, and other practices. It should also be noted, that typically you cannot have a branching and merging practice without a version control practice.

2.4 Benefits of CM

The perceived value and benefit of CM depends on the audience that is being addressed. Some of the main roles that benefit from the CM function may include management, development, CM, QA, and test personnel (note: there are also other roles that derive CM benefits). When CM benefits are stated in a presentation, ensure that the audience is considered.

2.4.1 Benefits of CM to Management

When discussing the benefits of CM for management, it is important to note that CM has an initial cost involved – both a technology cost and a personnel cost. This cannot be ignored since management will evaluate the importance of an item based on the cost/benefit perspective. With this in mind, consider the cost avoidance that CM provides. Some benefits are:

- CM may offer management a way to identify the cost of a change prior to making the change.
- CM offers a place to store and manage product assets. This may provide management with an understanding that the company's assets (a.k.a., products) are in a safe place. This avoids the cost of looking for lost assets.
- CM reduces maintenance costs. Once a release package is delivered, management may be sure that the application is under control, can be recreated, and avoids the cost of functional regression.

It is important to note that when you are discussing CM with management, you need to focus on the problems that can be solved. Gather the current issues and risks that CM may solve or reduce. The cost CM avoids may justify CM expenses.

2.4.2 Benefits of CM to Development Staff

When discussing the benefits of CM for development, it is important to provide them with the most streamlined process while still maintaining the integrity of CM. It is often better to start with a straightforward process, rather than a complex one. Consider gathering input from development as to what issues CM may solve and what improvements they would like to see with the CM process. Some benefits are:

- CM provides product integrity, reproducibility, and reliability. This lets development know that their changes are tracked and stored so that they do not have to reproduce the item and the items can be retrieved on demand. Effectively, it reduces the chances of losing code assets and the changes to code.

- CM provides a technology that allows for easy access and control of items. This ensures that there is a streamlined process and integrity of the code and, therefore, the released product.

- CM provides a window into changes and visibility into the release process. This lets development know what has changed, where, and when.

2.4.3 Benefits of CM for CM and QA/Test Personnel

In most cases, little effort has to be made to express the benefits of CM for CM, QA, and test personnel. However, it is important to identify a benefit for any CM function or process to ensure that it has merit. Some benefits are:

- CM provides traceability. This ensures that changes can be tracked from inception (requirement change or defect) to the completion of the change, therefore reducing effort to track the item.

- CM provides auditing capabilities. This ensures that CM processes are followed, and baselines and the changes to the baselines are identified.

- CM provides reporting capabilities. This allows CM status to be reported for visibility and opportunity for improving the CM system (technology and process).

2.5 CM Roles

Within the CM profession, there are several common roles. Within each role, there are various responsibilities and skills to clarify the role. If you analyze the way companies across the world apply CM titles, it becomes evident that there are no real standards. In fact, many companies use different CM titles for the same responsibilities. Inversely, the same title may include very different responsibilities from one company to another (and a plethora of titles and responsibility differences in between). Establishing a standard framework for the role and responsibilities therein (even if not the ones provided here) will help you and your company in the future. Included below are some common roles and their responsibilities.

Pit Stop

Many CM professionals have already been adapting CM for various methods and standards. They know that the implementation of CM is not a "one-size-fits-all". Adapting CM for Agile is just another area where CM professionals will adapt their implementation and roles without sacrificing the control and integrity that CM provides.

Configuration Management Manager

The CM manager is the primary role that establishes and leads CM for a product. This role may be held by a senior level CM professional, may be combined with some of the other roles below, depending on team size and expectations, and may support more than one project. This role can apply to traditional and Agile methods. The skills needed for this role include:

- Planning skills – the ability to establish a CM plan and program for a product team or organization ensuring the right level of CM.
- Management skills – if there is a team of CM professionals, the CM manager manages the team workload, leads team meetings, and supports the CM team on roadblocks and risks.
- Change control facilitator skills – the change control facilitator may lead the Change Control Board (CCB) in traditional methods or iteration planning in Agile methods to manage changes to requirements or stories and the production baseline.
- Technical writing & communication skills – ability to design CM procedures and templates and the ability to write draft Release Notes per release.
- CM Audit skills – ability to design an audit process per the method to determine the integrity of the release baseline and lead an audit.

Configuration Management Tool Administrator

The CM tool administrator is the primary role that manages the CM technology and all tasks associated with the technology. This role may be held by a senior to mid-level CM professional depending on how much technology setup work must occur (or a junior-level CM professional if the CM system is very stable). This role may be combined with the Build & Release Engineer role depending on team size and expectations and may support more than one project. This role can apply to traditional and Agile methods. The skills needed for this role include:

- CM technology skills – ability to maintain a CM technology, ability to upgrade, and ability to monitor and maintain CM technology.
- CM process skills – ability to understand CM processes and improve them.
- Analysis skills – ability to evaluate the current environment, gather needs, and propose a recommended CM solution (for CM implementations).
- Design/Architect skills – ability to define and design CM standards for the technology (for CM implementations).
- Scripting skills – ability to automate improvements.
- System administration skills – knowledge and ability to use the operating system(s) the CM technology runs on.
- Customer service and communication skills – ability to work graciously with users while resolving their issues.
- Training and Facilitation skills – ability to prepare CM technology and process training for users and the ability to deliver the training effectively.

Build & Release Engineer

The Build & Release Engineer is the primary role that manages all tasks associated with builds, migrations, and releasing software into production. This role may be held by a mid-level CM professional (or a junior-level CM professional if the build process and technology are well defined and very stable). This role can apply to traditional and Agile methods. The skills needed for this role include:

- Build Technology skills – knowledge of compilers, continuous build technologies, and build utilities like make and Ant.
- Build process skills – ability to establish build processes, understand parallel and continuous build concepts and how to implement them.
- Packaging Technology skills – ability to automate the packaging of build deliverables, database deliverables, and other deliverables needed to establish a run-time testing environment or the skills to perform this task manually.

- Migration Technology skills – ability to automate the migration of release packages from environment to environment or the ability to perform this task manually.
- Scripting/programming skills – ability to automate processes.
- Knowledge of product code structure – ability to understand how a product is architected to best design and build the product for increased build times.
- System administration skills with knowledge of the operating system(s) the code builds on.

Configuration Management Coordinator

The CM coordinator is the primary role that manages the CM processes for the group. This role may be held by a mid-level CM professional and may be combined with other CM roles. This role can apply to traditional and Agile methods. The skills needed for this role include:

- Change coordinator skills – ability to support the change control (for traditional) or iteration planning (for Agile) to manage changes to requirements and stories.
- Technical writing & communication skills – ability to design CM procedures and templates and the ability to write draft Release Notes per release.
- Defect tracking and requirements technology skills – ability to pull defect and requirements data for metrics and Release Notes preparation.
- Metrics skills – ability to establish and maintain value-added metrics and prepare metrics reports for review.
- CM Audit skills – ability to lead or participate in an audit to determine the integrity of processes and baselines.

CM professionals have a variety of titles today. Reviewing the CM responsibilities is a reasonable way to help prescribe the skill sets needed to handle the responsibilities. This can help differentiate between the various CM roles and help the hiring manager identify the right person for the CM job. The important point is to align the CM title with the responsibilities and skills. If what you need is a person who just does builds, then you need to hire someone with build skills calling the role a "build engineer." That way the name is reflective of the responsibilities and therefore the skills. From the skills needed, you can establish a better job description to identify the best CM professional to meet your needs.

In some cases, the CM professional handles a variety of different responsibilities that cross over the CM role boundaries. This may be the case if a CM professional joins an Agile team. A variety of other words may be included, from "coding" to "testing." Consider reading chapter 7 – "Adapting CM Practices for Agile" to get an understanding of adapting CM roles for Agile teams.

2.6 CM Mindset

The CM mindset focuses on the CM values. CM professionals typically have a need to ensure integrity of a product, by having control over the change and making sure tasks are complete. CM professionals focus on both the project and product level. The project level focus is to ensure there are enough controls to help the project stay on track and get released. The product level focus is to ensure there is integrity from one project to the next and on the multiple baselines that need support (e.g., current, new, bug fix). Because CM focuses on the product level, this becomes a good place to examine improvements over time. In general there are several focus areas that illustrate the mind of a CM professional. They are:

2.6.1 Thinking Modular

CM thinking focuses on modularity and in small building blocks. This makes it easier to group configurations when building blocks (i.e., configuration items) are uniquely defined. Thinking in a modular manner also makes it easier to construct and deconstruct a process, particularly when CM professionals are often asked to automate processes so they understand the checkpoints along the way as they script and code.

2.6.2 Thinking Integrity

CM professionals believe strongly in integrity. This includes both personal integrity in the manner in which CM professionals work and integrity in the product development they are supporting. Personal integrity implies that CM professionals believe strongly in doing the work the right way and feel accountable to ensure correctness and completion of the task. Integrity in the product implies that CM professionals feel strongly in having working processes that have the ability to control changes to the product and the ability to verify the baseline of code in which they are working.

2.6.3 Thinking "Get It Done"

CM professionals have a strong tendency to want to get the job done. In a 2007 study of Myers-Briggs Types Relative to CM Professionals, a surprising 79% of the CM professionals surveyed exhibited a leaning toward a judging preference. This preference indicates a willingness to make decisions and a need to complete tasks. This also implies a need to establish a level of structure. This may stem from the multitasking environment where most CM professionals work, where the completion of a task allows more of a focus on additional tasks. This 2007 study supports the same study done in 2003 where 76% were scored a judging preference (i.e., a need to complete tasks).

2.6.4 Thinking Improvement

CM professionals have a strong tendency to want to improve. They are always looking for ways to automate manual processes both for integrity and to simply find better ways of doing things. They tend to be forward-thinking insofar as they are motivated by perceived improvements in the future and less focused on the existing conditions today. There is always a better way. However, CM professionals only consider improvements that do not impact integrity of the product and the CM processes that support them.

2.7 Relationship of CM to Culture, Methods, & Governance

Most professionals in the software industry including Agile professionals recognize the need for Configuration Management. CM has been around long enough for people to have experienced problems when CM was either not in place or when the level of CM was insufficient for the needs of the work. CM values of identification, control, audit, and report are meant to ensure integrity of the product under development. These days, almost everyone has, at least, CM version control practices which include a version control tool and a simple check-out/check-in process. However, as with any engineering discipline, the level of the CM implementation (since CM is much more than just version control) will depend greatly on the culture along with the methods and governance that exist within the company. Think of it as having several gauges: the main gauge for culture, with two minor gauges for methods and governance. What methods and governance an organization has contributes to the culture, but they also indicate the level of importance an organization places on these areas.

Visibility into these three areas can help you gauge how readily the organization will accept CM, the level of CM they will accept, and the best approach for implementing CM into the organization. For that matter, these gauges can also help provide insight into how readily the organization will accept Agile, the level of Agile they will accept, and the best approach for implementing Agile into the organization.

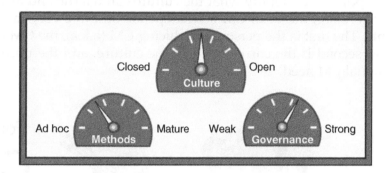

Figure 2-10   Adaption dashboard.

For example, if the culture is a closed one, the methods used are mostly ad hoc, and governance is lax, then it may be challenging to introduce CM practices into the organization. Even if the culture is open, but governance is lax and methods are ad hoc, it still can be challenging to introduce or improve CM practices. If the culture is somewhat open, the current methods used are mature, and the governance is somewhat strong, then introducing CM will be easier. In this case, there can be advantages in aligning CM with the current methods.

2.7.1   Relationship of Culture to CM

"Culture" may be described as the set of shared values, goals, and practices within an organization that make up patterns for the way people behave and work. Within a culture, patterns may be introduced in an ad hoc manner or driven by leaders within a company, but most often are somewhere in between. In very young companies, these patterns are being invented and constructed by the way people interact and are based on the needs of the company. In older organizations, these patterns have been well established and often continue to exist even when people recognize a need for change. In effect, inertia sets in. When people enter existing cultures, most attempt to identify the patterns and align with the culture while few will attempt to change the culture because of the effort needed to do so. The ability to change is directly proportional to how open or closed a culture is to accepting change.

When Configuration Management is introduced into a culture, it can take many forms based on the amount of CM functionality that can be introduced. As mentioned, version control is typically readily accepted. However, there is much more to CM than just version control. There is CM planning, build management, change control, problem management, branching and merging, release engineering, CM auditing, and CM reporting. It is important to identify what the culture can handle and also what it needs. Therefore, the form CM takes depends on three very important ingredients. The first is the person introducing CM (a.k.a., the CM professional) and second is the current state of the culture, and the third is the organizational CM need.

Figure 2-11   The path to a "right-sized" CM.

The CM professional will come with their own set of experiences in implementing CM. A wide range of experience in implementing CM is very helpful in implementing future CM practices. The goal of this person should be to identify the CM needs of the organization, identify the type of culture that exists, and how open the culture is to change. Then the CM professional should provide a form of CM that can be absorbed within that culture so that actual CM adoption will occur. It is best when a CM professional is flexible and has strong assessment skills so that they can determine the best form and level of CM and the best way to implement that level of CM. The biggest danger in implementing CM is when there are unrealistic expectations by either the CM professional or those within the culture. There are times when a CM professional is too enthusiastic and wants to implement the full array of CM functionality but the organization is not capable of adopting this level. On the other hand, there are times when an organization (e.g., its senior management) wants to implement a rigorous framework (e.g., CM for CMMI level 2) without realizing that the culture may not be ready or without preparing for the culture in this direction.

2.7.2   Relationship of Governance to CM

"Governance" may be described as a specific way in which leaders steer an organization. Governance implies defining mechanisms to help drive future direction and implies defining mechanisms that verify and validate that the direction of the company and goals therein are being met. Both pieces (mechanisms for driving direction & mechanisms for verification and validation) must be in place to have a strong governance process.

The more rigorous (or strong) the governance process (e.g., stage gates), the more likely that the goals of the organization will be met based on a long-term strategy. The more lax (or weak) the governance process, the more likely ad hoc decisions will get made that will lack long-term cohesion. A governance process also helps assure the clients that the organization is under control and managing toward their goals. Rigor in a governance process does not always equate to bureaucracy, but often this is the result. The goal in establishing and implementing a governance process is to keep it as lean as possible, avoiding too many levels of approval, too many process steps, and too much documentation. While there may be some level of budget oversight on IT, a lack of IT governance typically implies that the organization can acquire and implement any type of technology or IT process they want with little oversight or thoughts to economy of scale.

The way this relates to CM is that when there is governance in IT, this can be a natural conduit for driving CM change and ensuring change occurs. The value of CM as a whole or in parts can be determined and then deployed based on a managed approach whether it is a separate project or it is incorporated into iterations. Having governance ensures that CM is part of the big picture as it relates to using IT to the advantage of the company.

2.7.3   Relationship of Methods to CM

A "method" is defined as a systematic or structured way of implementing or accomplishing something. In the IT field, "methods" (a.k.a., methodology) refer to defined project lifecycle methodologies, practices, standards, and techniques that guide organizations in the way they should perform their work. The simple form of a method is a structure with phases (i.e., more traditional phased methods) or iterations (i.e., Agile methods) to get you from point A to point B. More complex implementations of methods include standards and practices that help you do specific things, templates that include the detail that is needed, and tools that help you perform certain tasks and functions.

The way this relates to CM is that CM is seen as an overall approach to enabling changes within a product line, and projects therein, used in context with most project lifecycle methods (both phased and iterative). CM includes various practices, some of which are used by most projects (e.g., version control, build management, problem management, and release engineering) because of their perceived value; other CM practices (e.g., CM planning, auditing, and reporting) are used by those organizations that follow frameworks and standards (such as CMMI, ITIL, IEEE, etc.).

The more mature the use of the methods within an organization, the more willing the organization is to adopt new value-added practices. Also, the more mature the methods are in the organization, the more likely there is a recognized need and acceptance of practices that ensure integrity of the product, in this case CM practices. With more maturity comes a likelihood that someone knowledgeable in the method will understand the importance of CM and be willing to help champion the CM change. In general, if an organization is mature in methods, it is very likely that they already have CM.

The less mature the methods, the more likely there is a cowboy "wild west" attitude. This cowboy mentality abhors structure, implying that CM practices will be ad hoc or perceived to be a nuisance. The only bright side here is that even those companies with immature methods often see the value of basic version control and typically build management. However, the form of the CM will vary greatly from group to group, making it hard for the CM professional to leverage reuse.

2.7.4   Avoiding Mistakes in CM Adoption

As you consider the adoption of CM, it is important to evaluate the culture of an organization, the strength of the governance structures in place, and the maturity of the methods being used. When these factors are not considered, mistakes are made that can impact the success of adoption. This data becomes valuable input into determining whether to initiate a CM adoption effort or what form of CM should be implemented.

If the culture is not open, then adoption efforts will often fail before they can start. If governance is weak, the adoption efforts will be ad hoc and something that is valuable can get mired in a conflict between personal bias and prioritized organizational needs. If methods are immature, then even if there is a good reason to adopt a good practice, the cowboy mentality may overrule any need for structure. In order to avoid starting in a bad position and incorrectly assuming certain factors within an organization, the evaluation of culture, governance, and methods by a CM professional can give you a strong basis from which to start. This can help you determine the form of CM that the organization can handle. The more the three gauges indicate a lower level, the more likely you will want to focus the CM efforts on specific CM needs. The more the three gauges indicate a higher level, the more likely you can initiate a more complete CM deployment focusing on several CM functions.

2.8   CM Resource Guide

There are numerous valuable materials available on CM to help with definitions and further knowledge and information. This section provides a small subset of these resources.

2.8.1   CM Books

- *Software Configuration Management Implementation Roadmap*, by Mario E. Moreira, Copyright © 2004, John Wiley & Sons Ltd. Provides the reader with tailorable step-by-step guidance for implementing CM with examples and templates. Both the guidance and templates will save you considerable effort, which pays back the cost of the book many times over.
- *Software Release Methodology* by Michael E. Bays, Copyright © 1999, Prentice Hall PTR
- *Software Configuration Management Patterns: Effective Teamwork, Practical Integration*, by Stephen P. Berczuk with Brad Appleton, Copyright © 2002, Addison Wesley Professional

Because there are other Configuration Management books on the market, consider visiting an online bookstore and perform a search on this topic.

2.8.2   CM websites

There are numerous CM-related websites available. The list included here is only a very small subset. However many of these links include numerous other CM links within their websites.

- CM Crossroads, online Community and Resource Center for Configuration Management – http://www.cmcrossroads.com/
- Institute of Configuration Management – http://www.icmhq.com/
- The Association for Configuration and Data Management – http://www.acdm.org/

Agile Primer

Agile methods for software development are one of the hottest changes in the methodology field. Agile is an umbrella term that includes various approaches, methods, and techniques that use short iterations and continuous customer feedback so that the project team can evolve the customer need (a.k.a., product). What the customer sees as progress is not the standard documents and status reports but instead tangible working product functionality. This approach allows the customer to reconsider and adjust their need until it is transformed into a valuable working product. Progress is not considered until a piece of functionality is built. Functionality equates to a value to the customer. This ultimately means delivering business value (what the customer really wants). Of course this implies that you have to continuously work with the customer to get there.

Agile methods provide a means of adapting quickly for teams facing unpredictable or rapidly changing requirements. Agile introduces a structured approach to software development to ensure the customer gets early and periodic views of their solution for continuous feedback, more assurance that they are getting a solution that solves their business need, and a working solution in typically a shorter time frame.

Implementing Agile methods impacts the culture because it relies on more than just implementing a process or new practices. Instead the organization needs to move away from the hierarchical command and control model, which includes ceremony (i.e., protocol) and requires approvals from the top down, and instead move to a more heterarchical world of a self-empowering team model moving empowerment and decision making to the lowest possible level, where most of the relationships and relevant data are present to make the best decision.

Pit Stop

Agile moves organizations and product teams from a hierarchical command and control world to a heterarchical self-empowering world moving empowerment and decision making to the lowest possible level.

This is a challenging change for many in management because it implies a loss of power and influence. It is also challenging for the masses of folks in an organization. On the one hand, it can be hard to change from a fairly rigid and directive culture where you know exactly what you are supposed to do day in and day out to a less structured culture where your role may change and where goals and requirements change. On the other hand, it can be hard to go from a "wild west" culture where people have little to no structure to a more structured and accountable culture of Agile. The fact is some people do not adapt to change from either direction.

With this being said, Agile requires all levels to better share leadership and assume the responsibility that goes with it. I called this "Collaborative Control". There will always need to be control but the question is where does the control come from? Collaborative control is defined by having the right people making the decisions, not just because a person has a title, but because they have the best insight into the change, opportunity, or problem. On one side of collaborative control is rigid command and control, where decisions are made at the top, and on the other side is no control, where decisions are ad hoc. In my opinion, collaborative control requires everyone to act like an adult: be responsible and accountable for their actions, listen, cooperate, and collaborate.

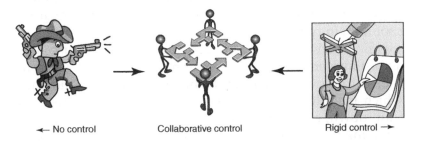

← No control   Collaborative control   Rigid control →

Figure 3-1 Striving for collaborative control.

Agile can be very effective when people take the method seriously and find the most pragmatic approach for their needs. Barry Boehm and Richard Turner's book, *Balancing Agility and Discipline: A Guide for the Perplexed*, offers strong evidence to this effect. Teams will have to be ready to provide an Agile climate in which it can thrive and benefit the company and businesses they serve.

Finally, because Agile truly does require changes in the culture, the adoption will take longer than when implementing a tool or process. The degree of difficulty gets harder when moving from having people learn to use a tool, to having them follow a process, to finally asking them to change their behavior. This is important to keep in mind especially as it relates to changing the culture of an organization.

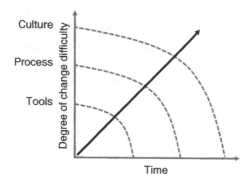

Figure 3-2   Degree of change difficulty and its relationship to the time.

There are people within an organization with varying levels of ability or desire to change, motivated by rewards, power, influence, and myriad other reasons. In order to change the behavior, people need to start seeing the benefit of the change and how it impacts their own circumstances. Will it make them happier, is it rewarding, will they receive more respect and support, is there a better sense of trust and fairness, and does it provide a stronger sense of accomplishment? This will need to be gauged as the implementation and adoption of Agile occurs. Within this Agile Primer chapter, you will find a section entitled "Moving to an Agile Culture" that focuses on targeting the sweet spot, actions for an Agile change, determining readiness, and measuring the change to Agile.

Information and details on Agile, its methods, techniques, and capabilities are found in many books and articles. The objective of this section is not to recreate the volumes of information on Agile, but instead to provide a concise summary for those in the CM and engineering fields in order to provide the context of what Agile is, while considering speed and sustainability.

3.1   Brief History of Agile

While more commonly known Agile methods arose during the 1990s, the predecessors to Agile methods are the incremental and iterative development (IID) approaches and methods that arose in the mid-1950s on military and space projects and into the 1970s on government projects. Many see Agile as a move away from the Waterfall methods that some believe are too heavyweight, slow, rigid, and bureaucratic, and do not adequately address the communication between customer and development team seen as a crutch by many hierarchical organizations.

Early IID projects may have been the result of adapting the Waterfall model to allow for smaller increments of delivery and more user interaction. However, over time it became clear that IDD was being applied and it became recognized in a published article by Victor Basili and Joe Turner in 1975 describing the ideas behind IID, entitled "Iterative Enhancement: A Practical Technique for Software Development".

Moving into the more modern area of Agile in the 1980s, the innovators include: Tom Gilb and his writing on "Evolutionary Development" and his article "Evolutionary Delivery versus the Waterfall Model"; Grady Booch and his book *Software Engineering with Ada*; and Bob Boehm and his article "A Spiral Model of Software Development and Enhancement."

Moving into the 1990s, we see a greater movement of Agile-type methods and techniques into the commercial world. Jeff Sutherland and Ken Schwaber introduced the notion of Scrum and time-boxed iterations (taken from the "holistic approach" by Hirotaka Takeuchi and Ikujiro Nonaka in the mid-80s). The notion of Rapid Application Development (RAD) was established as an iterative standard and it eventually evolved into the Dynamic Systems Development Method (DSDM), which has seen more adoption in Europe. Another method that grew out of RAD was Adaptive Software Development, established by Jim Highsmith and Sam Bayer in early 2000s. Rational Corporation (now part of IBM) with Phillippe Kruchten established the Rational Unified Process (RUP), which some see as heavy for an IID method but it earned a lot of attention since it provided the detail many companies were looking for when trying to move away from Waterfall. Ken Beck along with Ron Jeffries and Ward Cunningham established the extreme Programming (XP) method, which focuses on streamlined engineering practices. Jeff De Luca established an iterative framework, calling it Feature Driven Development (FDD), and Andrew Hunt and David Thomas established the Pragmatic Programming method. Note: More detail on various Agile practices will be given in a subsequent section in this chapter.

In the beginning of the 2000s is where we see the term Agile gain visibility. In 2001, a group of 17 Agile-related experts (later to be named the Agile Alliance) working with various methods (Scrum, XP, Crystal, DSDM, Adaptive Software Development, FDD, and others) came together, found common ground, and crafted the "Manifesto for Agile Software Development" (a.k.a., the Agile Manifesto). Starting with Alistair Cockburn who published the book *Agile Software Development* we start seeing the term Agile become used pervasively in the project lifecycle arena. Alistair also followed up with an Agile method of his own called Crystal Clear.

It was also in the 2000s that we saw a significant increase in companies using and adopting Agile methods within software development. Certification programs for Agile were established such as a Certified ScrumMaster (CSM) for the Scrum method. Agile methods continue to gain in adoption across many companies. More recent challenges have been implementing Agile in a distributed work environment where the project team members work at different sites. This challenge is being met by various Agile techniques involving collaboration practices and Configuration Management (CM) practices. In the 2010s, we see Agile move into the mainstream of software development methodologies.

3.2 Agile Values (a.k.a., Manifesto)

Now that we have a sense of the history of Agile, it is important to read and understand the values within the Manifesto for Agile Software Development (found at agilemanifesto.org). The Manifesto reads:

> We are uncovering better ways of developing
> software by doing it and helping others do it.
> Through this work we have come to value:
>
> Individuals and interactions over processes and tools
> Working software over comprehensive documentation
> Customer collaboration over contract negotiation
> Responding to change over following a plan
>
> That is, while there is value in the items on the
> right, we value the items on the left more.

One key factor to notice is that the authors are not saying there is no value in the items on the right, but their value is less than the items on the left. Anyone who disregards the items on the right are either cowboys or bandwagon enthusiasts who do not know better, or beginners who have not gained an appreciation of striking the right balance.

One perspective that helped me understand these values better is when I realized that the items on the left should drive the need and level of the items on the right. For example instead of starting with a predefined process for the team, the individuals on the team may examine their interactions and let this drive a more natural process. The same is true for customer collaboration. The team and stakeholders should use collaboration as the technique for establishing the needs and allowing needs to evolve over time through continued collaboration. While there will be a need to establish a contract, the contract should not drive to a static list of exactly what will be built but allow for flexibility in the collaboration to evolve the needs. Since it is human nature to evolve over time, then we should assume that needs evolve. A static list can get outdated fairly quickly. This is what makes customer collaboration so important.

3.3   Agile Methods

Now that we know some history on Agile, let us dive into detail into the more commonly known Agile methods. This includes (but is not limited to) Scrum, Extreme Programming (XP), Dynamic Systems Development Method (DSDM), Feature Driven Development (FDD), and Agile Unified Process (AUP). This section will focus on Scrum and XP in more detail since they may be more commonly encountered and are often used in tandem. The remaining methods will be covered with an overview for understanding. The purpose is not to compare them but to understand them.

3.3.1   Scrum

Scrum is an iterative and incremental process of software development. Scrum provides practices that are used to manage the project. Scrum is not an acronym for anything but is aligned with the Rugby scrum where the "team" moves the ball down the field to make progress. Scrum provides many of the Agile management practices for software development. Scrum is often used in tandem with XP, which provides many of the Agile engineering practices.

An important aspect to Scrum is that the customer can change their mind as necessary to ensure they are getting the product they want and need at the end. This approach recognizes that there will be changes and does not try to stifle this activity. Changes can be added to the Product Backlog at any time and re-prioritized. During the next sprint planning session, these new changes can be considered for the next sprint. It is important to note that once an iteration is started, there should be no attempt by the customer or team to change the requirements but instead allow the team to focus on the prioritized requirements from the sprint planning session.

3.3.1.1 Scrum Roles

On the Scrum project team, the main role is the ScrumMaster. The Scrum-Master acts as an Agile coach and project manager. This role is not characterized as an authoritarian but instead an enabler. On the team, there is also the "product owner" who represents the customers (and is the customer liaison) and the "team" that produce the functionality. In Scrum, the team is typically less than 10 members and is meant to be committed, empowered, and self-organized so they can make the best decisions to move forward since they are the closest to the challenges and work to be accomplished. The skills within the Scrum team include but are not limited to analysis, programming, design, and testing. These roles (ScrumMaster, product owner, and team) are lovingly known as the pigs because their "bacon is on the line" if things do not go well. This really gets to who is committed to the work. This is why the team must be empowered and self-organized.

In addition to these roles, there are roles outside of the core Scrum team where contributions and feedback are provided to the team. These roles include users, external customers, and managers. These roles are known as the chickens since they can contribute as a chicken contributes eggs but do not have as much riding on the line (i.e., their bacon) as the pigs do. Their contribution is limited to the sprint planning (i.e., requirements) at the beginning of each sprint and the review at the end of each sprint. They should have limited impact on the way the team does their work.

3.3.1.2 Scrum Practices and Artifacts

Here are some of the common practices you will see in Scrum.

- Sprint – An iteration is known as a sprint. Each sprint is typically 15–30 days long and the output is a functional software.
- Sprint Planning – At the beginning of each sprint, a planning session occurs. Within this planning session, both the pigs and chickens review the product backlog as input to what requirements should be worked on in the sprint. The customer may add new requirements but they should be prioritized against the current list of requirements. There will be further considerations beyond the highly prioritized requirements as to what will go into a sprint. For example, there may be dependencies from a high priority requirement to a medium priority requirement. There may be defects that need to be addressed in the sprint. Once the requirements are defined in this planning session, they are copied to the Sprint backlog where they are broken

down into tasks and where the team commits to the work. The work can now begin.

- Daily Scrum – During the sprint, there is a daily stand-up meeting known as the "daily scrum" or simply the "scrum." The scrum is a short time-boxed session about 15 minutes or less. It is meant to bring the team together in a timely manner, where the pigs discuss what they did yesterday, what they are planning to do today, and if there are any roadblocks preventing them from progress. The chickens may participate in a scrum but cannot speak.

- Backlog – The backlog is divided into two different types of backlogs. The "Product Backlog" is an artifact that the product owner manages that includes a list of prioritized high-level requirements. When there is an agreement in a Sprint planning meeting on what requirements should go into the next sprint, these requirements get copied into a "Sprint Backlog". In the sprint backlog, the requirements get divided into tasks and estimated for effort. There may be some negotiation of the number of changes if the estimated effort exceed the effort established for the sprint. Once requirements are defined to a sprint, that sprint is then frozen, meaning no changes can occur to the requirements.

- Burndown Chart – The burndown chart is a chart that communicates the daily progress or velocity within a sprint and what work is left to do. The information on a burndown chart lets the ScrumMaster know if the team is missing, meeting, or exceeding the progress goals for that sprint. The burndown chart should always be viewable by the team. Upon conclusion of the daily scrum, the ScrumMaster updates the sprint burndown to assess the progress in the sprint to determine if adjustments should be made.

- Sprint Review – The goal of this meeting, which is held at the end of a sprint, is for the project team to present to the stakeholders what was completed. It is meant to demonstrate to the customer the built functionality for feedback that can then be included in the next sprint planning session. What was not completed is also identified.

- Sprint Retrospective – The goal of this meeting which is held at the end of a sprint is to identify what went well in the sprint and what can be improved. The feedback from this review is captured and becomes input for improvements for the next iteration. The key participants should be the project team including the Product Owner. The ScrumMaster may facilitate this session.

For more information on Scrum, consider visiting www.controlchaos.com.

3.3.2 Extreme Programming (XP)

Extreme Programming known by its acronym "XP" is an Agile software development methodology that revolves around a set of engineering practices. From the customer perspective, XP believes that requirements changes are a natural part of the software development process. From the engineering perspective, XP believes in a rigorous set of engineering and coding practices. XP is often used in tandem with Scrum, which provides many of the Agile management practices.

XP emphasizes the customer and teamwork. The customer is the contributor of the requirements and may change them as they understand their needs more fully. The team focuses on building the product while continually engaging the customer, which reduces the level of risk of delivering the wrong product.

3.3.2.1 XP Roles

In XP, the team is typically 12 or fewer members and is meant to be committed, empowered, and self-organized so they can make the best decisions to move forward since they are close to the challenges and work to be accomplished. While there are various roles on an XP team, there is a strong emphasis on programming and testing.

The customer is the primary driver of the project and is the end user or is a representative for the end user. The customer provides business knowledge and should set goals for the project. The customer must always participate in the iteration planning to provide the stories or features needed for the product. The customer will also participate in establishing the acceptance tests to ensure the built features meet customer expectation. The developers on the team focus on the daily work, concentrating on the stories and converting them into executable and functional code. The developers should work with the customer to ensure they understand their expectations. They should estimate the stories and work based on a reasonable schedule to avoid burnout. Finally some XP teams (particularly the newer ones) will have a coach who will help them understand and execute XP practices. The goal of the coach is to lead by example.

3.3.2.2 XP Practices and Rules

XP provides practices and rules that revolve around planning, designing, coding, and testing. Some include:

- User stories are scenarios created by the customer. They are not meant to be detailed but provide enough information to help understand what the customer wants, typically written down on an index card. As a planning practice, user stories are also used to create estimates that are input to release planning. In addition, user stories are used as input in creating acceptance tests.

- Velocity is a measure of progress on an XP project achieved by adding up the estimates of the user stories that are finished during an iteration. As a planning practice, to make the velocity metric meaningful, velocity gets measured from iteration to iteration in order to understand potential velocity moving forward. Keep in mind that the initial estimate of effort per story may vary until the customer and team can estimate effort more effectively.

- Iteration planning is a planning practice where the customer determines the user stories to be developed that fit the estimate of effort as established by the velocity. During this planning session, user stories are divided into tasks written on index cards and posted on a bulletin board viewable by the team.

- Daily stand-up is a short meeting where members of the XP team literally stand up and communicate their progress. Remaining standing up keeps the meeting short.

- Refactoring is a very rigorous design practice where the programmers continually streamline the code by removing unused functionality, reduce redundancy, improve on existing design. Over time, refactoring reduces maintenance costs and improves quality by having more easily understood and better performing code.

- Pair programming is a coding practice where two programmers work together at the same computer while programming a user story or task. They take turns, one being the programmer or driver while the other is the reviewer or navigator. The intent is that, as one person is coding, the other person is continually inspecting the code and providing suggestions with the end result of increased software quality. This is not an easy practice to get working since it relies on the two programmers being able to work well together.

- Continuous integration is a coding practice where programmers should merge their code into the repository and code baseline whenever they have a clean developer build that has passed the unit tests. This will reduce large merges of code that can be problematic and allows other programmers to see the changes, therefore being able to integrate with the more recent code.

- Unit test is a very important test practice and considered critical to extreme programming because if the unit test is not established and run, the code cannot be considered complete. This is known as the done-done model where not only does the code need to be written and built (as appropriate), but it must also pass the unit test. In XP, the unit test typically follows a testing framework and highly recommends automating the tests.

- Acceptance testing is a testing practice that is created for user stories. The customer specifies test scenarios that are used to establish the acceptance test. The acceptance test is run upon the completion of the story to ensure it is implemented properly. Since the code that was used to implement the user story may be updated for that story or for other stories, XP recommends that acceptance tests are automated. This allows the test to be run any time the code gets changed to ensure the changes did not negatively impact the functioning code.

Pit Stop

The refactoring and continuous integration practices rely heavily on CM although they do not specifically call CM out.

It should be noted that XP is often combined with Scrum. For more information on XP, consider visiting www.extremeprogramming.org.

3.3.3   Other Methods that Support Agile

Aside from Scrum and XP, there are other methods that support Agile. A few are described here.

3.3.3.1   DSDM

The Dynamic Systems Development Method (DSDM) is an iterative and incremental method for Agile software development. DSDM is based on Rapid Application Development (RAD) that focuses on continuous user involvement. Prototyping is a key component of DSDM and is found throughout the activities within the project lifecycle phase.

Unlike other Agile methods that focus on just the project lifecycle, DSDM utilizes three phases, focusing on the pre-project, project lifecycle, and post-project phases. The pre-project phase focuses on commitment and budget. The post-project phase focuses on maintenance, bug fixes, and enhancements. In DSDM, you may iterate through the same activity several times before moving to the next.

The project lifecycle phase starts with a "study" activity focusing on feasibility to ensure that DSDM will work for the project and that it is accepted by management. This is a bit unusual since most Agile methods do not specifically have a step to verify if the method will be suitable and instead assume it will just work. However, ensuring that the methodology is aligned with the work and having management support are critical to the success of the project.

This is one of several of DSDM's success factors. DSDM specifically calls out the need to ensure management agrees to use the method and looks for a commitment moving forward. The other success factors are having customer involvement, an empowered project team, and a strong relationship between the customer and vendor. DSDM views the full picture of software development as areas to focus on because it is understood that any one piece that goes awry can lead to problems. It should be noted that DSDM may be combined with other methods and techniques like PRINCE2, XP, and Scrum. For more information on DSDM, consider visiting www.dsdm.org.

Pit Stop

DSDM, FDD, and AUP are Agile methods that specifically call out the importance of Configuration Management.

3.3.3.2 Feature-Driven Development (FDD)

Feature-Driven Development (FDD) is an iterative and incremental method for software development. FDD is model-driven and consists of five activities that focus on the modeling and development of features. The activities include developing the overall model, building a feature list, planning by feature, designing by feature, and building by feature. The first three activities are serial while the last two will involve several iterations. FDD also utilizes industry practices to support the method. This provides the follower of the method with established guidance to help them succeed. Some of these practices include developing by feature, individual code ownership, small feature team, inspections, Configuration Management (CM), and regular builds. These last two practices recognize the value of CM within FDD. For more on Feature-Driven Development, consider visiting: http://featuredrivendevelopment.org/.

3.3.3.3 Agile Unified Process

Agile Unified Process (AUP) is an iterative and incremental method for software development. AUP is a more streamlined and simple version of Rational Unified Process (RUP). In addition, AUP includes Agile practices like Agile Model-Driven Development (AMDD), test-driven development (TDD), change management, and database refactoring. In general, AUP focuses beyond building the functionality based on stakeholder needs, but also focuses on architecture and environments for the product under development. AUP provides a framework with four phases. They include the inception phase, where you focus on the scope, funding, and stakeholders; the elaboration phase, where you focus on architecture; the construction phase, where you iteratively and incrementally build the highest priority needs; and the transition phase, where you perform final testing and deploy the system into production. AUP includes disciplines that must be followed to ensure the team is meeting the needs of the stakeholders. The disciplines include modeling, implementation, testing, deployment, CM, project management, and environments. For more on the Agile Unified Process, consider visiting http://www.ambysoft.com/unifiedprocess.

3.4   Benefits of Agile

Why are teams turning to Agile methods? One reason is many software development projects have a poor track record of delivering on time, on budget, high quality, and what the customer wants. The question then becomes, what are the reasons for this track record?

- Software development is complex.
- It is not possible to know everything or most things upfront.
- Testing gets abused and minimized at the end as schedules get tight.
- Defining requirements in detail is impossible.
- Schedules are defined with very little information about the work.
- Requirements change.
- Processes are heavy with a lot of ceremony.

What are the impacts that arise from these reasons?

- Projects observe costly overruns.
- Features are not used by the customer.
- Schedules are missed.
- A lot of rework is required.

What does Agile provide to improve these conditions and results?

- Emphasizes continuous customer involvement and reduces the feedback period to ensure customers get what they actually want.

This approach ensures they continuously have insight into what functions are getting built and can respond with timely feedback.

- Ensures that requirements or stories are written at a high level and can be changed over time. This ensures that the team has a good general notion of the work and utilizes the iterations to focus on the details. Also, at the beginning of each iteration, requirements can be adjusted to the customer's needs.

- Considers scheduling a collaborative effort and should be adjusted by project team and customer, based on estimates of new and changing requirements, the track record of velocity, and the feedback from the end of iteration reviews and retrospectives.

- Ensures that writing test cases are done no later than the time that stories and requirements are being detailed. This ensures that everyone is aware of the acceptance criteria as functionality is being built and emphasizes the importance of testing.

- Provides an emphasis on unit testing and automated testing. Unit testing ensures that developers building the code have a criterion to determine if it passes. Automation testing increases the possibility of testing as much of the functional code as possible.

3.5 Agile Personality Types

When viewing the Agile world, it must be recognized that there are different types of folks who are in this space. Each has different motivations and it is important to assess this. There are seven types of people who are in the Agile space: Innovator, Champion, Workhorse, Bandwagon, Cowboy, Deceiver, and Denier. Whether you are a CM professional or an Agile professional, it is important to distinguish between them so you understand the person you are dealing with. In addition, people may move from one group to the next depending on how involved they get in the Agile space and their ability to adjust. Below is a figure that places the seven Agile personality types into quadrants with positioning being determined by the level of experience and positive or negative perspective toward Agile.

What follows are the seven Agile personality types discussed in more detail, highlighting their experience levels in Agile, their positive or negative perspective of Agile, the common roles that fit into a type, and details on their goals and motivations.

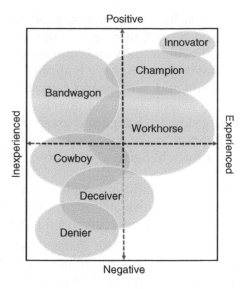

Figure 3-3   Placement of the seven Agile personality types.

3.5.1   Innovator

The innovators make up a small population of folks in the Agile arena who are very experienced in this field and are very positive yet pragmatic about Agile. These folks are the industry leaders and are motivated to improve and extend Agile.

The signatories of the Agile Manifesto would certainly fall in this camp as well as the many Agile writers, presenters, and authors. They are the folks who have conceptualized Agile into pragmatic methods and practices and have been evolving Agile over time. There are many others in organizations across the world who have actively practiced with Agile and have innovated and extended the capabilities of Agile into all areas of software development and adapted Agile into their work environments. Some common roles in this space are very experienced engineers who can construct methods and practices based on their working experience that extend the capabilities of Agile for their own organization.

3.5.2   Champion

A champion tends to know Agile well and is willing to advocate it in a very positive way across an organization. There are even some champions that may not be well versed in the practices of Agile, but have seen the benefits of implementing and using Agile methods. Some common roles in this space are Agile coaches, consultants, product owners, heads of software engineering, and project managers. They make up a small, yet core, leadership in the Agile community and communicate the real meaning of what Agile is and what it means to have it applied. They are motivated to educate others on Agile and understand how to get cultures (i.e., a cultural change agent) to accept Agile. Companies have very embedded cultures that are typically slow to change and grasp new ideas, so an Agile leader must have the ability to make culture change occur in an adoptable manner. In relation to culture change and adoption, Agile leaders need to:

- Make it very clear in what conditions Agile will work and avoid having folks say that it will work on any project. Communicate where there are challenges and share new ideas in the Agile space.

- Be able to generate buy-in with senior management, many of which are part of the bandwagon crowd, to initiate a new Agile culture (in pockets or throughout the company) and understand the notions of culture change. Positive cultural change involves understanding enough about the values and beliefs of the leaders of a company in order to improve performance. This requires analysis of the company culture, an ability to understand "change" patterns within a culture, and the ability to negotiate and facilitate change. This also includes the continual interaction with management to ensure they are engaged with the Agile direction.

- Be constantly ready to support product teams in utilizing Agile and to help remove obstacles, bottlenecks, and those Agile personality types (specifically cowboys and deceivers) that may get in the way of effectively deploying and utilizing Agile.

- Be ready to work with the more negative types (e.g., cowboys, deceivers, and deniers) to see if they are adaptable to moving more positively toward Agile. This can be by providing educational opportunities, changes in roles, and a change of projects.

- Avoid condemning and bashing other methodologies. Agile may get bashed on occasion and seen as a fad or a threat to another way of doing business. However, reverse bashing (even if in jest) only creates contempt and may impact acceptance. Be confident in the value of Agile.

3.5.3 Workhorse

The workhorse has learned about Agile by trying to implement it on their own or with some help from others. The workhorse is mostly positive about Agile but will be fairly honest on what works and what does not. The

common role in this space is the product team members that have implemented Agile methods and practices. They bring a pragmatic approach
to Agile, understanding the structure that Agile needs to thrive, by either
being bitten once already or by fully understanding the environment
needed for Agile.

The workhorse has worked in the trenches and really understands the
challenges of implementing Agile because their merit or bonus is typically
tied to their success. This group cannot afford to be idealists, but are realists
that learn the hard way when a new Agile culture collides with current
company culture. They learn the importance of facilitating change and
adapting. A lot can be learned from this group.

3.5.4   Bandwagon

The bandwagon crowd sees benefits in jumping on the Agile bandwagon.
Fads and trends rule the day, so if Agile is perceived to be "hot", then there
will be folks who will jump on the bandwagon. The bandwagon crowd
tends to be inexperienced with Agile but generally positive, especially
when they think it can help their own image. Some bandwagon folks are
middle and senior management who believe they can get ahead by aligning
with the hot new trend. They are very willing to "throw around" Agile
terminology to give the appearance of knowing the field.

The danger with the bandwagon crowd is that they act like they know
Agile well while not really understanding it and the culture change within
management that is needed in order for Agile to thrive. Another danger
with the management bandwagon is that they can just as easily abandon
Agile if they perceive a dislike from their up-line management and will
readily blame Agile if something goes awry. In other words, they go
wherever the politic winds move them. Sometimes bandwagon folks communicate inaccurate information without any bad intent (but it is incorrect
information all the same). Some bandwagon folks will see the value of Agile
and will become Agile workhorses or champions. However, most will not.

3.5.5   Cowboy

The cowboy sees Agile as an opportunity to abandon processes and
documentation so that they can enjoy the Wild West life. Cowboys are
the type of folks who are not necessarily negative about Agile because, in
many cases, they know that they can get away with pretending to be Agile
since many folks, particularly the bandwagon crowd, really have no idea
what it is. Ultimately, these pretenders can give Agile a black eye in the
organization, since others will believe from the cowboy's actions that Agile
means no process.

Pit Stop

Most Agile methods instill much more rigor and discipline than most cowboys can tolerate.

When reviewing the Agile Manifesto (see http://agilemanifesto.org/), the cowboys purposefully interpret the word "over" as "in place of." These individuals are smart enough to know that many do not understand Agile. They deliberately twist the true intent of the manifesto. For example a cowboy will reinterpret the Agile Manifesto value of "Working software over comprehensive documentation" into "Working software instead of documentation."

Agile does, in fact, value process, tools, documentation, and planning. However, these concepts are viewed differently in the Agile context in that they should not be automatically done for the sake of the process, tool, document, or plan, but as a need that arises from the individuals and interactions. A cowboy will always purposefully interpret the manifesto to mean that there should be no process, tools, documents, or plans, because it prevents them from doing whatever they want. In fact, there are cowboys out there who know a little bit about Agile, and just enough to know how to circumvent it.

A person with real Agile experience, whether it is the innovator, the champion, or the workhorse, will immediately see that the cowboy is not an advocate of Agile because as the cowboy does not advocate process, tools, document, or plans, they do not advocate any of the discipline that Agile applies, nor any of the Agile practices.

3.5.6 Deceiver

The deceiver will agree to the new terms and working processes of Agile but will silently attempt to sabotage the project in order to put the blame on Agile. A deceiver is negative about Agile because they may have been forced into a role on a team using Agile and did not want to lose any credibility by bad-mouthing the new direction. A deceiver will usually have some Agile experience because it may be thrust upon them.

If something goes wrong on the project, deceivers will be quick to blame Agile. Keep in mind that when you move to Agile, it can threaten some folks who have been used to playing a singular role (and doing it well) in a traditional method for years. Some deceivers may have enjoyed their singular role within a phased method and find the variable roles within Agile not to their liking and will begin to subtly rebel. There are some similarities between cowboys and deceivers in that both attempt to prevent the adoption of Agile. However, deceivers are the most dangerous because they undermine and obstruct the potential success that Agile may bring to an organization and they will attempt to hide any evidence of doing so.

3.5.7 Denier

The denier will deny outright any benefit to Agile. They are typically set against Agile from the beginning because they see that it will interfere with what they perceived to be their currently successful role within the company. They may also think that it will impact their reward structure in a negative way. Deniers typically do not have much Agile experience. It is actually better to have deniers than deceivers because you know where Agile deniers stand. Many times, it can be beneficial to listen to reasons why deniers dismiss Agile. The input from the deniers can help you understand their specific reasons for objecting to Agile (e.g., rewards, roles, loss of control, etc.). This input may help you look for a way to overcome the reasons, therefore strengthening the overall perception of Agile within the organization.

3.5.8 Summarizing the Types

When listening to people talk about Agile, try to understand their point of view. What is their Agile persona (Innovator, Champion, Workhorse, Bandwagon, Cowboy, Deceiver, or Denier)? Do they understand what they are saying? How much knowledge and/or experience do they have with Agile? How positive or negative are they with Agile? While employing Agile implies a cultural shift, the Agile community must continue to communicate the strengths and weaknesses. Knowing the people you are working with and their types can help you utilize their strengths or overcome the challenges ahead.

3.6 Agile Roles

Within the Agile world, there is a significant shift in roles and responsibilities. In a more hierarchical and traditional project, decisions are typically made in a hierarchical manner and roles are specifically established. In the Agile world, decisions are purposefully pushed down to the lowest possible level to the folks that have the most information and most to gain or lose from the decision. Also, there is a purposeful focus away from titles and roles. Certainly some team members will have strong skills in particular areas, but there is an emphasis on avoiding specific roles and sharing the work and the wealth. There is very concerted effort to create a team culture and move away from the blame-game culture. Therefore, when viewing the Agile world, it must be recognized that there are different types of roles with different responsibilities than the traditional projects. If you plan to follow a specific Agile method, then consider following the roles specified therein. Otherwise, review the following roles for a general understanding:

3.6.1 Agile Coach

- Helps initiate the Agile method and practices therein for the team.
- Coaches and trains the team on the methods and practices and mentors them as they gain experience, providing lessons and improvement opportunities.
- May coach more than one team at a time.
- Ensures that everyone is working well together and consistently following Agile practices.

Note: After one or two project releases, the Coach may move on to getting other projects up and running with Agile.

3.6.2 Agile Project Manager/ScrumMaster

- Trained and preferably seasoned in Agile project management, following an Agile method and practices.
- Collects and manages those stories prioritized in iteration planning sessions from the product backlog to the iteration backlog.
- Establishes and periodically produces the burn-down (or burn-up) metrics to indicate velocity.
- Facilitates the daily stand-up meetings.
- Manages the risk, issues, and defect logs. Also focuses on dependencies and constraints.
- Liaison with peripheral groups like architecture, operations, and test groups when there are dependencies to systems and infrastructure.
- A facilitator of the work. Acts as more of a shepherd for the team, moving them down the general path instead of telling the team what to do.
- Facilitates the retrospectives and will facilitate discussions when there are disagreements.
- Coaches and trains the team on the methods and practices and mentors them as they gain experience, providing lessons and improvement opportunities.

Note: Sometimes the Agile Project Manager/ScrumMaster also acts as the Agile Coach.

3.6.3 Agile Project Team

- Committed full-time team focused on completing the work for the project.
- The project team is made up of folks with skills in programming, analysis, testing, and design. The customer may also be a full-time and equally committed part of the team.
- Each may play more than one role and volunteer on any task that needs to be completed (affecting the true meeting of "team"). The goal is for the team to think of themselves in a more holistic way in order to optimize throughput, ergo always wanting to increase their velocity.
- Equally accountable and empowered to make decisions, determine estimates for stories, contributing in identifying risks, and articulating roadblocks.
- There will be other roles on the team focused on architecture, training, documentation, infrastructure, release management, and CM. While it would be good for these roles to be full-time, often there is not enough work involved for them to be continuously engaged.

Note: It is strongly recommended to include the CM professional and release manager in the daily stand-ups to ensure all CM needs are being met and for strong communication on build and release schedules, especially when it gets close to the release time.

3.6.4 Product Owner/Manager

- Owner of the product line and manages the product backlog.
- Collects and documents stories (a.k.a., requirements) from the customer into the product backlog and sets the priority of the stories based on business value.
- Must be continuously available for discussion on functionality and make quick decisions.
- Removes roadblocks and rules on issues where disagreements arise.
- Ensures there are active customers available for end-of-iteration reviews.
- Attends the iteration planning and retrospective sessions.

- Plays the role of voice of the customer (a.k.a., customer representative) and must be continuously communicating with the actual customer(s).
- Informs the team when there are changes in business conditions.

Important note: There will be some cases where the Product Owner and Product Manager are divided into two different roles. The Product Owner focuses internally with the development team. The Product Manager focuses externally with the customers to collect their needs and may play the voice of the customer role for the Agile team. If you have both a Product Owner and Product Manager, ensure they are continually in contact and define their roles in an Agile context based on the needs of the team.

3.6.5 Customer

- There may be a couple of levels of customer (full-time on the project and part-time external).
- A full-time customer should be continuously available to discuss functionality, contribute to the iteration planning sessions, play a role in testing within an iteration, and be active in the end-of-iteration review.
- Various customers can participate in the end-of-iteration review.

Note: It will be challenging to get the customer fully engaged and fully committed on the project. The continuous customer feedback provides the team with an opportunity for improvement. Sometimes the Product Owner/Manager plays the role of customer representative, acting as the voice of the customer.

3.7 Agile Mindset

Agile thinkers bring a different frame of mind to their work. In the traditional methodologies, the world is well planned with very specific milestones, and changes are constrained after a certain point. In Agile methodologies, the world is much more fluid, changes are dynamic, and in fact welcome. Traditional methodologies use a phased approach while Agile uses a continually evolving or sloping approach. In effective, traditional methodologies, there is a fairly fixed and pre-defined path, while in Agile the path is allowed to vary: it's a world where collaboration and sharing rule. You share tasks, you look to help others and proactively look for more work if you have free time.

3.7.1   Thinking Small

Agile thinking focuses you on short iterations and small increments. You believe in short iterations of 1 to 4 weeks. You time-box activities to ensure progress. This allows you to continually see progress. Also, think small or minimal documentation. Agile does not prescribe a certain length to any documents but it clearly advocates that you focus on working software over comprehensive documentation. The key here is to document what you think may help with collaboration or communication, but it should not be a form of a contract that specifies each item. Instead spend that time building the functionality and then allowing the customer to respond to it.

3.7.2   Thinking Business Value

Agile actively encourages the discovery of business value. Because the conclusion of each short iteration is reviewed by the customer, the project stays very close to what the customer finds valuable. In traditional methods, project timelines are typically very long (many months to even well over a year). The customer is typically engaged in the beginning (planning and requirements) and then toward the end (user testing). During the time in between, the customer needs may change and these changes may not get accepted during the change control period, often leading to a product that is less than ideal and some of whose functionality is unused. Agile helps you strive for a continuous reflection of business value all along the project lifecycle. This ensures that once the project is delivered, the customer finds the deliverable valuable and is ready to use it.

3.7.3   Thinking Continuous

A word you find in the Agile space again and again is "continuous". Dictionary.com defines continuous as "being in immediate connection". In the traditional methods, the world is well planned with very specific milestones and changes are constrained after a certain point. Agile thinking embraces a more fluid environment, in which dynamic changes are enthusiastically accepted.

3.7.4   Thinking Self-Empowered Team

By thinking as a self-empowered "team," it means that you move away from the command-and-control structure, where one person is telling the team what to do, and move into a self-directing structure where everyone participates in decisions and the direction of the project. Broadening the base of empowerment and pushing down the level of approval and decisions to the lowest possible level, i.e., reducing the need for numerous chains of approvals and decisions, can be a big change for many organizations.

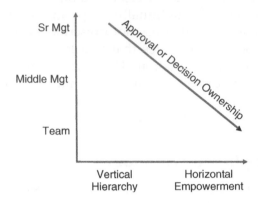

Figure 3-4   Culture change of approval and decision making with Agile.

This is effectively changing the culture from a vertical command-and-control model to a horizontal team empowerment model. This is much easier said than done. Therefore, prior to considering Agile, an assessment of the openness of the culture is critical.

Having self-empowered teams also means thinking beyond the individual successes and focusing on the team successes (you only succeed if the team succeeds). Individual rewards constrain collaboration. Rewards should be team based to drive this notion home. The "team" notion also means title, levels, grades, heroes, and egos need to be removed from team dynamics. Effectively hierarchy in the team should be removed as it can become a barrier to progress. Instead equality amongst roles should be promoted. Everyone in the team should be treated as an equal as this leads to more engaged team members. However, team members should be cognizant of the fact that some people do have more experience in certain areas than others and listen appropriately and use it to their benefit.

3.7.5 Thinking Collaboration

Communication and collaboration are very critical to having an Agile mindset. With collaboration comes the importance of listening. Listening can mean hearing and understanding what the other is saying, but it also means listening to what they are not saying. Sometimes a lack of a response may indicate that there is a lack of understanding. Instead of speaking up about the lack of understanding, some people choose to remain silent. There are those who remain quiet because they are learning and not necessarily looking to contribute. In either case, determining whether the silence is because of a lack of understanding or simply not being engaged should be probed. Another aspect of collaboration is being assertive. Quietly listening does not often lead to a building of ideas. Therefore, collaboration is a balance of being a good listener and being assertive.

3.8   Moving to an Agile Culture

The Agile structure may not be easily inserted into the culture of a more traditional and hierarchical company. Consideration should be made of what steps will help move the company toward an Agile culture. This will include the visible changes based on tangible actions that have been initiated to approach a change. Along with the visible changes, there will be social changes that are less tangible, such as the level of trust, fairness, and respect that will be sensed by the team. The combination of the visible and social changes will bring about the cultural change. However, initiating a "change in culture" is very hard to do. One method is to identify the outcomes of what you would ideally like to see in the culture and then initiate actions that will get you there. Also, it is important to give yourself a jump start by focusing on sweet spots where the change effort will more likely be successful.

Pit Stop

Success is a funny thing. On the one hand, success will draw people who also want to experience success. On the other hand, beware: Success also draws those that want to bring you down, since they do not want you to be more successful than them.

3.8.1   Targeting the Sweet Spot

When moving toward Agile, it is best to target the candidate product and projects therein where Agile has the highest rate of success. The characteristics below focus on the sweet spot. Keep in mind that Agile has been successfully applied to various sizes and types of projects, so your implementation should not be limited to sweet spot projects. However, if this is your first time, then serious consideration should be given to these sweet spot characteristics.

- Team is small – Most Agile methods tend to favor small teams typically no larger than 10. This way, team members get to know each other well and what they are working on, which increases communication.

- Team is co-located – This allows for continuous and synchronous communication between team members (a.k.a., face-to-face) and reduces the wasted time of seeking people out.

- Customer is readily available – This ensures the project team has direct access to the customer, who will continually provide feedback on the functionality leading to a product with strong business value.

- New interactive application – New products that are interactive (web applications) with customers and users can get more advantages from Agile's iterative approach.

- Willingness to move to Agile – This makes it easier to advocate the changes needed to utilize Agile methods effectively. Having the Product Manager, stakeholder and project team more willing to commit to Agile will make it easier to implement. You can learn more about how to gauge the willingness to move to Agile in the "Determining Agile Readiness" section below.

3.8.2   Targeting the Product Level

Moving to Agile is a culture change and a mental shift to an Agile mindset which is not trivial, and nor is the effort to implement Agile. With this in mind, it is best to apply Agile at the product level and not just target a single project. The effort to move a team to Agile may not be cost-effective on a single project, since a project typically has a shorter life and once it is done, any methods and practices are lost. However, if you make the commitment of moving to Agile at a product level, then each project therein can gain the benefit from Agile and subsequent projects within that product line can become more effective at using Agile over time. It takes time to fully grasp the concepts of Agile and apply them effectively. When a team gets a chance to learn Agile together and then hone it over time, their productivity and accuracy in estimating work will improve, particularly as retrospectives are implemented and the resulting improvement ideas are initiated.

In addition, the product manager/owner is a key contributor in making Agile successful. When implementing Agile at the product level, the product manager/owner contributes insight from the marketplace, information about customers, insights into the product road map, financial implications, current negotiations, and other details. This broader view and additional information ensures that the project team is building the right product.

3.8.3   Actions for Agile Change

To move to Agile, you can take one of two avenues. The first is a complete shift toward Agile on day one and the second is to make a gradual move toward Agile. The former strategy may be best employed when the product is brand new and you are starting from the beginning. The latter may be preferred when there is already a product team in place that has been working together using traditional practices. In either case, here are some Agile culture change actions you should consider. If you are making a complete shift toward Agile, then these actions can be tasks in an Agile implementation plan. If you are making a gradual move toward Agile, then select the actions that may be easier to do and then commence with additional actions over time.

3.8.3.1   Promoting a Dedicated Team

Agile advocates that folks on a team are dedicated to that project. The intent is for them to become a unit that is self-organized and self-motivated. This promotes the continuous collaboration that is a cornerstone for Agile. Team members cannot be multitasking between two or more projects or there is a significant productivity hit. Also by getting the people dedicated to the project it reduces the risk of over-committing the resources. Remember, Agile advocates people and interaction over process and tools. People tend to work best when they have one project to focus on.

3.8.3.2   Ensure Continuous Customer Participation

Project teams employing Agile must have easy and continuous access to the customer or customer representatives. This means getting time commitments from the customer. This can be quite challenging. The major point of employing Agile is so that the customer can get a continuous view of the evolving solution so they can adjust quickly as new business demands arise.

In a traditional method, the customer will contribute their needs then step away. For change control, it appears that the customer lobs balls of change onto the team without fully realizing the impact on the project. This relationship often becomes adversarial because the customer does not have the same level of continuous information that the team does, so the customer tends to only hear when things start going wrong or when their changes get challenged without understanding why. Effectively, when the customer and team do not work continually together, there appears a gap in expectations.

With an Agile mindset, the customer and team work continuously together. Having the customer (or representative) as part of the team is the best possible model. This way the customer is continually aware of the challenges, the need to expand on a need, and the complexities involved in change.

3.8.3.3   Advocating for an Agile Coach

When getting Agile implemented within an organization, it is best to identify and hire an Agile coach to help focus on strategizing and planning for the implementation of Agile on a product. The Agile coach will help facilitate the learning process, coach the team, help remove roadblocks, and initiate the Agile method and practices. When an Agile coach is not made available, it is very easy to revert back to traditional methods and command-and-control type approaches.

3.8.3.4   Promoting Co-Location

In order to have the most effective collaboration, it is best that folks are working as closely together as possible, applying face-to-face communications. Many project teams employing Agile have dedicated and centralized work areas known as co-location sites. Proximity promotes participation and collaboration. However, with the amount of distributed development that occurs within many companies, co-located teams are not always possible. The solution in this case is to advocate for distributed collaborative methods and tools that can help bring the team together, and to advocate that each site own a chunk of work to reduce the reliance on another site.

3.8.3.5   Introducing Agile Terminology

Companies typically have standard terminology for methodology, reporting, and hierarchy. Agile introduces new terminology, practices, reporting, and team structure. This requires some adjustment. It is important not to force the terminology across the company but instead to focus initially on the associates who will be working with the Agile methods. From there, through reporting, training, seminars, and workshops, the terminology will spread.

3.8.3.6 Promoting Agile Practices

Identifying and implementing a set of value-added and customizable Agile practices can help the newer Agile teams come up to speed with Agile more easily. The key is to ensure that people know that they should select the practices that are right for them and that they are expected to customize the practices specifically for their product and working situation.

Incrementally inserting Agile practices into a more traditional methodology can have some benefits for gaining acceptance with Agile. Agile practices like the daily stand-up, unit testing, continuous build, and others can be introduced into a project team with typically little disruption while showing some value.

3.8.3.7 Minimizing Project Reporting

It is important to note that Agile reporting is different from standard company reporting. Most traditional companies ask for Gantt charts to assess a project's progress. In addition, there are several more reports that organizations ask of the project which the project manager typically spends a bit of time creating and massaging. In Agile, the goal is to minimize the reporting so that time is spent on project work and very little on project reporting. Agile teams typically provide burn-down charts which are directly from the projects. There may be a need to establish a portfolio report with project roll-up data and it is recommended to pull this data from the project burn-down charts versus generating another set of reports.

3.8.3.8 Embracing Change

The ability to truly respond to change while achieving goals is at the heart of a successful Agile operation. As an iteration is completed, customer changes should be welcomed because this means that the team is getting closer to what the customer wants. It is important to encourage change while ensuring that the priority and effort is considered.

3.8.3.9 Praising Cancelled Projects

Praising a cancelled project sounds counterintuitive. Why would you want to support a methodology in which you praise the cancellation of a project? It sounds like failure, right? The short answer is that because Agile keeps the customer close at hand and provides working functionality at the end of each iteration, the customer can decide if what they see is what they really want. If it is not, there is a benefit of cancelling the project so no further money gets spent.

Pit Stop

Cancelling projects that are not perceived as adding value produces a dual benefit. It saves the company money and allows for reallocation of the resources.

There are times when a project gets delivered, but the customer does not really want the product and new buyers are scarce. Would it have made more sense to cancel the project much earlier to avoid wasting the money on an unwanted product? Instead, stakeholders should praise the team where money did not get wasted. It would also be of benefit for the project team to be working on something else much more in demand by the customer.

3.8.3.10   Removing Formality and Ceremony

Agile encourages the removal of processes that have high ceremony and low value. Good examples of this are the lengthy project reviews some companies hold based on expected protocol. The team or the key members must take productive time away from the project to build a set of project slides and spend time in the review. Another example is documenting a change request on a separate form, and then summarizing the change in a change log. It's better to track changes in a backlog instead. Sometimes there are bottlenecks and roadblocks that slow the team progress. For example, if an Agile team needs a test environment, there are times where there is a process with numerous steps that requires approval from many layers of management. This can hinder progress when the team is sitting around waiting for a test server. What typically happens is that the Agile project team spends time creating their own test environment from any available PC. This takes time away from building functionality.

3.8.4   Determining Agile Readiness

A key factor in the success of Agile is to determine if all parties involved are really ready and willing to accept and implement Agile methods. With reference to the "Actions for Agile Change" mentioned in section 3.8.3, another way you can use these actions is to re-craft them as a measure of how willing the stakeholder, product manager, and team are to implement these actions. If there is a high willingness to accept and implement these actions, then this product team is a good candidate for Agile. However, if there is low willingness to implement these actions, then they are not good candidates for moving toward Agile. Below is an example of a readiness survey. On a scale from 1 to 10, with 10 being the most willing, how willing are the stakeholders, product manager, and team to adopt Agile:

Table 3-1   Matrix to determine Agile readiness.

Readiness Action (includes only a subset of the actions for illustration purposes)	Score 1 = Low willingness 5 = Medium willingness 10 = High willingness
Promote dedicated teams	
Ensure active customer participation	
Advocate for an Agile coach	
Promote team co-location	
Total Score	

The total score should include at least half or more of the readiness actions having a score of 10 (or high willingness) and include no "1"s (or low willingness). If a low willingness is seen, you can continue to educate the product manager, stakeholder, and team on the advantages of Agile until they are at least at medium willingness.

3.8.5 Measuring your Move Toward Agile

A good way to know if you are really moving toward Agile as an organization or product team is to use the above actions and to re-craft them into a measure of success. For example:

- If the action is "Promote Agile Practices", the measure can be periodically counting how many teams are using 1 or more of the Agile practices.
- If the action is "Praise cancelled Projects", periodically count how many projects were cancelled when applying Agile and the potential cost savings by doing so.
- If the action is "Minimize Project Reporting", then compare the report size of those projects using traditional methods with the project applying Agile methods.

In addition to using the actions for measures, consider an overall satisfaction survey of those using Agile methods compared to those who do not. The satisfaction measures can focus on satisfaction from their work, how rewarded they feel, how empowered they feel, how respected and supported they feel, do they feel a better sense of trust and fairness, is there an improvement in their work-life balance, and does it provide a stronger sense of accomplishment.

It is recommended to initially keep the measures quiet to get a true baseline of the adoption. Measures are a double-edged sword. The key point of doing this is to know that Agile adoption is really occurring. Otherwise, you may get a lot of people pretending to follow Agile but in reality continuing to follow the same traditional methods they have used in the past.

3.8.6 Avoiding Mistakes in Agile Adoption

As you consider the adoption of Agile, it is not only important to evaluate the culture of an organization, but to also be aware of some common mistakes. These mistakes can impact the success of Agile. They include:

- Not having an Agile professional to help get you started. Agile professionals such as Agile Coaches and ScrumMasters are instrumental to evaluate cultural readiness, as well as product team readiness, to help determine the best starting position, and to have the ability to effectively begin an Agile implementation focusing on the right areas to ensure adoption. An Agile professional can also evaluate the cultural factors of hierarchy, empowerment, and role expectations to better assess the readiness of Agile.

- Allowing cowboy teams (those pretending to use Agile) to run loose, which sends the erroneous message to others that what they are doing is Agile when it is not. This can damage the reputation of Agile and cause you to spend time cleaning up the damage of setting the record straight on what is Agile.

- Not clearly positioning Agile within the organization. An interesting dynamic may occur when there is already an existing waterfall or phase-based lifecycle method. It is not unusual to see a battle between methods. This can cause a rift within an organization and it is best to ensure people understand that they have a choice between one or the other – or, as some organizations have done, go completely Agile. Management direction on this is important to reduce thrashing or bashing.

- Not adapting the governance model to support Agile. If the governance model has been only used for phase based methods, then there will have to be adjustments made to it to allow for less concreteness of needs up front and more variance to change as the project moves forward. Otherwise, it may force Agile teams to produce unnecessary documentation or force them into a partial phased approach.

3.9   Agile Resource Guide

There are numerous valuable materials available on Agile to gain further knowledge and information. This section will provide a small subset of these available resources.

3.9.1   Agile Books

- *Agile Project Management with Scrum* by Ken Schwaber, Microsoft Press, 2004.
- *Agile Adoption Patterns: A Roadmap to Organizational Success* by Amr Elssamadisy, Addison-Wesley Professional, 2008
- *Balancing Agility and Discipline: A Guide for the Perplexed* by Barry Boehm and Richard Turner, Addison-Wesley Professional, 2003
- *The Art of Agile Development*, by James Shore and Shane Warden, O'Reilly Media, 2007
- *Agile Modeling: Effective Practices for Extreme Programming and the Unified Process* by Scott Ambler, John Wiley & Sons, 2002
- *Software by Numbers: Low-Risk, High-Return Development* by Mark Denne and Jane Cleland-Huang; Addison Wesley, 2004
- *Crystal Clear: A Human-Powered Methodology for Small Teams* by Alistair Cockburn, Addison Wesley, 2004
- *Agile Project Management: Creating Innovative Products* by Jim Highsmith, Addison-Wesley Professional, 2004
- *Implementing Lean Software Development: From Concept to Cash* by Mary Poppendieck and Tom Poppendieck, Addison-Wesley Professional, 2006

Because there are other Agile books on the market, consider visiting an online bookstore and performing a search on this topic.

Pit Stop

A chicken and a pig decide to open a restaurant. The chicken says, "Let's serve bacon and eggs". The pig says, "No thanks, I'd be committed but you'd only be involved.

3.9.2   Agile Websites

There are numerous Agile-related websites available. This is only a short list. However many of these websites include numerous other Agile links within them.

- Manifesto for Agile Software Development (a.k.a., Agile Manifesto) – http://www.agilemanifesto.org/
- Agile Journal – a monthly journal that provides articles from various Agile specialists and perspectives – http://www.agilejournal.com
- Agile Advice – http://www.agileadvice.com/
- Agile Wikipedia – http://en.wikipedia.org/wiki/Agile_software_development

How CM and Agile Values Work Together

When we consider how CM and Agile can work together, we should review their specific values and blend them in a manner in which the implementation of CM for Agile addresses both sets of values. As you recall, CM principles focus on the identification, control, audit, and report of configuration items (CIs) and baselines that make up collections of CIs. In Agile the values include a focus on individuals and interactions, working software, customer collaboration, and responding to change.

The great news is that both CM and Agile focus heavily on responding to change. On the front end, Agile ensures there are customers available to provide their needs in a collaborative and continuous manner, while on the back end CM ensures there are the mechanisms and controls in place to be able to capture and track the change in an efficient manner. This is a powerful combination.

Figure 4-1   Agile & CM collaboration.

Think of CM as an enabler of change for Agile. CM is there to support the development efforts by ensuring the integrity of the changes so that the product team can focus on building functionality, knowing changes will be managed. With that in mind, a case can be made where CM enables many of the Agile values. Some examples:

- In order to achieve working software, many code changes occur when applying Agile. In order to manage the code changes and avoid regression, a streamlined CM infrastructure will enable this process.
- CM tools and process can promote collaboration amongst the team and with the customer. CM supports collaboration by offering mechanisms to enable refactoring, pair programming, and continuous integration and build.
- CM tools and processes respond to change. CM offers ways to ensure changes are tracked.
- CM tools and processes can promote reuse. CM provides mechanisms that enable the sharing of common components and code.

Pit Stop

As an enabler for change, CM provides the mechanisms that ensure the right thing (e.g., what the customer said they want through continuous validation) actually gets delivered to the customer.

4.1 Aligning Agile and CM Mindsets

Aligning Agile and CM is an evolution in melding speed with sustainability. Agile gives you the ability to build functionality in shorter cycles while CM ensures that what you are building can be recreated with integrity. The centerpiece of both Agile and CM is that each wants to ensure the "right product" is delivered.

- From an Agile perspective, the focus is to ensure that the customer gets the "right product" as quickly as possible.
- From a CM perspective, the focus is to ensure the team is confident that they produce the "right product" in a stable and repeatable way.

Agile is a contributor of getting to the right thing, while CM ensures you have the right product when it is delivered. Agile collaboratively extracts the stories (a.k.a., the needs) from the customer, while CM applies repeatable version control, build, and release processes to ensure the right product that was programmed is built, migrated, and delivered.

Figure 4-2   Delivering the right product.

4.1.1   Challenges of Aligning the Minds

It is important to understand that there will always be some CM professionals who will not readily adapt to changes needed for Agile methods. Even within the general software development world, there are some developers, project managers, analysts, and testers who cannot adapt themselves to Agile principles and methods and a few who do not see the importance of CM. As discussed in the introduction chapter, most Agile professionals understand the importance of CM to their work, but, there are some who do not. So what should we do to get people to adjust their thinking?

For the rest of us, it is important to advocate the values of CM and Agile and the alignment between the two. Look to see if there are bad relations between the Agile team and CM in the past. Often it is because one side tried to exert their will over the other, with neither side understanding each other.

It is also important to understand that there will always be people who will not accept Agile for several reasons. One reason is because they have been rewarded for following the traditional methods for years. Another reason is that they think that Agile is simply a way to get rid of discipline. And yet another reason is that some people feel very confident, experienced, and comfortable in their current roles and will not want to adjust to the notion of Agile because they may lose their identity.

Pit Stop

The reward system must change for effective Agile adoption to occur. First it must change from individual to team-based reward. Second, people should be rewarded to follow Agile and impacted when they revert back to the traditional methods.

Remember, people don't really like change so there must be motivators offered to both advocate and bring about change. For the people who continue to be rewarded for following the traditional methods, the reward system must change to favor the use of the new methods. For those who think that Agile is a way to get rid of discipline, they need to be educated on what Agile is and the discipline and structure that comes with it. For those who are comfortable with their current roles, ask them to experience an Agile project while giving them the option to get back to their old roles. Of course, there will always be folks who will not adapt to Agile. This does not make them bad; it is simply a fact.

Agile tends to look at coding as a design and construction activity, since they are done simultaneously, while the traditional approach is to think of coding as a construction activity. In most Agile methods, the construction phase starts with the build activities that focus on the compilation and code generation of the code into executables. Since build will be utilized much more in Agile due to the short iterations, automating the build cycle reduces the effort of building and promotes frequent integration.

4.2   Supporting Agile and CM Values without Sacrifice

The balance for Agile professionals is to value long-term thinking just enough to reduce or avoid the risks of unanticipated impacts. This could be stories or requirements that did not get prioritized correctly, architectural impacts, or impacts of changes from dependent applications. Having this long-term view may reduce rework and waste. The key is just enough forward-thinking to avoid the impacts but not too much to have it impact the progress and incur debt.

The balance for CM professionals is to see the value of lean thinking and streamlined processes that reduce steps and effort. The key though is to eliminate as much waste as possible without impacting the CM values. A CM professional has to realize that an Agile mindset sees things in short iterations and expects a high degree of interaction.

Agile requires more freedom and collaboration for design. CM requires identification and control of changes. To align Agile and CM in this case, a reduction of any heavyweight processes where there are approvals required to check-out or check-in, when there are lengthy build and test cycles, or when waiting for the next baseline of "good" code, must occur. The inverse implies that Agile must maintain a sufficient level of tracking to ensure integrity of the product. An example is to support the freedom and collaboration of Agile and the control of CM, by automating the build and test process as much as possible. This reduces the wait time and need for manual intervention, while increasing the integrity and stability of the process.

Agile professionals can take advantage of the longer CM view by regarding the change as not just to the code but possibly to the corresponding hardware, along with upgrades to systems and tools, updating of data, dealing with multi-site updates and issues, changes to business process that must be rolled out, training time needed by end-users, and many others.

Where there is some similarity in view is that Agile professionals view development as an incremental design of functionality, which is a very modular way of thinking. CM professionals also think in a modular way, having to understand how to do incremental builds and the modularity of the code baseline. This can help both understand each other.

4.3   Value of Retrospective to CM

A common Agile practice that can be applied to CM is the retrospective. Known to many as a "lesson learned," this is the practice where at the end of each iteration, it is recommended that the team take some time to reflect on what went well and what could have been done better. Specifically, the team lists the opportunities for improvement, prioritizes them, then identifies one to three of the opportunities (depending on the effort of the improvements) to initiate in the next iteration. The benefits of doing this include sharing amongst the team as well as the continuous focus on improving team dynamics, working processes, and overall quality.

Pit Stop

End-of-iteration retrospectives are a great place to identify if there are areas within CM to improve for the benefit of the Agile team.

So how can CM benefit from this? Applying CM processes and tools should not be thought of as a one size fits all. In many organizations, the bandwidth for CM professionals to adapt CM to the team's needs is often challenging. Whether the product team inherits a CM infrastructure or is implementing a new CM infrastructure, there are benefits to conducting periodic retrospectives. Particular focus should be given to where CM processes can be streamlined and more traditional CM practices can be adjusted to align better with Agile while still maintaining the values of CM.

The first way in which CM can benefit from a retrospective is when a CM professional is considered a core part of the product team that is implementing Agile. During the retrospectives, the team can identify where things are going well and where there are opportunities for improvement. Should there be areas where CM is doing well or has an improvement opportunity, then the CM professional can make notes and also learn how high a priority it is. If it is the top one to three and gets chosen as an improvement task, then there will be a team focus. However, even if it is not chosen as a top task for improvement, the CM professional should note it and work on it as there is time.

The second way in which CM can benefit from a retrospective is when the CM professional helps the Agile product team over time but is not considered a core part of the team. In this case, if the CM professional does not get invited to the retrospective, they can request to see the opportunities for improvement. However, it does not hurt for the CM professional to ask to attend the retrospectives at the end of each iteration, even if they remain an observer.

4.4   Agile Perspective of CM Practices

In order to align Agile and CM perspectives together, it is important to understand what CM and Agile professionals each think about CM practices in their field.

4.4.1   Value Ranking of CM Practices by CM Professionals

At first glance, one may think that CM professionals consider all CM functions as having near equal value. However, from the results of a study conducted through CM Crossroads ("Comparing the Relative Values of CM Practices" by Mario Moreira) where CM professionals were asked to rank order from a list of CM practices, I learned that this is not the case. CM professionals tend to find themselves in a situation where there is a lot of work to do and often a lack of resources, forcing them to prioritize their work based on their own perceived value of the practice, those of the teams they support, and the organizations they are in. Below is the result of this study generating the rank order (lowest ranking equates to highest value) of which practices CM professionals find of greater value:

From survey responses, change control (3.09 mean) and version control (3.35 mean) practices are perceived to be of the highest added value to the work CM professionals provide. Since one of the core functions of CM is control, it may be no surprise that these two top the list.

Table 4-1 Value ranking of CM practices by CM professionals.

CM Practice	Mean Ranking
Change control (most value)	3.09
Version control	3.35
Branching/Merging	3.83
CM planning	4.87
Build management	5.11
Problem management	5.46
Release engineering	5.82
CM Reporting	6.57
CM auditing (least value)	6.58

The third in order is the Branching/Merging (3.83 mean) practice. Since the Branching/Merging practice is closely aligned with version control, this may account for the closeness in ranking. The branching and merging practice may also have more importance due to the distributed development that is occurring in many organizations and the need to allow teams to work independently from each other. The next two that are closely grouped are CM Planning (4.87 mean) practice and build management (5.11 mean). Auditing and Reporting bring up the rear in perceived value by CM professionals. It is not surprising that CM Audit is considered the least value-added practice. The majority of CM professionals are CM tool administrators and/or build and release engineers, who are highly technology focused, while CM Audit tends to be a fairly process-focused activity. While I do not consider this conclusive data, it is certainly data to "chew on."

4.4.2 Value Rating of CM Practices by Agile Professionals

It is important to get direct input from Agile professionals on the value of CM practices. In a study conducted in the *Agile Journal* in 2009 ("Importance of CM Practices to Agile Professionals" by Mario Moreira), Agile professionals were asked to score (from 1 to 10, with 10 being the highest value) what they perceived to be the value of CM practices. The following are the results which include the average score of perceived value and the percentage with a 9 or 10 score (receiving the highest value):

Table 4-2   Value ranking of CM practices by Agile professionals.

CM Practice	Average Score	Percentage of 9 & 10 Scores
Build management (most value)	9.21	72%
Version control	9.13	80%
Branching and Merging	8.33	60%
Change control	7.92	48%
Release engineering	7.54	28%
CM planning	7.50	40%
Problem management	7.42	44%
CM audit	6.42	20%
CM Reporting (least value)	6.00	20%

It is not surprising that build management had the highest average score overall since continuous integration and build is a highly valued practice in Agile. Version control is seen as highly valued with 80% of the Agile professionals scoring either a 9 or a 10. Branching and Merging is next and considering that a big part of continuous integration assumes merging, then this high score is not surprising. Most interesting is that the CM practice with the fourth highest score is change control. In the survey, there was a short description of change control that said "(managing changes to baseline)". With this additional piece of insight, it may not be surprising that Agile professionals find change control of relatively high value, since they know the value of managing the integrity of baselines.

Not surprisingly, CM reporting and auditing are perceived as of least value. Agile tends to find reporting beyond the basic burn-down charts of little value and believes that auditing is just an extra step that is unnecessary when the team works continuously and closely together. While I do not consider this conclusive data, it is certainly data to "chew on."

4.4.2.1   Agile Perspective of CM Tools in General

It may be interesting to discuss the importance of CM tools for Agile teams. The Agile Manifesto has four values (the details of which can be found in the Agile Primer section). One value says "People and interactions over processes and tools". What this means is that the people and their interactions should drive the appropriate level of processes and tools and that a tool or process should not drive how people work and interactions occur.

While most Agile professionals do not let CM tools drive their interactions, they do understand the value of CM tools. With that in mind, A study was contacted in both the *Agile Journal* and on "LinkedIn" by

Mario Moreira, where Agile professionals were asked the following question: How important are CM tools for Agile projects? Five categories were provided as choices: Extremely Important; Very Important; Somewhat Important; Not Very Important; and Not Important At All.

With over 200 responses, the results from this study clearly indicate that CM tools are considered important for Agile teams. When combining the number of respondents who answered either "Extremely Important" or "Very Important", the result was a dramatic 94%. This is quite an amazing number. Parsed out, this includes 75% of the respondents answering "Extremely Important" and 19% answering "Very Important". I wonder if there are any other tools where 75% of Agile professionals would regard as being extremely important to their work. While I do not consider this conclusive data, it is certainly data to "chew on." The following figure illustrates the spread of answers across all five categories.

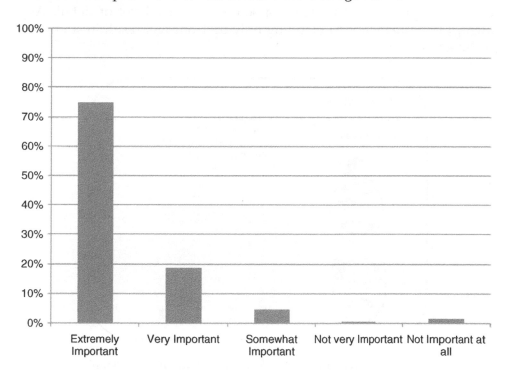

Figure 4-3 Importance of CM tools (e.g., version control) for Agile projects.

4.4.2.2 Agile Perspective of CM Planning

CM planning has value for Agile teams but not as a stand-alone CM plan document and certainly not in a big-effort up-front approach. In general, traditional planning approaches are not aligned with Agile. Most software professionals understand the need for CM on their product and are keenly aware of the control it provides, particularly when rapid change occurs. However, the challenges Agile professionals have with CM planning are two-fold.

The first challenge is to what extent we need to implement everything entailed in a typical CM plan. For most Agilists, implementing everything detailed in a CM plan will appear to be overkill. When pushed to implement it all, Agile professionals will push back. They will see some CM areas as valued added, but not all.

The second challenge is that Agile professionals reject the notion of "big effort up front" (BEUF). Traditional planning tackles planning in a BEUF manner, which is deemed to be an anti-pattern in Agile as this may lead to creating the wrong solution because you or the customer may not know enough up front to define a solution in any level of detail. Any attempt to implement CM planning fully up front will result in strenuous pushback.

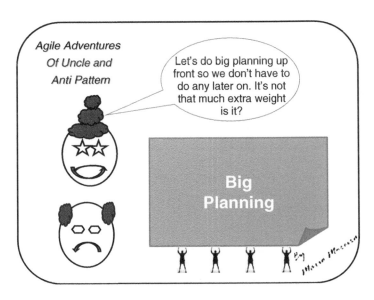

Figure 4-4   The Agile Adventures of Uncle and Anti Pattern – Big Planning.

So the question is, how could CM planning be established in a more incremental way? Agile professionals perceive value in many of the components within the CM plan and maybe a more iterative approach to CM planning work may be more acceptable. Possible solutions are presented in chapter 7 – "Adapting CM Practices for Agile."

4.4.2.3 Agile Perspective for Version Control

Version control technology is typically seen as very high value by teams following Agile methods in order to manage the frequent changes that occur within each iteration. As previously indicated in this chapter, version control was scored as one of the highest value CM practices by Agile professionals.

The check-out/check-in procedure has value as it relates to understanding how to best use the version control tool, but not as a stand-alone procedure document. The team certainly wants to learn how to check-out/check-in code and other associated features. A procedure may be best placed in a brief training guide used to train folks on this process. This combines the procedure with training. In addition, it's best to investigate if the tool comes with help test or built in training.

4.4.2.4 Agile Perspective for Build Management

As previously indicated in this chapter, build management is seen as high value by teams following Agile methods and very high value when continuous build is involved. This allows for the continuous build and integration of development and promotes sharing of the latest changes amongst the team.

While more frequent builds gained recognition in the recent past, with the advent of the Agile methods, frequent builds became a standard pattern. This was not by accident but instead by design. There was a realization that a continuous integration and build process provides quicker views into integration and build problems and quicker turnaround in getting the problems resolved.

In general, most Agile professionals see continuous build as the only way to build. It is a cultural leap that may seem counterintuitive to some. While it may appear that continuous build may be continuously disruptive, Agile professionals find that continuous integration and build output provides the team with valuable information on the health of the product that well justifies the effort of resolving the very small integration and build problems.

A build procedure has value but not as a stand-alone procedure document. This may be best placed in a brief training guide used to train folks to ensure they know details of the build scripts and commands. And finally, Agile professionals expect to see build technology in use that automates the process. This reduces the time programmers need to focus on build activities so that they can focus instead on their coding work. For more details, see chapter 7.

4.4.2.5   Agile Perspective of Change Control

Change control procedure has little value in Agile – at least as change control is traditional perceived. Change control is not needed per se because in most Agile methods, once a set of stories, requirements, or changes are decided for an iteration, that set of changes are effectively set in stone for that iteration. Keep in mind that an iteration is typically only 1 to 4 weeks so the need for change is rarely needed since the team knows that the next iteration is coming very soon and that during iteration planning the change can be introduced. In general, the notion of change control becomes much less formal and is transformed into the iteration planning activity at the beginning of each iteration.

4.4.2.6   Agile Perspective of Problem Management

Problem management technology (defect tracking, etc) has value in Agile. Since Agile methods motivate the development and coding practices as early as the first iteration, defects will be found much earlier in the process than in the latter phases of the traditional project lifecycle. This implies a strong need to have a tool by which defects can be captured and a process to track them to closure. If there is not yet a problem management tool available for the new product line, then having a manual process or implementing a tool will be needed almost immediately.

Problem management procedure has value but not as a stand-alone procedure document. The team certainly wants to learn about the defect tracking system and how to open and manage defects, particularly since some defects will become part of the work for iterations. This may be best placed in a brief training guide used to train folks on this process to ensure they know details of the build scripts and commands.

4.4.2.7   Agile Perspective of CM Audit

Audit procedure has little perceived value by teams following Agile and few will have a desire to establish a stand-alone procedure document. In fact in many organizations that do not have formal CM, few audit processes exist. Organizations that do require baseline audits and other audit activities will need to identify ways to streamline this activity so that if there is an organizational requirement for audits, this need is met without impacting the progress of the product team following Agile. If there is an audit team, then they can audit the baselines, comparing them with the master backlogs for baseline verification. If audit must occur, the more automated the process the better.

Keep in mind that there are Agile practices, like pair programming, refactoring, retrospective, and the continuous validation, that constantly focus on quality. These practices provide the team with a deep knowledge of the direction of the code baseline and the contents within. Of course, they are not the same as an audit, but some adaptation may be worked out. Possible alternatives are presented in chapter 7.

4.4.2.8   Agile Perspective of CM Reporting

CM Reporting (a.k.a., Status Accounting) procedure has little perceived value by teams following Agile. In Agile, reporting is typically minimized to the burndown charts to indicate progress. Beyond this, additional reports are seen as bureaucratic. If there are already common CM reports expected from the projects, then there will need to be a discussion on how to best retrieve similar reports or how to minimize the need for additional reporting. Automating this process is recommended. Often reporting is driven by organization or industry standards depending on what is needed. However, CM reports and metrics that highlight waste and help the team reduce waste may be seen as advantageous and value-added.

4.4.2.9   Agile Perspective of Release Engineering

Release technology has value in Agile. Release tools provide both migration and installation functions that are readily needed when iterations are short and migrations and installations may be continuously occurring from development to test environments. Release technologies can also help in the automation of migrating code.

Release procedure has value but not as a stand-alone procedure document. The team certainly wants to understand the migration and release process as it relates to their work. This may be best placed in a brief training guide used to train folks on this process to ensure they know details of the migration and installation commands.

Approaching Infrastructure for Agile

The primary focus of Agile methods is in building product functionality. Only some Agile methods focus on how to establish the infrastructure the team needs and most with very few details. Building out the architecture and infrastructure are critical to the success of product development. For a team using Agile, it can be challenging to get infrastructure set up, especially as there are instant demands on it because the team almost immediately begins actual development. This chapter is geared toward infrastructure and operations personnel that support Agile teams and will provide several modern options on getting infrastructure set up for new product teams following Agile. Also, if you are moving from a traditional method to an Agile method, this chapter will provide guidance on adapting the current infrastructure to better support Agile.

I have seen many Agile projects, particularly those focused on brand-new product lines, struggle with getting their infrastructure up and running. Much of the reason for this is that the time and effort needed to get infrastructure established far exceeds the time it takes to start development using an Agile method, effectively the first iteration. Typically the approach used to establish infrastructure is ad hoc and often not always aligned with the needs of the product. Therefore, a task must be identified to establish infrastructure. The question is, how to best approach the establishment of infrastructure for a project using Agile methods? We do not want to build excessive infrastructure that may constrain us in the future, yet we want to establish enough to keep us stable and productive.

Infrastructure refers to the technical structures such as environments, tools, and the processes that are used to support the product. Examples of infrastructure-related components include servers, network, development, requirements, Configuration Management (CM), build, defect tracking, and test tools used within the product development context. When following a traditional methodology, infrastructure for a new product typically gets defined and established within an architecture and infrastructure phase of the first release. The challenge is to find how to establish infrastructure for a project following Agile methods when you must shift from a phased approach to an iterative approach, when there is an almost immediate demand for infrastructure, and when the infrastructure personnel work in a hierarchical organization.

5.1   Guiding Principles for Approaching Infrastructure

Let us start with some guiding principles that will help frame an approach better suited to implementing infrastructure for Agile teams.

- Applying Agile implies that we move away from big effort up front (BEUF) for establishing the infrastructure and instead evolve it over time, so that it is not an overwhelming effort for the first project and ensures that the infrastructure is closer to our needs as the project team uncovers them over time.

- The establishment of the infrastructure has dependencies on architecture. Architecture helps define the technology stack that forms the building blocks for infrastructure.

- The infrastructure should be constructed to suit Agile, moving away from phases and hierarchical processes and services, where typically much ceremony and permissions are required, and instead moving toward a more continuous and "heterarchical" world; (the opposite of "hierarchcal", where the world is flat and people are empowered at the lowest possible level) where knowledge and function and the constant building of these are the mode.

- The project team using Agile methods must continue their development work to deliver functionality and business value per Agile principles as the infrastructure gets incrementally built.

- There are more ways to establish infrastructure then simply trying to build it ourselves. While physically owning and establishing infrastructure allows for more control over the infrastructure, consideration should be given to "renting" infrastructure in the clouds (a.k.a., the Internet). There are advantages to each approach, owning or renting infrastructure, and a comparison may be in order.

5.2   Considerations for Approaching Infrastructure

What are some areas to consider when establishing an infrastructure that supports Agile while not obstructing the progress of the Agile team that must deliver value? They include the following.

5.2.1   Iteration 0

While it is important to focus on the task at hand, it is also important to understand the context of your working situation. The same is true when you are developing a piece of code. To build that code module, it is important to have an understanding of the other code modules and how they all work together. Having a high-level understanding of the product and its objectives helps the team understand the direction they are going even if they have to look at the horizon every now and then.

In order to get an idea of the context of infrastructure, it is important to envision the infrastructure needs of the new product, knowing that things are subject to change. Within an Agile framework, this may be best served by implementing an iteration 0 approach that focuses on a high-level infrastructure model. The goal of infrastructure envisioning is to identify the initial scope of the infrastructure, assess feasibility of technologies, and establish a reasonable go-forward direction. From here, it is important to understand that while we have a reasonable go-forward direction, we will continue to revisit the direction and adapt as appropriate.

An iteration 0 provides the glimpse of the horizon without getting bogged down in the details. When a product is brand new without any architecture, requirements, design, and infrastructure, then there needs to be a place to have high-level discussions of these areas so that we have a general idea of the direction we are heading and the feasibility of the work.

5.2.2   Agile Team as Customer of Infrastructure

Another consideration is understanding who the customer is and being aware of the customer stream to know where value comes from. This includes two different groups who need to work together to adapt the infrastructure to the Agile method being used. The first group is the project team who is using Agile to deliver working software for the end-user (the ultimate customer who receives the business value). The second group is the infrastructure team who improve the infrastructure. Interestingly, the Agile project team becomes the customer for the infrastructure team, just as the end-users are the customers for the Agile project team. Just like the standard practice where it is extremely beneficial for the customer to be part of the project team for continuous feedback, the same holds true where a member of the project team should be on the infrastructure team. This is important to understand because the project team is the group that must assess the value of the changes so that the infrastructure team knows which changes are perceived to be most valuable and which to work on. The customer stream (the string of provider-to-customer relationships until we get to the end-user) in the figure below illustrates these relationships.

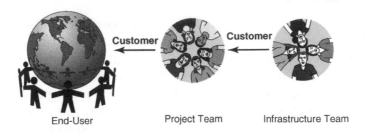

Figure 5-1   Customer stream.

5.2.3   Architecture Envisioning

Within some Agile frameworks, there are models that describe an iteration 0 or inception phase where there is time spent imagining what the product framework looks like by investigating high-level requirements, design, and architecture. These three engineering fields can help provide content to the infrastructure framework, but none more so than architecture. Architecture helps provide construction guidance for the infrastructure. This is particularly true since infrastructure has become more complex due to integrations amongst tools, connectivity across systems and domains, and standards being applied across environments.

Leveraging the Agile Model Driven Development (AMDD) framework established by Scott Ambler can help drive the evolutionary establishment of architecture, starting with envisioning the architecture. AMDD focuses on establishing models (i.e. architecture) before writing source code. However, the key is that a "just barely good enough" model is needed to move the development effort forward and not an extensive and detailed model. Over time the architecture and design models will evolve in a way that more closely aligns with the actual needs of the product as they become more clearly known. Within the AMDD framework, one of the outcomes of architecture is a technology stack. One representation of this stack is the physical model that articulates the layers within the infrastructure, such as the platform, programming languages, tools, and more. This becomes input to infrastructure envisioning. However, the local challenge with architecture is that there are many architecture models and viewpoints that are used so it is important to understand the model and viewpoints within the company where you work.

Some infrastructure layers are mandatory (e.g. server and desktops). For the sake of this illustration, I will call this the platform layer. Some layers need to be defined early (e.g., database, programming, reusable components) since they may be utilized early in the project when using Agile. I will call this the development layer. Some layers support individuals and interactions in their day-to-day work (e.g., collaboration, CM, test, etc.). I will call this the support layer. For the sake of this section, I am keeping the layers simple. As a point of reference, I have crafted this figure based on my experience to illustrate a simplified architecture framework, while highlighting the infrastructure stack. Again, the various layers within an infrastructure stack may be different within your company so it is important to identify the infrastructure view within your organization.

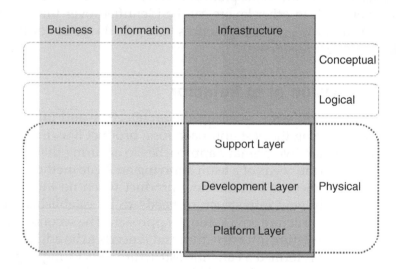

Figure 5-2   Simplified architecture framework highlighting the infrastructure stack.

In some cases, the infrastructure stack is made up of interdependent legacy systems and if there is a corporate IT roadmap listing standard tools, this may constrain the choices for envisioning the infrastructure for the new product. However, this is not always a bad thing. If this new product must integrate with legacy products, then this helps assure easier integration. For example, if the existing legacy architecture and infrastructure applies the .Net framework, then introducing a Java Interface Layer (or JIL) framework may add extra work, including bringing new skills into the company. Typically legacy constraints occur at the platform and development layers.

It is beneficial not to let predefined tools, components, or environments constrain the interactions of people, but instead to allow the way the team optimally interacts to be a means to help drive the better infrastructure choices as far as it is feasible. When the Agile Manifesto says "Individuals and interactions over processes and tools," this is an example of not allowing the tool to drive or constrain the interaction. A suggested approach is when you start projects using Agile, to see how individuals and interactions start to gel into working processes, then use this information to help identify tools that may be suited for the work (as appropriate). This is particularly true in the tools found in the support layer.

The end product in the short infrastructure envisioning exercise should include a high-level infrastructure stack list of technologies within their respective layers as they relate to the architecture framework. While you should not expect to fill in all layers, there are some layers you cannot ignore. An example of this is the platform layer, where servers and desktop live. However, tools in other layers can be identified over time after it is clear what Agile processes and practices best suit the needs of the team. Then a tool may be considered.

5.2.4   To Envision or to Refactor

As you move forward with assessing the architecture and infrastructure needs and determining the best approach for a product line, first consider what exists. There are two primary approaches to ensuring that the infrastructure is tuned to the needs of a team applying an Agile method. The first approach is when there is a brand new product when no infrastructure exists and a wholly new infrastructure needs to be established. This is termed as an "infrastructure envisioning" approach. The second approach is when there is an existing infrastructure and it needs to be adjusted for an Agile method. This is termed as an "infrastructure refactoring" approach. Which infrastructure approach should be considered will depend on when the team is adopting the Agile method. Let us explore the two approaches in more detail.

5.3   Infrastructure Envisioning

Much like architecture envisioning, "infrastructure envisioning" is a term used to describe imagining infrastructure that does not yet exist and applying a pragmatic approach in getting there. Infrastructure envisioning takes this a step further, in that we spend a short cycle to flesh out the vision by understanding our high-level infrastructure needs. Output from establishing the architecture in whole or in part is input to this effort. Infrastructure envisioning relies on a short iteration (iteration 0) that will allow us to have insight into the infrastructure needs, focusing on platform and development layer components and direction. From there infrastructure envisioning applies an incremental approach to the continuous establishment of an effective infrastructure.

Pit Stop

"Infrastructure envisioning" is an approach coined by Mario Moreira that applies an iteration 0 to establish a vision of the high-level infrastructure, and then applies iterations to build it out over time. This may be of benefit for Agile teams on new product development efforts.

As we will look at infrastructure envisioning more closely, we will utilize the guiding principles for approaching infrastructure to ensure we are moving in a more Agile manner.

5.3.1 Initiating an Iteration 0 at the Beginning

It is beneficial to consider using an iteration 0 cycle at the very beginning of the effort to review any architecture or high-level requirements input that may be available and set a strategy on how to move forward. Because you are setting up an infrastructure from scratch and the many infrastructure components therein (CM, testing, development, architecture, database, release engineering environments, and other engineering spaces) are significant, it is worth initiating an iteration 0. Within this 1- or 3-week cycle, the goal is to better understand the infrastructure needs and what approach may be taken. Some areas to focus on are rounding out the technology stack needs, considering the infrastructure approaches (renting in the clouds, owning on premises – more on this later in this chapter), identifying dependencies, and then determining the work that needs to be done to get infrastructure up and running.

5.3.2 Thinking Iterations

It is important for infrastructure to emerge based on the needs of the product team. Applying an iterative and incremental model with continuous adjustments (as applicable) helps lead us in this direction. It allows us to limit "infrastructure debt". Borrowed from the concepts of design debt and technical debt by James Shore, infrastructure debt refers to building beyond our need such that when functionality evolves, any incorrect or extra infrastructure becomes a constraint or waste to the functionality the customer wants and can eventually impact progress. Identifying dependencies to help in the prioritization process of what to tackle and allowing the needs to drive the infrastructure while minimizing the constraints allows us to apply a more evolutionary approach. This is also the time to consider separating the work into smaller, more consumable chunks.

Pit Stop

"Infrastructure debt" refers to building infrastructure beyond the need such that when the functionality evolves, any incorrect or extra infrastructure becomes a constraint or waste.

What are some strategies that can help with establishing infrastructure in an iterative and incremental manner? Within a project timeframe, you may not be in a position to build a fully functional and automated infrastructure. Instead, focus on the areas that reduce risk and are perceived to be of high value (priority) to the project team using Agile (the customer of the infrastructure). After each infrastructure piece is delivered and effectively implemented, acquire feedback on the infrastructure functionality as input for adjustment and prioritization for the next iteration.

When following an iterative approach, it is important to manage risk because it provides lead time into potential problems that can slow velocity. By identifying and assessing infrastructure-related risks, the more serious risks can be appropriately mitigated. This ensures we do not waste time up front focusing on lesser risks and also do not waste time later on resolving a problem that could have been prevented if a mitigation of the greater risk had occurred.

Prioritization of infrastructure needs allows the project team using Agile and those involved in establishing the infrastructure a means of knowing how much value certain components and tools are to the infrastructure and then implementing them in a just-in-time (JIT) approach. As an example, a server and desktops typically are high priority needs without which work cannot get done, so they should be available when the project team is ready in the first iteration. However, prioritization of other tools in the support layer may be a lower priority until such time as the effort to implement them is outweighed by the need to have them in place.

Another example of this is CM tools. Sometimes on new projects, people avoid or use a very simple CM tool. However as code starts to change frequently and many people work with the same code modules, there is a potential to start deleting other people's changes. In this case, the effort to recreate lost changes is considered waste and greatly impacts velocity. At this time in the project, implementing a competent CM tool may become a high priority.

By employing prioritization and JIT, we can ensure we do not build out too much infrastructure too soon, therefore limiting our infrastructure debt. Otherwise an "inventory of infrastructure" becomes shelf-ware until such time that it is needed. In addition, there may be changes that occur to the direction of the project that make the shelf-ware infrastructure of less value or constrain future infrastructure direction.

5.3.3 Tasks in Product Backlog or Infrastructure Backlog

When implementing infrastructure, two different groups need to work together to establish the infrastructure for the Agile method being used. As previously mentioned, the first group is the project team using Agile to deliver working software for the end-user (the ultimate customer receiving the business value). The second group is the infrastructure team who establish the infrastructure. The project team is the group that must assess the value of the changes so that the infrastructure team knows which infrastructure changes are perceived to be of most value and which to work on. There are two approaches in managing the work involved in infrastructure envisioning.

Pit Stop

The task of forming an infrastructure team can be very challenging if the organization is not used to Agile and the iterative approach it follows. The services provided by infrastructure support functions typically align with a more phased or task driven approach.

The first approach upon the conclusion of an iteration 0 is to include the infrastructure work as stories and/or tasks within the Agile team backlog and prioritize the work as you would stories for functionality. The work that is prioritized which focuses on infrastructure then gets assigned to the infrastructure professionals that support Agile. Upon the conclusion of the iteration, it is reviewed with the Agile team as the customer of the changes. This is a good approach in that it keeps all of the work in one backlog, but often Agile teams prefer to only include stories that focus on building functionality into their iteration backlog. However, if the effort is to establish a full infrastructure, it may involve including too many infrastructure stories or tasks into the Agile team backlog.

The second approach is to apply an iteration 0 that provides a go-forward strategy for infrastructure. Then to work with the infrastructure group that supports the Agile team and form an infrastructure sub-team to drive the work in an iterative manner from a separate infrastructure backlog. This sub-team would include appropriate members from infrastructure and a member or two from the Agile team who act as the customer, much like Agile requires the customer to be available when building functionality.

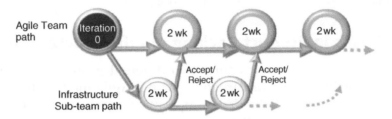

Figure 5-3   Infrastructure envisioning starting an iteration 0 and separate work path.

Then both the Agile product team to build functionality and the infrastructure sub-team to improve infrastructure will work in parallel. The infrastructure sub-team will utilize regular end-of-infrastructure iteration reviews with the product team to validate readiness of the changes. At some point, the infrastructure work will diminish and any remaining work can be moved to the Agile team path. The figure above illustrates this scenario.

5.3.4   Reflections on Infrastructure Envisioning

The benefit of infrastructure envisioning is that in a short timeframe, it provides a high-level framework of the infrastructure for the new product that is aligned with both the high-level requirements and architecture. The benefit of an incremental approach is that it utilizes the important aspects of minimizing risk and considers value for prioritization, while at the same time spreading out the effort of establishing an infrastructure over time based on the JIT needs of the project team.

5.4   Infrastructure Refactoring

The previous section focuses on the brand new or newer product lines where new infrastructure is needed. With Agile gaining acceptance in the legacy product space, teams are moving away from their company's traditional (a.k.a., waterfall or phase-based) methods and moving toward Agile methods. In these cases, the product team that begins to use Agile methods is typically inheriting an existing infrastructure that was constructed for a traditional approach.

At first glance, this may not appear to be a major issue, but very soon the team learns that the infrastructure is not well suited for Agile and changes must be made. For example, the build process is slow and occurs only on a weekly basis, producing numerous broken builds. The project team realizes they need either continuous builds or at least nightly builds to minimize the merging effort and reduce the rate of broken builds. Sometimes the infrastructure is specifically designed to a certain way of doing things to reinforce the best practices yet makes it challenging for people to move to a new way of doing something. Ultimately, the infrastructure should be a reflection of the method being used.

As there is a focus to change areas to better align the infrastructure and associated processes to Agile, the project team must continue their development work to deliver functionality and business value per Agile principles. How can this team solve the problem whereby they must continue to deliver value, but must also make changes to their infrastructure to reduce problems and gain velocity? One suggestion is to utilize a newly coined termed I call "infrastructure refactoring."

As many folks know, within Agile there is the practice called refactoring. As Martin Fowler describes it, "Refactoring is a disciplined technique for restructuring an existing body of code, altering its internal structure without changing its external behavior. Its heart is a series of small behavior-preserving transformations. Each transformation (called a 'refactoring') does little, but a sequence of transformations can produce a significant restructuring. Since each refactoring is small, it's less likely to go wrong. The system is also kept fully working after each small refactoring, reducing the chances that a system can get seriously broken during the restructuring."

Similarly, when confronted with a stodgy infrastructure for an existing product line which has not been aligned for Agile, infrastructure refactoring can provide such advantages. Infrastructure refactoring initiates a "restructuring of the existing infrastructure." It should occur in a series of small changes to preserve the overall integrity of the infrastructure and the existing release processes for the product line. When an infrastructure of an existing product is changed, the change must ensure that the product team can continue its development without any significant downtime. The infrastructure must be kept working after each small refactoring, reducing the chances that an infrastructure can get broken during the restructuring and, *ergo*, injure the ability to support the existing streams of development for the product.

Pit Stop

"Infrastructure refactoring" is an approach coined by Mario Moreira that applies a series of small changes to the infrastructure of a product team in an incremental manner to preserve the integrity of the infrastructure and ensure that the product team observes no downtime.

The goal of infrastructure refactoring is to take the existing infrastructure that may be more complex and support a phased approach, and instead streamline and simplify it so that in supports a more iterative and Agile approach. The product owner should be the primary driver of this work but may assign a more technical representative from the Agile team to focus on the strategies and the work ahead. As we look at infrastructure refactoring more closely, we will utilize the guiding principles and considerations for approaching infrastructure to ensure we are moving in a more Agile manner.

5.4.1 Iteration Planning or Iteration 0

Depending on the size of the refactoring that needs to occur, there are two possible paths in approaching the work. If the infrastructure refactoring changes are smaller in nature, then it may be appropriate to identify and prioritize the work in an iteration planning session within the team backlog. If the potential number of infrastructure changes that are involved (requirements, CM, testing, development, architecture, database, release management, and other engineering spaces) are significant, it is worth initiating an iteration 0. Within this 1 or 2 week cycle, the goal is to better understand the number of changes and place them into a backlog. Then prioritize the changes, assess the impact of the changes, identify the dependencies of the changes on other areas, and then determine the work that needs to be done to get the changes to occur. The dependency identification will help in the prioritization process of what to tackle first, second, and so on. This is also the time to consider breaking up the work into smaller consumable chunks. This helps establish an expectation of how much can be accomplished in each refactoring task.

5.4.2 Thinking in Iterations

Since refactoring implies a small series of changes, it is beneficial to think of changes in relation to iterations. Therefore another strategy is to use an

Agile approach of short iterations (e.g., 1 or 2 weeks), first having identified and assessed a small enough chunk of work that can be managed within this timeframe. Toward the end of the iteration, the team validates the change per a standard Agile iteration. At the end of the iteration, the Agile team and product owner decides if the infrastructure change is acceptable and is ready to go live and start being used by the team. If not the change can be bundled with the deliverables of the next iteration(s) and then released together when acceptance occurs.

5.4.3 Tasks in Product Backlog or Infrastructure Backlog

There are two approaches in managing the work involved in infrastructure refactoring. The first approach is to include the infrastructure work as stories and/or tasks within the Agile team backlog and prioritize the work as you would stories for functionality. The work that is prioritized and focused on infrastructure then gets assigned to the infrastructure professionals that support the Agile. Upon the conclusion of the iteration, it is reviewed with the Agile team as the customer of the changes. This is a good approach in that it keeps all of the work in one backlog, but often Agile teams prefer to only include stories that focus on building functionality into their team backlog. Also, it is rare for infrastructure personnel to commit full time to an Agile team as they are instead part of an infrastructure team. As previously discussed, Agile works best when team members are committed to the team, to ensure the focus remains on the work identified and prioritized by the team, and not part of an infrastructure team that may be juggling a number infrastructure requests.

Pit Stop

There is often a challenge in getting members of the infrastructure team to be fully dedicated since infrastructure work tends to be multitasking in nature. Per Agile principles, the more dedicated the infrastructure resources, the better the ability to utilize the iterative approach.

The second approach is to inject an iteration 0 that is separate from the Agile team work to get a better understanding of the go-forward strategy for infrastructure. Then the infrastructure group that supports the

Agile team forms a sub-team and drives the work in an iterative manner from a separate backlog. This sub-team would include members from infrastructure and a member or two from the Agile team who act as the customer, much like Agile requires the customer to be available when building functionality.

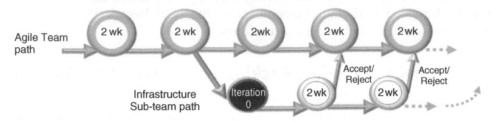

Figure 5-4   Infrastructure refactoring injecting an iteration 0 and separate work paths.

In this scenario, the Agile team may slow progress for an iteration and instead participate in the iteration 0, which simply focuses on an infrastructure change strategy and identifies the initial changes. During iteration 0, the Agile team discusses the various areas of infrastructure that are constraining productivity with the infrastructure personnel. Then the Agile team iterates to build functionality and, in parallel, the infrastructure sub-team iterates to improve infrastructure. The infrastructure sub-team will utilize regular end-of-infrastructure iteration reviews with the product team to validate readiness of the changes. At some point, the infrastructure work will diminish and any remaining work can be moved to the Agile team path.

5.4.4   Reflections on Infrastructure Refactoring

When you find yourself in a position where you inherit an existing infrastructure and find that it is not well suited for Agile processes, consider the infrastructure refactoring approach. Introducing strategies like an iteration 0, thinking in iterations, and running the infrastructure work in parallel with the project work may help you get to an infrastructure that is much more closely aligned with the team's needs. The infrastructure refactoring approach helps you focus on a series of small changes in order to preserve the overall integrity of the infrastructure and existing release processes. This reduces the risk of breaking the infrastructure, therefore allowing those working in the current development stream, the maintenance stream, and the bug fix stream to continue to be productive, deploy changes to production, and continue to deliver continuous value.

5.5 Owning on Premises or Renting in the Clouds

In the context of beginning new product development using Agile, there are instant demands on the infrastructure. Given that when applying Agile, you start coding almost immediately, how do you get the infrastructure set up quickly? Even when you implement an iteration 0, it still does not leave you with much time to establish an adequate infrastructure. When you are in an established company, it may seem easy to set up infrastructure when it appears plentiful. However, even in these scenarios company resources may be tight, making it challenging to set up infrastructure for a new product team. When you are small company and have little to no funds, then what are your options? By moving the development action to the beginning as Agile does, you squeeze the time it takes to get your infrastructure set up.

Unlike the past where organizations and product lines spent considerable time and large amounts of capital to establish local infrastructure, the future presents us with other options. They include (but are not limited to) renting everything in the clouds (on the Internet), owning the server and renting space in the clouds (hosting service provider), and owning everything locally and on premises (within your company).

All of these options come with a set of advantages and disadvantages. While there are many factors in determining the best choice for an organization, there are two driving factors. The first is how much budget exists for the product team. This includes the ability to purchase the infrastructure that is needed, including servers, software, data center space, and staff. The second factor is how much control a product team or organization wants to have over their infrastructure. This includes how much perceived sensitivity there is to the product under development and data therein, and how much direct control is desired over access to the infrastructure. Based on your budget and ability to buy infrastructure and the control level you want, it can help you determine a more suitable approach.

With the advent of Agile methods, there is now a third driving factor that may drive the choice. I have seen many Agile projects, particularly those focused on brand-new product lines, struggle with getting their infrastructure up and running. Much of the reason is that the time and effort that is needed to get infrastructure established far exceeds the time it takes to start development in the first iteration. With new cloud infrastructure and co-location options, the "establish product infrastructure" game has been changed. The following figure illustrates a model for considering your choices based on the level of control desired and budget in place.

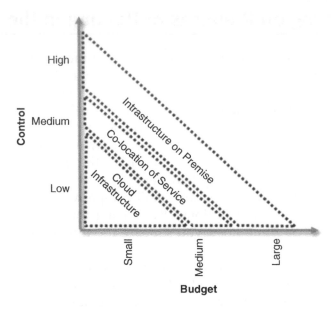

Figure 5-5   Infrastructure approaches based on budget and control.

So, the question is, should you physically own infrastructure, rent space and own servers, or rent infrastructure in the clouds? It is important to better understand each option and assess your circumstances and needs before formally deciding on an approach.

5.5.1   Renting in the Clouds

Renting or leasing from a cloud infrastructure is a more recent concept and option that some organizations are utilizing where the infrastructure (servers, software, etc.) is effectively in the Internet cloud. This service is sometimes known as cloud computing but has a variety of other names, each with slightly different focuses and approaches, including software as a service (SaaS) sometimes known as the application service provider (ASP) model, platform as a service (PaaS), and application infrastructure provider (AIP). You have a hosting service provider that may provide hardware, tools, software, network, etc. that is available to subscribers. It follows a pay-per-use approach that may be seen as utility computing, since you are charged for the portion you are using.

The advantage of renting the cloud infrastructure is that it helps minimize capital expenses and lower up-front costs, since you do not have to buy hardware, software, and other components. Effectively the infrastructure (e.g., servers, software, etc.) becomes more of an operating cost instead of a capital expenditure. Another advantage of this approach is that you do not have to establish and manage the infrastructure. This includes not having to hire and manage IT staff for maintenance and upgrade work. However, with this being said, it is important to have people on your staff that know how portable the data is that is being hosted and how easy (or challenging) it is to get it off the cloud should the service provider go out of business.

This infrastructure will include the same type of infrastructure and network components that a locally owned infrastructure would include and in some cases have servers that have some of the database and tools already installed. This approach can be particularly advantageous when you are a start-up organization that has not yet released a product or are early in the product business. It may not be right for mission-critical applications and in a situation where data is highly confidential. In general, the size and newness of company and product line is a factor where renting in the clouds can be advantageous.

A distinct advantage for those who are Agile proponents is that the cloud infrastructure provider approach enables users to only use what they need, something that is directly in line with Agile. This "use what you need" approach minimizes infrastructure debt and allows the product team to adjust and scale to their need in a just-in-time manner.

The biggest disadvantage is that there may be security, control, and privacy concerns. Remember, when renting space in the clouds via a provider service, all of your product code, data, and documents will effectively be sitting on someone else's systems (i.e., the service or platform provider). It is important to ensure there is security-related software, network, and protocol that support this service from authentication to access control. Interestingly enough because cloud service providers know this is a concern for many, security measures are often well managed in these environments. Finally, it is important to gauge the profitability of the cloud infrastructure service provider you select. If the service provider goes out of business, it may be difficult to get your data exported and hosted by another provider. Understand how portable your data will be to another platform and ensure you have backups readily available in another location.

Other disadvantages with this approach are that the ability to customize the infrastructure and software therein is reduced, that many of the integration issues may remain if there is a high degree of complexity in the working environments, and that there is less control over the skill level of the support staff, meaning sometimes they will be experienced and quick troubleshooters and other times they may not.

When using this approach, it is important to ensure that the cloud infrastructure provider being used has: prescribed service levels; established backup, recovery, and fail-over processes; is able to meet regulatory compliance standards; has the ability to allow you to scale up, provision, and instantiate quickly, and has other factors for support, load balancing, and performance. Another factor that should be considered before selecting a cloud infrastructure provider is their financial status, such as their cash position, spend rate, profit margins, etc.

When using either the physically owned or rented cloud approach, you should have an application architecture and network diagram established which includes the platforms, operating environments, interfaces, services, and locations (physical or cloud). The specifics of the design will help you in defining the physical infrastructure to purchase or the cloud infrastructure to rent. With owning the physical infrastructure, there needs to be more in-house expertise in establishing the architecture, infrastructure, and network design. With renting from a service provider in the cloud, in most cases the provider can help you with this and walk you through the process of your design needs.

Not all cloud infrastructure providers offer the exact same set of services. They each provide aspects of cloud infrastructure services. Consider performing a search on "cloud infrastructure" or the various incantations of the services (e.g., SaaS, ASP, PaaS, AIP, etc.) to identify current cloud service providers.

5.5.2   Owning Server and Renting Space (a.k.a., Co-location as a Service)

Co-location as a service refers to renting space in the clouds from a service provider in order to physically host your hardware. This is also slightly different from cloud infrastructure where you rent a service that provides you access to infrastructure without necessarily knowing the details behind it.

You would utilize this option because you want to have the ownership and control of the box and content therein but do not have the budget to establish a physical data center on premises, therefore minimizing expenses. This includes not having to hire and manage data center staff to support this facility.

This approach can be particularly advantageous when you are a small company or start-up organization that has a website that you rely on for revenue but you are not in a position to establish a data center on premises. Other advantages of a co-location service are that they typically provide scalability bandwidth based on your need, generator backup, and remote console access.

A distinct advantage for those who are Agile proponents in a startup or small company, is that you do not have to spend time establishing a data center, but instead focus on the development of the project. It allows you to minimize data center infrastructure debt and scale to the space needs over time.

The biggest disadvantage is that there may be security and control concerns. Any servers you own are in someone else's data center. It is important to ensure there is rigorous security access into this facility. However, because it is the primary business of this service provider, there will most likely be fairly extensive security access control. You also want to ensure the data center staff are experienced troubleshooters and quick to resolve connectivity and network performance problems. Finally, it is important to gauge the profitability of the co-location service provider you select. If this service provider goes out of business, it may be difficult to get your server out of the service provider's data center. Understand how portable the data on the server is and ensure backups are readily available from another site, especially if this server is hosting production data.

Co-location is most advantageous when the service is within your location. With this in mind, consider searching on "co-location" within your region.

5.5.3 Owning on Premises

Physically owning infrastructure is the traditional approach and is still the prevalent method of infrastructure for product teams. For many it is perceived to be the safer more, secure approach and is better suited for organizations that want to have total control of their infrastructure. Owning the infrastructure also means that you have the capital to purchase the hardware, software, databases, network, and other components needed to host product development, testing, and production.

Even when you consider physically owning infrastructure, you may have multiple sites of development. You have choices to place infrastructure at each site or share infrastructure at one site. In addition, owning your infrastructure means having the full breadth of administration, upgrades, maintenance, license management, and security that goes with supporting infrastructure. You also have to focus on performance, scalability, and integration and it implies that you hire staff to manage the infrastructure.

Owning on premises does not mean you have to set up the full infrastructure (servers, data center, etc.) each time a new product is envisioned for development. Organizations can use strategies similar to "in the clouds" options. These can include hosting a provisioning model, implementing an internal Platform as a Service (Paas), and sharing common support services (e.g., common CM or testing environments and tools). In the PaaS option, there are new choices where you can establish the platform locally.

It is wise for organizations to share space in existing data centers much like the co-location as a service option. Also, some organizations may utilize a "renting in the local cloud" option, meaning that the organization can establish infrastructure co-ops that already have many of the infrastructure needs of a product team. The reality is, most product teams have fairly similar infrastructure needs (platform, development environment, CM tools, test environments, etc.). Organizations would be wise to deploy an infrastructure service model to make it quicker and easier for new product lines to get their infrastructure established. This can be particularly advantageous to new product lines utilizing Agile methods.

5.5.4   Reflections on Premises or in the Clouds

As you consider each of these approaches, take a good look at the amount of your budget, need for control, and even the development methodology you are considering. These factors can help you better evaluate the infrastructure model that is best for your needs. While lesser in importance, there are other inputs that can be factored into your decision whether to own or rent. These include the consideration of the various development support tools that may or may not be available including, version control, test, and defect tracking. Their availability may lean you toward one model or the other.

Consider reviewing chapter 9, "Evaluating Tools Suited for Agile" for more details on how to objectively and effectively evaluate these choices. Owning or renting are considerations that can affect the tool that is selected. Ultimately, it is good to know that while there are choices that keep you on the ground (on-premise infrastructure), you can also reach for the sky (cloud infrastructure)!

Approaching the CM Implementation for Agile

There are different ways to approach a Configuration Management (CM) implementation. Most will include the core CM practices with some type of version control, build management, change control, problem management, and release engineering. If a team is starting a new product development, this may be a good set of CM practices to start with. From there, Agile teams should add those CM practices that they deem valuable. If a team is shifting to an Agile method, then there may be several CM practices already in place. The goal in this case is to adapt them to align with Agile values while still retaining CM values. This can be approached either incrementally (the recommended approach) or as a whole but not before assessing the need of the team.

Reflecting back on the previous chapter that discusses the approaches to implement infrastructure for Agile, we will consider similar approaches for CM. The first approach is CM envisioning. This is where there is a brand new product line and new product team that does not yet have a CM infrastructure (practices and tools). The second approach is CM refactoring. This is when there is an existing CM infrastructure and it needs to be incrementally adjusted for an Agile approach.

6.1   CM Envisioning

"CM envisioning" is described as visualizing CM for a new product line. In CM envisioning, we take this a step further in that we spend a short cycle (a.k.a., iteration 0) to flesh out the high-level CM needs of the product. If you already have an iteration 0 occurring for architecture and infrastructure envisioning then consider including CM envisioning. When we look across a product lifecycle, it is important to determine what CM infrastructure is needed to ensure that product development is effectively supported.

Pit Stop

CM envisioning is an approach coined by Mario Moreira that applies an iteration 0 to establish a vision of the high-level CM infrastructure and process needs, and then applies iterations to build them out over time. This may be of benefit for Agile teams on new product-development efforts. CM envisioning may be combined with the iteration 0 that focuses on architecture and infrastructure envisioning.

If you are only looking to prototype a product without formally releasing it, then having little or no CM process and technology is worth the risk. However, when a company is building a product, they typically expect it to last as many years as possible and contribute to the profitability of the company. This implies that if they can sell it, they hope to have numerous releases of the product. Immediately after the first release begins the onerous task of maintaining an existing release in the field while developing a new release of the product internally. In order to stay in business, it is critical to avoid regression of product functionality. The focus becomes establishing an effective way to manage multiple code baselines while eliminating regression in the product. Configuration Management provides that solution.

6.1.1   Strategizing for the Whole with Iteration 0

While it is important to focus on the task at hand, it is also important to understand the context of your working situation. In order to get an idea of the context for CM, it is important to envision the CM needs of the new product line while understanding that things are subject to change. Within an Agile framework, this may be best served by implementing an iteration 0 approach where you can focus on the high-level CM model. The goal of CM envisioning is to identify the initial scope of CM, assess feasibility of the various CM practices and tools, and establish a reasonable go-forward direction. From here, it is important to understand that while we have a reasonable direction, we will continue to revisit the direction and adapt as appropriate. An iteration 0 provides a glimpse of the horizon without getting bogged down in the details.

As part of the scope and context, it is beneficial to consider your options and your starting position. Do you want to own infrastructure on premises, rent it in the clouds, or share it with someone else? During iteration 0, the pros and cons of each can be discussed and considered to better understand the go-forward direction.

6.1.1.1   Owning CM Infrastructure on Premises

Physically establishing and owning CM infrastructure is the traditional approach and is still the prevalent method for product teams. For many it has been perceived to be the safer, more secure approach and is better suited for organizations that want to have total control of their CM infrastructure, *ergo* their code assets. Owning the infrastructure also means that you have the capital to purchase the hardware, software, databases, network, and other components needed to host product development, testing, and production.

Owning on premises does not mean you have to set up the full CM infrastructure up front. Instead, use an iterative approach during implementation. Also, the CM infrastructure can be established during the first release or after the first release. The best approach for your needs depends on how quickly the CM infrastructure should get set up.

The advantage of building the CM infrastructure during release 1 is that the team can take advantage of the CM tools and processes to feel confident that the rapid code changes and builds that Agile introduces are controlled. The disadvantage is that resources are applied to infrastructure tasks versus getting the product to market. This can be a critical challenge to startup companies. Then it may be best to focus effort on getting a product to market and establishing market share to avoid bankruptcy.

The advantage of building CM infrastructure after release 1 is that it allows the product team to focus on building the product. The disadvantages of this approach are that the team does not have the benefit of CM control (version and build) and lack of CM can immediately impact subsequent releases. When the second release is under way, the focus on CM becomes very critical, since some form of parallel development is needed immediately to focus on release 2 while maintaining and patching fixes to release 1. If key elements of CM are not in place, it can take more time to solve problems and get the next release out due to the increased risk of overwriting or losing existing code and bug fixes, therefore causing regression in functionality that can impact the market share of the product in the future.

6.1.1.2   Renting CM Infrastructure in the Clouds

A CM infrastructure may not be feasible for most startup companies who do not have the resources to do this work and are initially focusing on getting a product to market. Renting or leasing CM services from a cloud service provider is a more recent concept and option that some organizations are utilizing. In this instance, you have a hosting service provider that provides CM tools and infrastructure for the team.

The advantage of renting the cloud infrastructure is that it helps minimize capital expenses and lower up-front costs since you do not have to buy hardware and tools. Effectively the CM infrastructure becomes more of an operating cost instead of a capital expenditure. Another advantage of this approach is that you do not have to establish and manage the infrastructure. This includes not having to hire and manage IT staff for maintenance and upgrade work. However, with this being said, it is important to have a CM professional on your staff to help you manage code baselines, builds, and releases and to verify the integrity of the code being hosted in the clouds.

A distinct advantage for those who are Agile proponents is that the cloud infrastructure provider approach enables users to only use what they need, something that is directly in line with Agile. This "use what you need" approach minimizes infrastructure debt and allows the product team to adjust and scale to their need in a just-in-time manner.

A disadvantage with this approach is the limited ability to customize the CM infrastructure and process. However, configuration options are often provided. A perceived disadvantage is that there may be security, control, and privacy concerns. Remember, when renting space in the clouds via a provider service, all of your product code will effectively be sitting on someone else's systems. Interestingly enough because cloud service providers know this is a concern for many, security measures are often well managed in these environments. It is also important to gauge the profitability of the cloud service provider you select. If the service provider goes out of business, it may be difficult to get the code hosted by another provider. Understand how portable the code will be to another platform and ensure you have backups readily available in another location.

When using this approach, it is important to ensure that the cloud provider being used has prescribed service levels, established backup, recovery, and fail-over processes, is able to meet regulatory compliance standards (as necessary), has the ability to allow you to scale up, provision, and instantiate quickly, and other factors for support, load balancing, and performance.

6.1.1.3 Sharing through CM Co-op Environments

In general, I have seen new product development using Agile methods struggle with getting their CM infrastructure up and running in the early stages of the project. A way to partially solve this problem of getting a new product into a stable CM environment can be to establish CM infrastructure co-ops. These co-ops provide readily available infrastructure that can be quickly leveraged for use.

There are some CM tools that are storage (a.k.a., repository) platform independent meaning the storage (code, files, etc.) can be hosted on a platform that is separate and different from the platform on which the new product is being developed. These CM tools will have clients that can run on a variety of platforms while the storage servers can be on a different platform.

Having a CM co-op can literally save a product team a majority of the time is takes to set up a CM environment. Instead of dealing with what server the storage will be placed on, the installation of the CM tool on the server, and the setup of the working processes, the product team can focus on the remaining tasks of establishing a code repository on a previously set-up server and then set up the client front-end on either a centralized server or locally on workstations.

Particularly if an organization is planning to implement Agile in a big way, having a CM co-op environment can literally save the many product teams hundreds of hours each on getting CM established.

6.1.2   Implementing Incrementally

In the CM world, there is a requirement to ensure that CM principles are being followed. However it may not always be reasonable to build out all CM functions at one time for a product and in many cases only some CM functions will ever be implemented. The time and effort required would sink the project at hand. This is particularly true when you are building out the CM infrastructure on premises. Instead apply the basic "lean" principles by flowing value from demand. In this case, this would mean understanding CM well enough to prioritize the CM functionality, then deliver it incrementally to the project following Agile. Keep in mind that this approach can be beneficial for projects following traditional methods as well.

The incremental deployment approach of CM functionality focuses on spreading out CM tasks over a period of time based on the perceived value and resources available so they can be more easily accomplished and offered to the product team on a just-in-time basis. This ultimately provides a balance between funding, resources, and risk management. The goal then is to focus on introducing the perceived high-value CM functionality iteratively during release 1 and focus on the lesser-valued CM functionality at a later release. Often a company or product team does not have the means to implement full CM, so they end up implementing very little. In order to reduce project risk, introducing some elements of CM during release 1 can be a wise decision. This may be considered the just-in-time approach, which is more aligned with the Agile perspective.

6.1.3   CM in Product Backlog or CM Backlog

The effort to envision and then establish a CM infrastructure is not trivial. Nor is the number of tasks involved in this effort. Much like approaching infrastructure envisioning, you can approach work that is derived from CM envisioning in similar ways. The first approach is to include the CM work as stories and/or tasks within the product backlog and prioritize the work as you would stories for functionality. The CM tasks that are prioritized are moved to the iteration backlog and get assigned to the CM professional that supports the product team. Upon the conclusion of the iteration, the completed CM functionality is reviewed with the team as the customer of the changes. This approach is recommended when the CM professional is part of the Agile team. However, this may be challenging due to the number of CM tasks that may need to get included in each iteration backlog.

The second approach is for the CM professional or group that supports the product team to form a sub-team and drive the work in a parallel stream of tasks from a separate backlog while doing so in an iterative manner. This sub-team would include a CM professional or group and a few members from the product team who effectively act as customers, much like Agile advocates that the customer (or customer representative) be available when building and validating functionality. This approach is recommended when the CM tasks are numerous or when the CM professional is not considered part of the Agile team.

6.2   CM Refactoring

When you are on a product line that has decided to move from a more traditional method to an Agile method, revisiting of the existing CM practices may be in order. In this case, the team is inheriting an existing CM infrastructure that was constructed for a phased method. At first glance, this may not appear to be a major issue, but very soon the team learns that some of the CM practices as currently implemented are not well suited for Agile and changes must be made.

When confronted with CM infrastructure and processes that have not been aligned for Agile, CM refactoring can provide advantages. CM refactoring initiates a "restructuring of the existing infrastructure and processes." It should occur in a series of small changes to preserve the overall integrity of CM for the product line. When CM is modified, the change must allow the product team to continue its development without any significant downtime.

Pit Stop

CM refactoring is an approach coined by Mario Moreira that applies a series of small changes to CM infrastructure and process for a product team with existing CM in an incremental manner to preserve the integrity and ensure the product team observes little or no downtime.

The key to adapting CM for Agile teams is identifying where ceremony can be removed from CM, where existing CM practices can be streamlined and adapted to better fit the Agile working processes while still retaining CM values.

6.2.1 Iteration Planning or Iteration 0

What happens when the CM infrastructure already exists for a product and then the methodology changes from a phased approach to an Agile approach? This is where a re-engineering of some CM practices may need to occur. Possible CM changes to suit Agile may include changing the use of an existing tool, introducing a new tool, changing how environments are used, and changing existing practices. The product owner should be the primary driver of this work but may assign a more technical representative from the product team to focus on the strategies.

Depending on the size of the CM refactoring that needs to occur, there are two possible approaches. If the CM refactoring changes are few and smaller in nature, then the work can be identified and prioritized in an iteration planning session and worked on in an iteration. If the changes appear to be significant, then consider injecting an iteration 0. Within this iteration, the goal is to better understand the number of CM changes and place them into a backlog, prioritize the changes, assess the impact of the changes, identify the dependencies of the changes to other areas, and then determine the work that needs to be done to get the changes to occur. The dependency identification will help in the prioritization process of what to tackle first, second, and so on. This is also the time to consider dividing up the work into small sizes. This helps establish an expectation of how much can be accomplished in each refactoring task.

6.2.2   Think in Iterations

Since refactoring implies a small series of changes, it is beneficial to think of changes in relation to iterations. Therefore another strategy is to use an Agile approach of short iterations, identifying and assessing a small enough chunk of work that can be managed within this timeframe. At the end of the iteration, the product team reviews the changes and along with the product owner decides if the CM changes are acceptable and ready to go live into the working infrastructure to start being used by the team. If not, the change can be bundled with the deliverables of the next iteration(s) and then released together.

6.2.3   CM in Product Backlog or CM Backlog

The effort to refactor an existing CM infrastructure will vary per scenario. Much like approaching infrastructure refactoring, you can approach the work derived from CM refactoring in similar ways. The first approach is to include the CM work as stories and/or tasks within the product backlog and prioritize the work as you would stories for functionality. The CM tasks that are prioritized are moved to the iteration backlog and get assigned to the CM professionals that support the product team. Upon the conclusion of the iteration, the completed CM functionality is reviewed with the Agile team as the customer of the changes. This approach is recommended when the CM professional is part of the Agile team and when the number of CM tasks are manageable.

The second approach is for the CM professional or group that supports the product team to form a sub-team and drive the work in a parallel stream of tasks with a separate backlog while doing so in an iterative manner. This sub-team would include a CM professional or group and a few members from the product team who effectively act as customers, much like Agile requires the customer (or customer representative) to be available when building and validating functionality. This approach is recommended when the CM tasks are numerous or when the CM professional is not considered part of the Agile team.

6.3   Automate, Automate, Automate for Agile

A key to Agile is making as many of the interactions and processes as lean as possible, therefore reducing the steps programmers and CM professionals need in interfacing with the CM system. One answer is automation. Any process that is operational, meaning the same steps are run again and again, can be automated.

When using Agile methods, it is best to automate any process that is repeated by enough people where the team will see a cost and time benefit. Ultimately the benefit is in reducing the time it takes for the rest of the team to work through that process. The maturity curve in getting to automation for those processes that are used repeatedly follows a general pattern.

- First you tend to see people figure out the manual process, typically in an ad hoc manner. While ad hoc, this can nevertheless help in having discussions on the process.

- Second, once people see that a number of others have a need to do the same thing, then the repeated process typically becomes documented and shared. By "documented," this does not just mean in a text document, but means it can be documented in any manner that you and the team find of benefit (e.g., Wiki site, man pages, training materials, etc.). The document can then be distributed to the team, therefore reducing the need for one person to train others.

- Third, someone realizes that there can be effort savings by automating the process because enough people are doing it. Simple metrics could be created to ensure that the value of the automation in effort savings is worth the cost of establishing the automation. Assuming there is perceived value in the automation, this initiates an effort of taking that documented process and turning it into code, which in turn gets generated into a working program or tool. This tool then gets communicated to the team, depending on the extent of the explanation, and then inserted into the team's working processes.

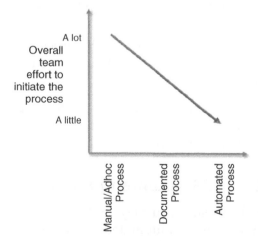

Figure 6-1   Tracking maturity of process automation to effort.

While it initially may sound counterintuitive from an Agile perspective where there is less of a focus on documenting processes, as you can see in the figure and the recent discussion above, there can be strong benefit for having a documented process when it is known to be repeated by many. At the "documented process" level, this saves time for one person explaining the process to many, or for many people attempting to figure it out themselves. At the automated process level, this can significantly reduce the effort of the team that repeatedly uses the manual process, therefore reducing effort, potentially increasing team velocity, and in the long run reducing costs.

What are some general benefits to automation? These may include:

- Automation makes actions less error-prone, assuming the automation is defined, designed, coded, and tested effectively.

- Automation eliminates idle time, which is considered a waste in lean thinking. When one step is done, the next one immediately begins.

- Automation reduces the need for troubleshooting a particular process (e.g., initiating a build, entering a workspace, etc.) because it avoids the need for someone to figure out their own way of doing something, which may result in some complex discussions with the troubleshooter on what process was actually followed. Sometimes this leads to more time taken because the troubleshooter must do some mind-reading due to the fact that sometimes people do not want to completely confess to their mistakes.

- Automation makes things maintainable and repeatable. When an action is automated, it ensures that the next time someone wants the item that the automation provides, it can be easily implemented and described.

- Automation makes it easy to improve the process. It provides for a known process baseline from which to improve the automation if updates are needed.

As you consider the deployment of Agile, realize the importance of automation and consider making it a key goal when processes are repeated, since productivity gains can be achieved.

6.3.1 Benefits of CM Automation to Agile

On an existing product team, you may find that there are steps in many CM processes that are not yet automated. This may include setting up a repository, setting up clients, creating a workspace, accessing a workspace, performing builds, conducting smoke-ests, etc. You will discover that many of these processes are constantly repeated and can be automated with a minimal amount of effort. While it may require initial effort, the benefit is that it will save the team considerable time in the future, leading to improved productivity and increased velocity.

Consider for a moment the build process. Developers will build their updated code quite possibly several times a day to ensure it builds and unit tests properly. Imagine if this build process was manual. It may only take about a minute of effort to run each step in a manual build process, but it may take several minutes of duration because the developer spends time waiting for the next step to run, *ergo* not allowing the developer to focus on other tasks. Context switching is a big time sink, especially for those who do not multitask well.

For the sake of argument, let us say the developer uses 2 minutes or 120 seconds in duration focusing on executing the various steps of a build process. When the build process is automated, it only takes 10 seconds of time in both effort and duration for the same developer therefore saving 110 seconds.

Now, saving 110 seconds (less than 2 minutes) may seem like trivial time savings in relation to a day. However, imagine that the developer builds 4 times a day for 22 working days in a month. Now the 110 seconds becomes 9680 seconds or 161 minutes. This is more than a 2.5 hour saving for 1 developer in a calendar month. Now imagine that there are 10 developers, each saving 2.5 hours a month. This is 25 hours of productivity saved which could be put to better use elsewhere. This is just one example of automation in CM. There are also automation opportunities in other engineering disciplines, like test.

As the product team gets up and running, the lack of automation may impact a team's progress and velocity. In fact, over time, given the continuous nature of building, migrating, and testing code and the increasing size of the code base with new functionality, a lack or minimal amount of automation may start to impact velocity fairly quickly in a negative way. Please understand that at a certain point, velocity may remain constant even with automation, but you can be certain that the team's velocity will begin to drop when no or minimal automation is achieved. The figure below illustrates this point.

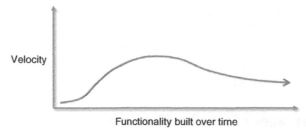

Figure 6-2   When no or minimal automation remains constant on a project following Agile.

6.3.2 Chunks, Iterations, and Increments

When a person shovels snow, the process typically involves taking a lightweight shovel and shoveling a little bit of snow at a time, making progress, and depositing the deliverable of snow to the side of the driveway or sidewalk. While you are working, you can work around cars (a.k.a., obstacles) and adjust direction as necessary.

Now imagine doing this with a very large shovel which is the width of the driveway. You can only move the large shovel in one direction and just a little bit at a time, making very little progress, not able to adjust, having little visibility of what is up ahead, and not making a delivery until the end.

While this sounds funny, this is how many software development projects operate. They try to take on the whole effort, progress seems very slow, visibility into the effort is minimal, and no one can utilize the outcome until the very end. For many, they have found a better way. They chunk up a large effort into manageable chunks or releases, define releases as increments and iterations, and divide iterations into bite-size tasks. Customers see progress, management has visibility, and the team has a sense of continuous accomplishment.

Pit Stop

With Agile, the customer sees real progress in the form of working functionality instead of progress in the form of a status report and specifications.

When a company moves toward Agile methods, there is even more of an emphasis on smaller chunks of deliverables, both within the context of a release and within the context of an iteration. As mentioned, Agile has a goal where the product team delivers functional deliverables at the end of each iteration. While this does not mean that you release at the end of each iteration, it does mean that you may release the deliverables so most aspects of release readiness will apply at the end of each iteration, like they would at the end of each release. This enables the customer to gauge the benefit of continuous change. By working in smaller chunks, the customer gets an opportunity to view the functionality at the end of each iteration and then can reassess their needs.

6.3.2.1 Advantages of Smaller Chunks and Increments

There are advantages to delivering in smaller increments and frequent releases. The customer actually gets to see working functionality being built before their very eyes and can more adequately respond with changes. More importantly, the customer builds a better understanding of their requirements in a gradual manner. And probably most importantly, the customer reduces the risk of getting a product they do not want and increases the chances of getting a product they really need. This can be especially advantageous when the business or product domain is new and the customer does not yet have a clear understanding of their needs.

Estimation and planning becomes a lot easier when thinking smaller. Estimating and planning large chunks of work is hard and has not proven particularly effective. It is hard to estimate the future when there are changes happening across the organization that are beyond the control of the project. It is hard to estimate when requirements change. It is hard to estimate up front when you have little sense of team velocity. Working in smaller chunks helps understand the pace of work.

Pit Stop

When considering estimation on a large project when there is much unknown up front, it may be worth taking a page from famed mathematician John von Neumann: "There's no sense in being precise when you don't even know what you're talking about."

A technique that can help you manage work in smaller chunks is known as "time boxing". Time boxing focuses work on short iterations or increments and can be used to divide out the work on a project into smaller chunks. Agile uses the notion of an iteration of 1 to 4 weeks where the deadline is fixed but the amount of requirements (or deliverables therein) is adjusted per team velocity and prioritization by the customer. The advantage of this technique is that over time, it becomes much easier to estimate the future work. This is because you can capture the velocity of past work ("actual") and use it as a basis for more accurate estimation in the future, particularly because you always know the period of time is fixed. Another advantage to this technique is that by expecting a deliverable at the end of each time period, it reduces the procrastination and lack of visible progress that tends to occur in long projects where deliverables are not expected for some time.

6.3.2.2 Disadvantages of Smaller Chunks and Increments

As you consider moving to projects with shorter release schedules or moving to Agile with regular iterations, it is important to understand that there is an impact to moving to smaller chunks of work. At a high level, there is a cultural shift in the way development occurs and it's a big adjustment for many. Smaller activities and shorter cycles imply a need for greater customer involvement. Customers (or the product manager/owner) must be readily available for the end-of-iteration review. Customers must be more frequently ready to provide input on requirements as they see the product being developed. Some customers are not ready to accept more frequent product releases within their organization. However, it is still good practice to continually get customer feedback even if they do not want to install a release. This customer involvement at least continues to ensure that when they are ready to install the product, they will get something closer to their actual needs.

Smaller activities and shorter cycles imply a great need for a testing process that can handle the frequent changes and ergo some level of automation. In addition, smaller activities and shorter cycles imply a need for a more rigorous set of controls to ensure changes are truly captured and you stay on the path. This is where CM must be adapted to handle a much more rapid pace of change. Smaller activities implies smaller change sets with much more frequent check-ins and a higher volume of change, This implies more focus and pressure on the CM technology and process. The CM system must be able to accommodate the continuous check-ins, builds, and merges and ensure the process is optimized for small continuous changes and can handle the continuous check-in, merge, integration, build, package, and test in an error-free way.

6.3.3   Location, Location, Location

In real estate, there is a saying that identifies the three things that best sell a house. They are "location, location, location." It is possible that these are the same three things that make Agile work best, in this case "co-location, co-location, co-location." But here it is not a singular definition of the word co-location, but instead it is polysemous (i.e., has multiple meaning). There is co-location of the team, co-location of the infrastructure, and co-location of the functionality under development.

6.3.3.1   Co-location of Team

The first meaning that comes to mind when discussing co-location amongst Agile professionals is co-location of team members. The definition of co-location of the team is the degree to which you can place the team in reasonably close proximity taking into account the factors of staffing and communications as they relate to potential success rates for the project. The ideal situation is to have the full Agile team together in one Agile team room. Many Agile professionals advocate this as a way of efficiently working together. Interaction can be immediate with little or no formality or dependency on technology. Decisions can be made and progress can continue.

Co-location implies that team members can communicate directly, face to face. Agile advocates face-to-face communications wherever possible because this is typically the leanest type of communication, where no additional tools or processes are needed. In a recent "Agile Practices and Principles Survey" by Scott Ambler, he asked Agile professionals what is the most effective communication strategy and the winner both within the team and with stakeholders was face-to-face communications. Teleconferencing and videoconferencing were also evaluated within this survey but neither came close to the preference of face-to-face communication.

Pit Stop

Agile advocates face-to-face communication because it is the leanest type of communication between people. In a recent study by Scott Ambler, face-to-face communication was identified as the most effective communication strategy.

There are many reasons for face-to-face communication being a big advantage for teams. Initially team members find that being close to their peers allows for continual communication with each other in an informal manner. In a world where pertinent information may be discussed in hallway conversations, it is not surprising that informal communication is a common means for sharing information and learning a lot about what is going on around you.

This continuous feedback that is promoted by face-to-face communication allows teams to adjust and refine ideas on a continuous basis that ultimately is a benefit and value to the product under development. In a recent study done by Damon Poole in his "Agile Development Thoughts" blog, Agile professionals responded to the importance of co-location for Agile teams and 76% said its value is such that it is foolish not to use it.

But while there are advantages to co-location for Agile, there are also disadvantages. It can be a struggle for those who are used to working from home or office and enjoy a quiet working environment or like to be left alone for long periods of time. This implies that noise and continuous interaction may be a problem for some. Also, this implies that the team agrees to a core set of working hours to enjoy the benefit of face-to-face communication. These are some aspects where Agile may not be the right working environment for some people.

Another disadvantage is that co-location practices do not support "near-shore" or "off-shore" team members. However, Agile can work in a distributed environment. In fact, in the real world, most companies are more distributed than ever. Methods, processes, practices, tools, and techniques must be viable in a distributed context or they will eventually cease to exist. The good news is that Agile is working in distributed environments. However, there is tangible impact to the success rate based on how distributed the team is. In a study conducted by Scott Ambler, he identified the success rate of Agile teams in different team scenarios. In teams where everyone was co-located, the rate of project success was at 83%. When team members were distributed close by (near-shore), but not in the same room, the success rate dropped to 72%. When teams were extensively distributed (in different cities and countries where off-shoring is common), the success rate dropped to 60%. The good news is that this highlights that projects can utilize Agile in a distributed development scenario, but they have to accept and manage the risk of such a scenario impacting project success.

6.3.3.2   Co-location of Infrastructure

This brings us to the second meaning of co-location. In this case, it refers to the ability to co-locate infrastructure and tools therein. The definition of co-location of infrastructure is the degree to which the infrastructure is in close proximity to the team and how it relates to the budget of the team, the local or distributed nature of the team, and the best CM approach for the code repositories to support the team.

When you take advantage of co-location of infrastructure, this simply means that you attempt to locate your infrastructure as close to the team as possible. The ability to co-locate the infrastructure with the team is dependent on how co-located or distributed the team is and what budget there is available to allow for more creative options. If you have a co-located team with a budget then owning and co-locating the infrastructure on your premises may be an advantage because of the control and performance benefits it provides. In a near-shore scenario (e.g., same floor, building, or nearby building), those that are nearby can typically use the on-premises co-located infrastructure with adjustments to appropriately scale the network bandwidth needs. In an off-shore scenario (with team members in two or more distant locations) where members are distributed, co-location of infrastructure with the team may not be viable and not necessarily advantageous, so going with a cloud infrastructure service where you rent infrastructure may be advantageous because of the cost benefits it provides.

In a distributed and off-shore scenario, this becomes more complicated particularly when bandwidth can become a significant factor. If the team is low on budget, then renting in the clouds may be the only viable option. If the company has budget and support staff, then a way to compensate for this is to locate infrastructure on-premises in each significant site so that the local team members can utilize the infrastructure locally for their more demanding needs, like continuous development, building, and testing.

6.3.3.3 Co-location of Functionality

The third meaning of co-location is co-location of functionality, or more precisely, the code under development. The definition of co-location of functionality is the degree to which the code is well structured (i.e., architected) such that it is easy to identify the various pieces of code that establish a specific function. The manner to which the code is structured has an impact on the options for how the local or distributed team can work with the code and the CM capabilities available.

Does the code design follow a component-based architecture where it is clear which code module or collection of code aligns with a specific function? Or is the code poorly architected, making it difficult to identify where functions are really coming from or worse yet, meaning that the function requires numerous unrelated yet dependent sets of code in order to be built? In this case, refactoring may be in order.

When the code is well structured in a component-based architecture, it is then much easier to allocate work to certain groups knowing that each group can have ownership of that work with little concern for impact by others. This can be very advantageous to any development team that is distributed. In this case, when the code is well structured, it becomes easier to allocate certain chunks of code to the off-shore site knowing that the merging effort will then be trivial because the different sites are working on different parts of the code baseline. If the code is not well structured and the dependencies not well understood, then members of a distributed team could be creating large merge activities with the result of potentially overwriting other's code changes during the merge process.

There are benefits of having a well structured and component-based architecture. First, the better structured the code, the better the opportunity to reduce merge conflicts. Second, as the team is more distributed, the more likely you will need a branching structure or have a replication solution of the code baseline so that each site can work separately from the other. If the code is poorly structured and there is a lack of knowledge of where certain functionality comes from this will have a direct impact on the amount of code that will need to be replicated to another site or the size of the distributed branch that will need to be established. If the code is well structured and functionality understood, then only that part of the code baseline needs to be replicated or branched.

6.3.3.4 CM Considerations for Co-location and Agile

When you add CM to the mix of co-location, it can help in several ways. In relation to co-location as a team, CM can help improve collaboration by providing another framework for communications. Work is represented as a check-out to a set of changes that align with the work on the requirements list, backlog, and/or defect list. A good CM tool will provide a GUI that allows insight into the branches and check-outs that are occurring on those branches. When it comes time to check the code back into the project branch, a good CM tool will have strong merging capabilities that will announce when merge conflicts occur, therefore providing the developers that must resolve the conflict with both the awareness of the conflict and the means to have a successful merge.

In relation to co-location as infrastructure, CM can provide you with some options to help you consider the best approach to accessing code. As you add CM into the mix of discussions on co-location of infrastructure, there are several factors to consider. They include:

- If you have a local on-shore team that is in one Agile team room or on the same floor, the closer you place the CM system (repository and tools) to the product team, the more you minimize performance or transaction challenges.

- If you have a near-shore situation where the team is located in close proximity, some within the same room or floor, and some nearby (in the building or buildings nearby), then it is still best to have the CM system as close to the majority of the team as possible. Even if there are several members of the team in another building, it is best if they can connect directly to the CM system if possible, or if not, then use a remote client approach or web interface to access the code. In this circumstance, it is best to avoid a replication solution where you would replicate the repository to the other site. However, in all cases, performance and transaction time should be measured and tested to find the most streamlined solution.

- If you have an off-shore situation where you have one part of the team in a local on-shore or local near-shore situation but the rest of the team is located off-shore (completely at another site), then you may need to apply a solution involving a replication of the repository. In this case, it may be best to have replicated repositories of the code so that each group can work independently from each other without relying on the other's systems and the network in between. At regular intervals, you will have to sync up the repositories so that each sub-team has the latest code baseline. After merging, there should be a build and test of all newly merged changes so that there is an assurance that the changes are valid. If the code is well architected in a component-based structure, then a replicated solution may be reasonable as long as there are no or very few dependencies between components. Please note that it is still worth investigating if the off-shore team can directly connect to, remote client into, or web interface with the CM system. In all cases, performance and transaction time should be measured and tested to find the most streamlined solution.

Ultimately the three "co-location" aspects must work together. How you structure your code, where your team is located, and where the infrastructure is located are interdependent and should be considered in tandem to give you advantages in cost (best location for equipment), performance (most effective code structure and code access methods) as well as efficiencies in streamlined processes (branching, merging, and collaboration).

Adapting CM Practices for Agile

Many software development teams are using Agile practices. When adapting a practice for a specific team, it becomes a best practice for that team. This is because a best practice represents the best approach for the team given the context and forces in play. The key to adapting Configuration Management (CM) practices for Agile teams is in understanding the context and forces in play that lead to a practice that is best suited for Agile. The context is the situation the team is in (iterative vs. phased) and the forces are the pressures, constraints, and goals (e.g., the need to eliminate waste) that can impact the solution. Considering these helps lead to the creation of the best practice for a team.

Pit Stop

A practice becomes a best practice when it is tailored to address the needs of a specific team given the context (i.e., situation) and forces (i.e., pressures, constraints, and goals) in play.

For Agile, CM practices should be streamlined, the CM responsibilities should be realigned in an appropriate way to better fit the Agile working processes. While those with the Agile mindset are more likely to consider these adaptations, please note that many of these changes can be done for traditional methods as well and gain similar benefits.

Implementing Agile is best suited to the product level. This way the product team receives economies of scale by implementing Agile at the longer product lifecycle level versus at the short-lived project lifecycle level. When Agile is implemented at the product level, each project leverages the Agile practices and benefits therein. This allows for the continual improvement of the Agile practices initiated in the end-of-iteration retrospectives.

CM is also best implemented at the product level so that you can take advantages of economies of scale and apply consistent CM for all of the projects therein. Each project under the product banner takes advantage of CM practices and can hone the CM practices incrementally with each release.

Pit Stop

Both Agile and CM are best suited to the product level. This way the product team receives economies of scale by implementing these for a product lifecycle. It also ensures that the method and practices are consistent from project to project.

The importance of the various CM practices will depend on the context and forces in play on a particular team or organization. This section will provide the latest approaches, ideas, thoughts, and guides on how to best adapt CM for Agile needs. From this guidance, it is incumbent on you to craft a practice that is best suited for your team (a.k.a., your best practices) given the context and forces in play.

7.1   Adapting to Continuous Integration and Build

The term "continuous integration" refers to the process of integrating code frequently (or on demand) to reduce large integrations, complexity, and pain in the future and to make functional software readily available for testing and the customer. Establishing continuous integration and build will provide development with immediate feedback on the success or failure of changes via a build and smoke test of the product and reduce large integration efforts. While the term "continuous" is catchy, there is not really an on-going integration. Instead in the context of integration, the term "continuous" implies an on-demand and as needed process.

The notion of continuous integration and build takes a different mindset where the team needs to constantly be thinking in smaller bite-size tasks that allow for frequent check-in and build. In order to design and implement this value added practice effectively, there are some elements that must be considered.

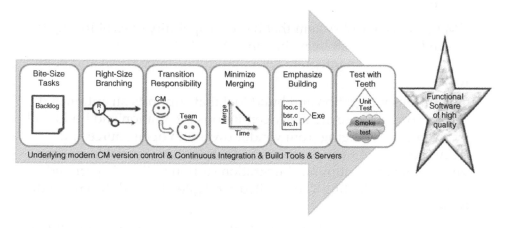

Figure 7-1   The road to a successful continuous integration & build practice.

Entrance criteria for an effective and lean continuous integration and build process include:

- The ability to specify the right "bite-size" level of story or requirements tasks that represent changes that allow for granular and frequent code changes. This implies that the Agile team can understand the stories well enough to divide them up in small and consumable tasks which allow the programmer to make changes frequently and incrementally.

The key components to initiate an effective continuous integration and build process include:

- Right-sized branching strategy that reduces risk yet ensures code stability where people can work in a stable workspace without being impacted by changes of others on a regular basis.
- Shift in roles and responsibilities of who performs merging and building.
- Minimizing the merge process through continuous integration.
- Emphasizing building in general and understanding the build levels so it is clear who the target of the build is. Builds can occur within a private workspace and within shared branches like the mainline or project branches.
- Testing with teeth by establishing and conducting unit testing at the individual programmer level and then smoke testing after the integration build level.

Underneath all of this, there is a need for infrastructure to support a continuous integration and build process. The two primary elements of this include:

- CM version control system that has the capability of establishing the desired branching strategy, has an automated and intelligent merging capability, and can integrate with continuous integration and build tools.

- Continuous integration and build tool that supports an automated build process. There are many continuous integration and build tools on the market, ranging from vendor owned to open source and freeware tools. As you evaluate the tools that are available, ensure you review the continuous integration section in this chapter and chapter 9, "Evaluating Tools Suited for Agile" toward the end of the book.

It is important to note that tools (both version control and build) are critical in the support of an effective continuous integration and build process.

Pit Stop

Both CM and Agile use the acronym "CI" in a meaningful way. For CM, the acronym "CI" stands for "configuration item." For Agile, the acronym "CI" stands for "continuous integration."

With the advent of continuous integration and build, Agile and CM professionals can adapt traditional build management approaches to provide the customer with continuous working functionality for continuous feedback. More frequent builds with fewer changed files reduces the amount of time wasted on debugging problematic builds with a large number of modified files. Building frequently also lets you and the customer know where things stand as a mark of value delivered. Integration helps ensure the integrity of the code baseline. When you have multiple people working on the same code, continuous integration raises merging issues to the forefront more quickly for more expedient resolution.

7.1.1   The "Continuous" Cultural Shift

A very interesting cultural shift occurs when the concept of "continuous" is ingrained in the culture and method. Agile embraces continuous change and those practices that support this. In more traditional cultures and methods, practices are set up to maintain the status quo and constrain change. This is why Agile often has challenges getting adopted in more traditional companies. This is not really a clash of methods, but instead a clash of cultures. The method used reflects the way the culture works. Some cultures are heavy in ceremony, governance, and multilevel approval. Agile will have challenges with this type of corporate culture.

In an Agile context, what we see in CM and the build space is a fundamental shift in the way we build software. The build process moves from an event-based integration process to a continuous integration process. In other words, no one needs to hold onto large amounts of changes for a major integration effort or declare that builds will occur nightly, weekly, even hourly. There is no ceremony needed. We move away from the infrequent and often painful integrations (a.k.a., merges) and move to an integration and build process that becomes part of the team's daily activities.

Pit Stop

Within an Agile context and with the advent of continuous integration and build, build should be seen less as an event-driven model, but instead as a continuous model since build activities are pervasive in each iteration.

When you integrate and build all the time, integrations and builds become non-events. As an example, when code gets continually promoted based on successful private builds and unit tests, an integration and build at an integration level becomes automatic and trivial (e.g., with minimal merge and build problems). Then the results of a successful build routinely become candidates for test and release if they pass the defined tests (integration, system, performance, etc.) and meet the customer need in the end-of-iteration reviews.

The primary benefit of continuous integration and build is that the changed code provides immediate feedback whether it runs correctly with the rest of the code in the integration branch (the project release branch or main branch). When code sits in a programmer's private workspace, no one else can see it, nor can it be accessed by other programmers. Much like the concept in Agile where value is only realized by working functionality, the same is true with continuous integration. Progress is only realized when the code has been integrated into the active codeline where others realize that it exists. If not, it does not exist as far as others are concerned.

Pit Stop

In Agile, value is realized by working functionality. With continuous integration, progress is realized when the code has been integrated into the active codeline where others realize that it exists and can integrate with it.

The longer the programmer goes without integrating their code, the greater the possibility of large merge efforts which lead to greater effort to integrate and more disruption to other team members because they have to then integrate a larger change to their own work. Even more problematic is that the longer you wait, the more this increases the chances of complex merge conflicts, since others may start working on some of the same code to complete other pieces of requirements or stories. This problem leads to a double impact of programmer's velocity and productivity. Why? Because the effort that is required to resolve the merge conflict takes up not only more of the first programmer's time, but also requires another programmer (whose code is associated with the conflict) to shift gears out of their working flow to now focus and resolve the merge conflict.

7.1.1.1 How "Continuous" Adds Stress and Load to CM

The continuous actions of check-in and build introduce a new challenge to CM. A continuous integration and build practice places considerably more stress and load on the CM version control and build systems. In other words, there will be a significant increase in check-outs, merges, check-ins, and builds. Having more modern, faster, and automated CM tools with underlying infrastructure that can support these continuous actions is important to the success of this practice. As the continuous notion gets introduced to the project, you need to ensure focus on tools. In addition, infrastructure is considered so there is an appropriate balance between velocity and infrastructure (tools and servers). You do not want too much infrastructure that introduces infrastructure debt, but nor do you want to have insufficient infrastructure that will impact velocity and productivity of the team. This topic will be discussed further in chapter 8 – "CM Tool as a Strategic Agile Partner."

7.1.2   Right-Size Branching for Agile

The primary branching consideration for Agile is to keep it simple. The first impulse is to say Agile teams should work only from the main branch. However, right-sizing the branching strategy is the key. Branching can be inappropriately applied when not well understood (either too minimally or too heavily) and factors are not considered. Some Agile teams are getting larger and more distributed and may have more complex branching needs then initially realized. Agile teams should consider the most efficient branching approach. For some, it is challenging to know where to begin.

When considering a branching and merging strategy and corresponding branching model, it is important to involve the Agile team since this strategy directly impacts product development. The team should be part of the branching strategy decision process. They should be aware of the branching factors, branch types available, the pros and cons to branching, and have knowledge of the effort and risks involved in branching.

It is also important to note that the CM tool being used plays a key role in the branching and merging capability and whether it can support the desired branching strategy. Some CM tools are better at branching and merging than others. It is important to select and use a CM tool that can support the needed strategy.

7.1.2.1   ABCs of Branching

A branch represents a stream of an active development baseline that is independent of other streams but will have a common history. Within a branching model, the "root" development baseline may be known as the "trunk" and sometimes it is referred to as the "main branch" or "mainline." A new branch can be based on the trunk or another branch and is known as the "child" of the "parent" branch. When a new branch is created from the trunk or another branch, it shares a common history and ancestry.

The items within a "child" branch (whether physical or virtual) are initially identical with the parent. But over time, the items in the child branch will evolve and become different to the parent due to the active modification, creation, or deletion of the items within the branch. However, the opposite can be true. When the main branch (parent) has more than one child branch from it (e.g., the project release branch and patch branch), then the main branch may evolve with the latest supported patches which cause this baseline (the main branch) to become different from the child branches (e.g., the project release branch). The parent is also known as the child's backing stream or branch (i.e., the branch the child promotes into). Below is an example of the parent-child relationship in a branching structure.

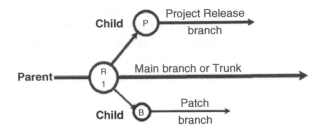

Figure 7-2   Example of the branching parent-child relationship.

A discussion should occur on balancing the team velocity with product risk when considering the branching and merging approach. What is interesting is that either working on mainline or on branches can increase velocity and can increase risk depending on your situation. Working on the mainline means that you are impacted more frequently when check-ins occur to mainline, therefore increasing the risk of ever getting your own code changes to be stable. Working on a branch allows you to work in isolation from others and not be impacted by their changes until you are ready. On the one hand, working on a branch may increase merging activities, which increases the risk of extra merging effort. On the other hand, some programmers enjoy working in isolation and may not merge for a long time, which introduces the "big merge" problem that can result in complex merging, extra rebuilds, and extra testing.

It is a good exercise to examine what branch types are possible so you are better informed to discuss branching strategies. In general, all branches are technically considered integration branches since all can have files integrated (or merged) into them, including the main branch. As you consider the factors and your needs for branching, consider reviewing some common branch types:

- Main branch (a.k.a., trunk or mainline) – the "root" development branch in which all other branches are based. The trunk is the "parent" of all branches. The project can work off the main branch. It is important to understand the three primary approaches for utilizing the main branch.
  - Active – the main branch can be the main codeline where the team actively checks out and checks in their work. This may be preferred

when teams do not require isolation from each other. If used in this manner, mainline will always hold the latest active code under development. Labels can be used to distinguish between levels of changes and builds.

○ Milestone – the main branch can be used as a backing stream to stabilize and test periodic milestone integrations from child branches (QA milestone, etc.).

○ Release & Patch – the main branch can be the backing stream for the project release branch. In this scenario, the main branch only holds the latest production code that has either been delivered as part of a release or as part of a patch (or similar).

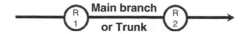

Figure 7-3   Illustration of the main branch.

▪ Project Release branch – a branch used to hold project-specific work which is isolated from the mainline. This could be used to construct the next release of the product or a platform-specific version of the product. "Branch per project release" is a common branching strategy when you want to align the branching strategy with releases.

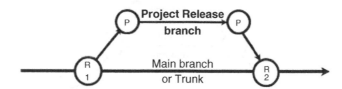

Figure 7-4   Illustration of the project release branch.

▪ Task branch – a branch meant for a subset of developers who need to work on and integrate with the same set of functionality without disturbing others. This could include component-specific work or work on volatile code so it does not impact others until it is sufficiently built and tested appropriately. This type of branch can be temporary in nature, but used so that the changes can be tracked. For example, if new development occurs on the project release branch and the build breaks, it may take days to fix. In this case, a task branch based on the latest good code may be useful in the mean time to continue development as the project release branch code gets fixed. A task branch is often backed by a project release branch or main branch.

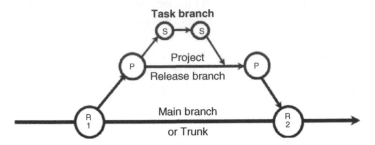

Figure 7-5   Illustration of the task branch.

- Site branch – a branch that may be used when there are other sites involved in development, particularly when the other site has a medium to high number of developers. It can mirror a project release branch if the other site is working on the same project and it is usually backed by a project release branch. A site branch isolates work but still allows for merging and integration to the project release branch.

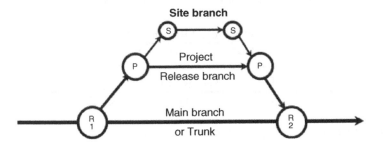

Figure 7-6   Illustration of the site branch.

- Patch branch – a branch that is used to perform bug fixes or maintenance to an existing release. Any changes in this branch should not only be merged "in" to the main branch (assuming this is where the latest production release exists), but in most cases, they should be merged "out" to any new project release branch so that the fix is included in the new release, therefore minimizing regression in functionality and stability in the code baseline of the next release. This can be a kind of task branch when a subset of the team is focusing on

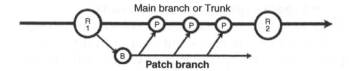

Figure 7-7   Illustration of the patch branch.

bugs, or if only one person is working on the bug fixes, then a private branch is sufficient.

- Private branch – may be used to isolate individual developer's changes from each other. This may be backed by any branch (site branch, task branch, project release branch, or main branch).

7.1.2.2   Private Workspace

A private workspace is an isolated work area that is defined as the check-out location for a programmer. This provides a programmer with a personal work environment that is separate and stable and where they can manage their changes before they introduce them to the rest of the team. It is my strong recommendation that in all cases, whether working on the main branch, a project release branch, a bug fix branch, site-specific branch, or shared branch, that each programmer should work from a private workspace.

Because the private workspace is an isolated setting, it allows the programmer to make changes, build, and unit test to success prior to promoting to the backing branch. By stabilizing the work in the private workspace, this enhances the stability in the backing branch for greater success of the project. Keep in mind that the CM goal of a private workspace is to work on coding activity with confidence and safety and the goal for Agile is to regularly promote the code when it is ready into the backing branch. Neither wants you to isolate yourself from others for long periods of time. Another benefit of the private workspace is that it ensures velocity by allowing the programmer to work at the pace they desire and accept the new changes from the backing branch when they are ready, therefore minimizing any impact to their velocity.

Up to this point, we have been talking about the private workspace in its generic sense without any structure surrounding it. Private workspaces come in two forms: A private workspace that lives outside of the version control system that is supported by a filesystem location as the touchdown space, and a private workspace that is supported by a private branch from within the version control system.

Private Workspace supported by a Directory

The "directory-based" private workspace structure is simply a filesystem directory where the check-out operation deposits the file. While the CM version control system knows you have it checked out, the file is effectively outside of the system with no ability to track incremental changes. However, the programmer can work on constructing functionality, building it, and unit testing the executables as appropriate without impacting those using the shared backing branch.

The advantage of this approach is that it can be set up easily by specifying the touchdown location outside of the version control system. Another key advantage is that it may be the easiest to maintain. From a programmer perspective, getting access to code is just a check-out away.

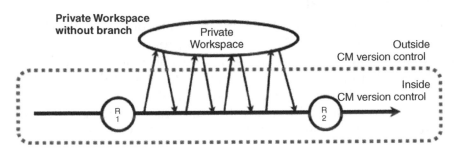

Figure 7-8   Private workspace without a branch.

The primary disadvantage of this approach is that while it is a good practice to check in regularly, if you do so before the code is stable, then it can disrupt the stability of the backing branch and those that use it. In general, only mature. well-tested code can get checked back in. Most programmers take days if not weeks to construct the requirement into a working code module (or collection of modules) and are hesitant to check in their changes to preserve them since it can disrupt their backing branch on which the full team relies. The ramification is that the programmer's changes are kept on their computer and if not backed up daily, this increases the risk of losing changes. If the workspace is on a backed-up server, this minimizes the risk of losing changes when not checking in so frequently.

In addition, it is a good practice to merge all of the latest code from the backing stream "out" to your private workspace so that you can ensure your changes work with the latest stable code. A challenge when checking out to an outside workspace is that if a file already exists in the workspace, it will recognize this as a conflict but not necessarily know how to merge it appropriately since it cannot assume a common ancestry. The same is true upon check-in. Depending on the version control system, it may find it challenging to compare what you are checking in from the outside workspace with what is currently in the backing branch. It will assume a common ancestry based on the check-out action earlier and assume that the file is effectively a child. If the file in the backing stream has changed, then the merge can be even more difficult. As discussed, regular check-ins are encouraged in order to reduce the risk of losing changes but ultimately this type of "outside" private workspace does not encourage regular check-ins, since it introduces risk into the backing branch unless what is checked in is actually stable code (i.e., successfully built and unit tested appropriately).

Private Workspace support by a Private Branch

The recommended approach for a private workspace is one backed by a private branch. This has the advantage of having a personal workspace to work in without distractions, and the ability to check-in unfinished code into a private branch on a frequent basis, reducing the risk of losing any changes while not impacting the backing branch where others may be working. This is because the private branch provides isolated version control for the programmer so that they can control their unfinished changes and have the ability to retrieve older versions of code (even hours before) if they find that their current group of changes is not working. This approach also ensures that the ancestry is known, which benefits future check-ins and merge-promote operations. If this approach is appealing, it will be important to find a CM version control tool that can support private branches.

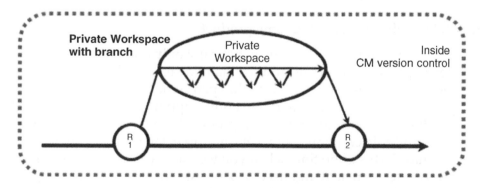

Figure 7-9   Private workspace with a private branch.

As programmers promote their completed code into the backing branch, other programmers can update their private workspace with the latest in the backing branch from time to time to keep in synch with the current state of the parent. The distinct advantage of using a private workspace backed by a private branch is that it allows you to update your private code baseline in an automated manner while supporting automated merging (unless there is a merge conflict between the same file on different branches). When a merge conflict occurs between the backing branch and what is in the private workspace, it can be resolved in the programmer's private workspace first without holding up the check-in and merge action to the backing branch. A process should be set up to ensure this is done efficiently and with integrity. A minor disadvantage is that when you want to get the code back to project release branch, you have to check in to your private branch, then promote it to the project release branch.

7.1.2.3   Factors for an Agile Branching Strategy

The goal of this section is to provide you enough information to establish a lean branching structure. In general, Agile teams starting brand new product development may begin on the mainline (a.k.a., main branch). This initially works well when Agile teams remain small, co-located, and work in a self-managed manner with excellent communication amongst team members. In this case mainline becomes the "active" line of code because there is no code in production yet.

Your ability to craft an effective branching structure is dependent on several factors. These and other factors should be considered in tandem so that you understand the benefits and risks of branching and so that you have a thoughtful and effective branching structure as an output. As you approach your strategy, consider the following factors and a branching strategy may emerge.

Parallel development for the same product

- When a product is in its infancy, typically only one active line of development is occurring and the mainline or main branch typically meets the needs. However, what happens when you release the product into production and must now support the released product and the development for the next product? What happens when you have multiple customers and, *ergo*, multiple versions of software to maintain? This is the time when you technically have several active lines of development and need to seriously consider a branching strategy. It may make sense to have a branch for each active line of development (one for the new release, one for the bug fixes, etc.).

Quality of Architecture and Design

- How well structured the code is depends on how well architected and designed it is (e.g., component based with distinct code modules designated for functionality). Poor code structure makes it difficult to reduce the amount of code being touched. For example, if the login functionality is sprinkled throughout the code base and not well known where it is, then you may need to branch in order to fully understand what you are working on while not impacting the velocity of the rest of the team members. While branching will not help you overcome a poor design, it will allow you to keep your work separate from others while you figure it out. In this case, it is better to spend time establishing a better system of architecture and design, which may include refactoring. But if the code is well structured, this reduces multiple people touching the same code and reduces the chances of modifying or removing a change during a merge that someone else has made. The better structured the code, the less likely you need a branch. The use of a private branch to resolve quality design issues may be more advantageous than initially thought.

How work is allocated

- Agile teams are self-managing and work collectively on the code base. Team members commit to work within the context of the functionality they know well. When work is allocated by functional area and the code is well structured, this minimizes the need for merging. The more likely it is that people are touching the same code, the more this increases the need to merge, which may require additional effort and the need for branching. If you are faced with this situation, it may necessitate the need to have a private workspace on a private branch. This approach will also reduce the merging effort since tools that can establish private branches often come with merge automation.

Number and volatility of new features

- When you are working on a fairly stable product, minimizing the branching structure may be appropriate. However, when you introduce a new feature that is volatile, then introducing a branch for this new feature work may be appropriate. If there is a general volatility across the code base, then applying a private workspace with a private branch will help reduce breaking the backing stream and introducing bad changes into everyone's work. Private workspaces isolate developers from the volatile and any bad changes that are introduced early on in the project lifecycle. However, if you have two or more programmers working on the new volatile functionality, then a task branch may be needed. This allows the two or more programmers to share each other's changes without impacting the rest of the team.

Size of the team

- If the team is small (7 +/− 2), then mainline development with each team member having a private workspace (preferably with a private branch) is very reasonable. The smaller the Agile team is, the more likely that there is good communication amongst the team members and everyone knows what others are working on. As the team expands, it may be necessary to allocate work to team members in order to reduce the amount of merging.

- The smaller the team, the more likely you can work on the mainline. However, even with a small team, once you have more than one stream of work, you may still need to have branches for each stream of work (new release, current release bug fix, etc.). If your team gets larger, there may be a need for branching, but this depends on how well you communicate with each other. Good communication reduces the need for branches in some instances.

Distributed nature of team

- How distributed your team is may have an impact on your branching strategy. If the team is mostly co-located with a couple of people near-shore and even off-shore, then initially using the mainline with private workspaces is suggested. If the team is half co-located on-shore and half co-located off-shore, then it may be beneficial to have a site branch so each team can own the work in their branch. However, if the work is clearly allocated in such a way that everyone is working on separate code modules, then initially working from mainline with private workspaces may work.

Pit Stop

It is recommended that Agile teams initially minimize the branch strategy and work off the mainline with a private branch. However, it is a good exercise to continually consider the factors that can introduce risk. For example, once you place a release into production, branching may become necessary.

7.1.2.4 Understanding Codelines

A codeline is effectively a configuration set of code. While a codeline can be directly associated to a branch, it is really a specific view of the contents of a branch or set of branches. A codeline can be static and it can be dynamic (i.e., active and evolving). The more likely it is that you'll use the mainline as your backing branch, the more you should be aware of the ways to define your codeline. However, this can apply to any variation of branch usage. Here are several ways in which a codeline type may be defined:

- LAG – In most cases, this configuration set is associated with the latest and greatest (LAG) code on a particular branch (i.e., the latest versions of files on the branch are included in the configuration set and represent a codeline). In many cases, product builds are built with the latest code and this assumes that all the check-ins have been properly built and tested. This may be the case for projects applying Agile.

- PIT – In some cases, the codeline is defined by code on a branch at a point in time (PIT) sometimes referred to as a static codeline. Some CM systems allow you to establish a view of the code from a date within the branch context. Instead of seeing the latest codeline on the branch, you would see a date-specific configuration set. This may be used because the last successful build of the product occurred three days ago so we want that codeline. Sometimes, you can branch from there to create a new line of development.

- Label/Tag – In many cases, the codeline is defined by a label function that tags the specific versions of code in the version control repository to form a configuration set that represents a milestone. This is similar in nature to the PIT codeline but includes a labeling step and preferably a label-naming convention for what you want that label to represent (e.g., build1, QA3, etc.). Sometimes, you can branch from the label to create a new line of development if needed. For an Agile team, the label approach is particularly effective when you are working from the main branch. This way, the label approach allows you to tag the good builds, QA-passed codeline, or production codeline, while allowing the programmers to continue their work on the LAG codeline.

- MP – In some cases, you may need to have some files come from one branch and others come from another branch. This is known as a multi-path (MP) configuration set. An example is that in the context of a private workspace with branch, you can set the codeline to include the latest files from the project release but supplement it with the latest foo.c file that programmer 1 is working on in his workspace, and the latest bar.c file that programmer 2 is working on in his workspace. This new codeline includes all of the files in the project release branch plus the programmers' latest foo.c and bar.c that eclipse the same files from the project release branch. Why would you want to do this? If you want to attempt a build with your latest changes and what programmers 1 and 2 are working on (i.e., foo.c and bar.c respectively), then this can be done without asking programmers 1 and 2 to check in or promote foo.c to the project release branch (a.k.a., backing branch for all programmers). For an Agile team, the MP codeline approach can be another way to share code without having to set up a shared branch off the main branch or the project release branch.

The more modern CM version control systems allow you to create a codeline type through a configuration set construct in an automated manner. However keep in mind that the older CM tools do not have this capability.

It is important to note that in most cases, people use the LAG codeline on a branch for continued development. This is because it is the easiest to use and maintain. PIT and labels are used to identify milestones (a.k.a., static codelines). Labeling is fairly common in the version control practice to identify "good" working sets of code. And as mentioned, the MP codeline can be another way to build and test with someone else's code without having to promote the code to the next integration branch (the shared, project release, or main branch).

Armed with codeline type information and the various elements of branching, it may be beneficial to establish a codeline policy to support the branch strategy so the team understands how to use codelines. For example, a codeline policy would govern how a team checks out, checks in, merges, and promotes the code to the mainline based on the type of private workspace programmers have. This policy can go hand in hand with the branching strategy so that the team knows what branches will be used and rules for each branch.

7.1.2.5 Branching Scenarios

This section illustrates some of the common branching scenarios. These are not meant to be standards in branching but provide examples from real-world scenarios to better craft a branching strategy for your needs. In a nutshell, the primary reason to branch is if there is a need for concurrent or parallel development. As soon as you are successful enough to place a release into production and have customers use the product, you may immediately need an active branch to provide support and bug fixes.

However, most likely you will also begin the active development of the next release with new functionality. Once you have an approach, consider preparing a branching model to share with the team so that they can visually grasp the strategy.

Please understand that there is no one right approach and it is important for the team to discuss what is best, based on the factors previously discussed including the team size, volatility of the code, where the team is in the product lifecycle, interactions amongst the team, and other factors. The goal is to establish and implement a lean branching strategy that is good for the current needs and can adapt to further needs. In addition, much like Agile, you can use an iterative approach in evolving your branching strategy.

Working on Mainline (a.k.a., Main Branch or Trunk)

This is a branching strategy that should be initially considered for all Agile teams that are beginning new product development, provided they need only one line of active code development which is typically the case. In fact, it is a good branching strategy for any new product development that initially has only one active codeline.

The mainline represents the main branch. When working on the mainline, teams check-out code into their private workspace. The programmers modify the code, compile, unit test, and eventually integrate (check-in or check-in and promote) their work back into the mainline in order to incrementally construct the functionality needed for the release in progress.

When mainline is the active line of development for the team and the LAG codeline type is applied, it is highly recommended that developers have a private workspace where they can work on their changes separately from others. The best approach when working from the main branch is to have a private workspace preferably backed by a private branch if this is feasible. This way, the programmer can isolated their work but frequently check into their private branch and regularly promote to the active main branch.

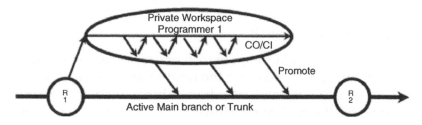

Figure 7-10   Working off the main branch with a private branch.

There are advantages with this approach. The first advantage is that this is the easiest branching option to set up and maintain. Next, it is best for small, co-located, and collaborative teams. The primary disadvantage is that it is susceptible to a chaotic check-in of non-working code, which slows the velocity of the entire team. The more people work on mainline, the greater the chance that someone will check-in a module without appropriately testing or produce merge conflicts which may result in a break in the LAG codeline. If you have code in production and working on the main branch, then you must have an effective way to distinguish what is production-ready code and what is not (e.g., by labeling).

Working on a Project Release Branch

This branching strategy is introduced when there is a need to have an active project release codeline together with the need to use the main branch to hold the combination of production releases and patches. This approach is used to develop the next release of the product or a platform-specific version of the product when the mainline is meant for milestones or production release and patches.

Another reason to utilize the project release branch is when the team needs to stabilize the release. When the code is stable, it can be merged back into the main branch. While working on a project release branch offers you the safety of separating active work from the main branch, it requires the additional effort of merging to mainline and the rebuilding and retesting that occurs.

The disadvantage of this approach is that it requires merging from the project release branch to the main branch. However, if there are any changes introduced into the mainline from other branches (e.g., bug fixes from a patch branch) and they are merged out to the project release branch and built and tested with the latest development, then the merge back to the main branch should be trivial. In addition, in order to support active branching, you need a modern CM version control tool that has the capability of performing branching and intelligent merging.

Working with a Patch Branch

When a team working on the main branch or project release branch puts a release into product, there becomes the need to actively begin supporting the release to correct bugs and introduce enhancement and maintenance improvements for the customers. However, at the same time, active new development on the next release starts to occur. In this scenario, the creation of a patch branch will provide the team with an isolated codeline to correct the defects while allowing the rest of the team to work actively on the functionality of the next release. The advantage of this approach is that it provides an isolated codeline for active bug fixes and maintenance.

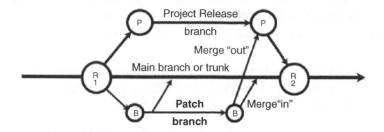

Figure 7-11   Working with a patch branch.

It also provides you with the ability to merge from the patch branch "in" to the main branch and "out" to project release branch. The primary reason you want to ensure you merge changes "out" from the patch branch to the project release branch is to guarantee that the corrected defects, enhancements, and maintenance changes to the product also get into the latest code of the next release currently in the project release branch. This minimizes the regression that can occur when bug fixes are not integrated effectively into parallel project work.

Aside from these three branching scenarios, there are many others. A site branch may be used that is backed from a project release branch and there can be task branches used for volatile features being newly developed. Many smaller Agile teams may have a simple scenario of working on the main branch with private workspaces. However, some Agile teams are getting larger and more distributed and may have more branching needs. You should determine the best approach for your team's needs but ensure you are driving the approach in a lean manner. Keep in mind that "lean" does not necessarily mean the most simple since the simple approach can introduce more risk and instability. Limiting yourself to one line of code (working off the main branch or trunk) or creating too many lines of code can impact the amount of effort involved in branching and merging and the amount of testing that is needed to manage changes. Finding the balance is the key.

7.1.2.6   Branching Challenges

As you approach a branching strategy, be aware of the branching challenges that may arise. They include:

- Dangling branches – when branches have been created for unknown reasons with no clear purpose.

- Generational branches – where there are generations of branches (children branches attached to parent branches, attached to grandparent branches, attached to great-grandparent branches and so on) many of which have never been merged back.
- Inherited Danger branches – where the unstable code within a branch is shared with other branches. This has the effect of reducing productivity since instead of one person fixing the unstable code, now many people are left trying to fix their working software while limiting their ability to work on new changes.

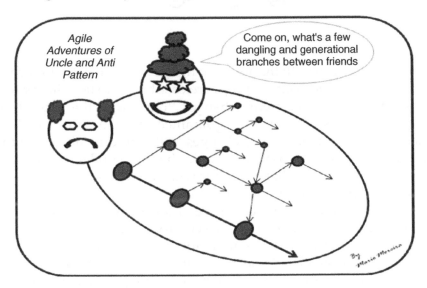

Figure 7-12   Agile Adventures of Uncle and Anti Pattern – Dangling Branches.

7.1.2.7   Branching Summary

To summarize, consider the following steps:

- Understand the branch types. Learn what the different branches are for and their advantages and disadvantages.
- Understand the factors that can help you determine the best branching strategy for you.
- Decide the level of risk you are willing to accept as it relates to the stability of the various branches you are using.
- Prepare a branching model so that those you support can visually understand the branching and merging strategy and where they are working. Walk-through a scenario using this model.

With this information, a branching strategy that is best for an Agile team can be designed with the type of branches needed, based on factors that can reduce risk, reduce effort, and increase stability. Having a long-term branching strategy in place can help you manage change now and into the future. As with Agile, your branching strategy can evolve over time to fit your needs.

7.1.3 Shifting Responsibilities for Merge and Build Activities

Within the context of continuous integration and build, there occurs a shift in roles and responsibilities in both the merging and building activities. In a more traditional method, CM professionals tend to have the majority of the responsibility for merges and builds. In an Agile context or companies striving for more agility, the responsibility moves to a shared effort between CM and development and sometimes is tilted toward development (with appropriate CM oversight).

This is actually a good thing since with continuous integration, there is typically a much higher volume of merge and build activity. In this case, when a change gets promoted to the mainline or project branch, an automated merge and build will occur. The key here is that automation should play a big part of this process since the activity level will be high and it is important to reduce errors introduced by manual steps that may hinder the velocity of the team.

7.1.4 Effective Merge for Agile

As part of the continuous integration process, a programmer checks in code. As long as the programmer checks in code to their backing stream frequently, they tend to avoid merge conflicts. But if the programmer waits too long and someone else changes the same code modules in the meantime, then a merge conflict will occur. Part of the reason for initiating the continuous integration practice is to reduce or avoid merging by more frequently checking in and promoting code. The more you merge, the less is the effort not only in the merging activity, but in the resulting rebuilding and retesting of the same code. However, it is important to understand the merge process so that we can use it effectively and understand how it ties into continuous build and integration.

A merge is an action that compares two files from the same ancestry and combines them back into one file. For example, version 5 of foo.c resides on the main branch. Programmer 1 checks out foo.c and begins working on it. Because it is a sizable change, she works on it for four weeks before checking it in. In the meantime, Programmer 2 comes along and checks out foo.c and modifies it for a quick change and checks it back into the main branch to create version 6 of foo.c. Now along comes Programmer 1. She is finally ready to check foo.c back into the main branch. Upon the check-in action, the version control system notifies the programmer that a merge is required.

If there are no logical lines of conflict and you have a CM version control tool that is capable of automated merging, then the merge will proceed in an automated manner, producing version 7 of foo.c. Then an automated build will be run as part of the continuous integration and build process. If there are merge conflicts (Programmers 1 and 2 both have changes to the same line within foo.c), then it is highly recommended to stop the merge action and instead merge version 6 of foo.c out to the private workspace of Programmer 1. This ensures there is adequate time to resolve the merge conflicts since Programmer 1 must talk with Programmer 2 to ensure that both sets of changes are included in the upcoming new version of foo.c. Then additional time will be needed to rebuild and retest the combined changes in the private workspace to reduce the risk of breaking the mainline. Once the merge conflict has been resolved in the private workspace, then a check-in can occur creating version 7 of foo.c. An automated build will be run as part of the continuous integration process.

The ability and extent to which merge occurs is dependent on the CM version control tool. A quality CM version control tool will recognize the need for a merge upon check-in and inform the programmer. More sophisticated CM version control tools will provide an automated and visual three-way merge window with a view of what areas within the code need to be merged, so that it's possible to see the changes and the code around these areas. In the example above, the three-way merge will compare version 5 (a.k.a., the original version or parent) and version 6 (changed version from Programmer 2) with the version that Programmer 1 is working on in her private branch. With a window for each version, the programmer has all of the information she needs to make an informed decision of what should go into version 7.

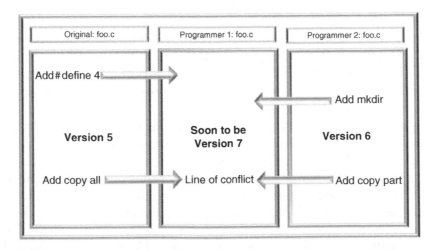

Figure 7-13   Example of a three-way merge screen.

As illustrated in the example above, if the merge compare reviews the changes between the two files and there are no logical lines of conflict, then this is considered a trivial merge. In this case, modern CM tools with an automated merging feature will require no human intervention for the merge. However, if there are logical lines of conflict (e.g., the same lines in each file have changed and differences must be resolved), then human intervention must occur to select and edit in the correct line changes. In general, the more automated the branching and merging capability, the easier and more productive the team can be.

A goal for an Agile team is to keep merging to a minimum, particularly avoiding merge conflicts. As discussed above, there is extra work involved when merge conflicts occur. Below are some common ways to minimize merging for Agile teams:

- Apply a lock to the file that you check out so that no one else can check it out. This also communicates to others that someone already has a file checked out. Also, if someone does have a file locked, then this can lead to discussions of how to make both changes to the file in a more orchestrated manner.

- Allocate code changes to programmers based on components (assuming that the product is architected well in a component-based manner). This is a bit against the grain of collective code ownership but may be worth it if numerous merge conflicts are occurring. However, you may also find that some programmers prefer working on certain parts of the code based on their domain knowledge, so this may be reasonable.

Pit Stop

The most challenging part of merging is merge conflicts (i.e., the same logical line in each file has changed and differences must be resolved). From an Agile perspective, this should be minimized.

7.1.4.1 Merge Challenges

As you approach merging, be aware of the merging challenges that may arise. They include:

- Merge Avoidance – when the team chooses to avoid merging because of the challenges that arise. The fact that they perceive challenges in the first place indicates a problem.

- Continuous Merge – when the team spends more time merging than working on new development or bug fixes. This may occur because multiple people are working on the same pieces of code.

- Event Merge – when the merge is so huge it becomes an event for the project team. Typically this type of merge occurs at the end of a project where merging was very infrequently done. This results in having the whole team wait around while the merge occurs, and often producing numerous merge conflicts, build problems, and testing problems, *ergo* slipping the schedule at the end.

7.1.5   Effective Build for Agile

When approaching the continuous integration process, the build activity is a critical step. In the context of continuous integration, the integration build process immediately follows the check-in/promotion of the code. The primary reason for the build is to compile, translate, and/or link source code in a certain order to generate executable code that can run on a computer.

Because continuous integration emphasizes continuous feedback, the build results are part of such feedback. They allow the programmers to get immediate feedback as to the success of the build and identify problems sooner, therefore minimizing larger build issues further downstream. Build problems are more easily analysed when only one change has occurred. If you wait until 20 changes (a.k.a., check-ins) have occurred it can be a greater challenge to identify who made what change, particularly when more than one check-in focused on the same set of code.

Upon conclusion of an integration build, the results should be communicated to the Agile team if the build compiled properly. If the integration build compiles and smoke tests successfully, then those who own a private workspace can update it with the latest "good" code from the successful build. However, careful consideration should be given as to when project team members need to update their private workspaces. In most cases, this should be left open to the programmers unless a significant change was made, when everyone should begin updating their workspace with the baseline.

7.1.5.1   Build Levels

To minimize or eliminate discrepancies of various builds on a project, all levels of build should have a similar process. What this means is that the individual build process used in the private workspace should follow the same build process used in the continuous integration build as people check-in to their backing stream. Therefore when code moves from the private workspace to the backing branch (e.g., mainline, project branch, etc.), the build process is the same to ensure that it will continue to build successfully. What are the various build levels? The various levels of build include:

- **Private build** – A private build is described as an individual programmer working in isolation (e.g., in their private workspace) who builds their code separate from others. The idea is that a change to code is built and unit tested locally before it ever sees integration into parent branches (therefore reducing downtime). The continuous build of the main branch or project release branch should only be a final verification build with little risk of build errors. The local build in a private workspace should never be broken prior to checking in or promoting into the parent branch. Synchronizing recent changes (when appropriate) into the private workspace helps ensure the developer is building and testing against the LAG (latest and greatest) working versions of code. Note, this implies that what is in the parent branch is stable.
  - In Agile it is imperative that you establish the private build process early on, since Agile methods initiate development (*ergo* building and integrating) in the first iteration, so all programmers build in the same manner. This ensures that all code can be built together and any build and execution issues can be corrected quickly. As a CM professional who establishes the build process, it is important to work with members of the Agile team (most likely development and test personnel) to ensure that their considerations are included.

- **Integration build** – An integration build is described as a build in a integration branch (e.g., on the main branch, project branch, etc.) where programmer's check-in or promote their code changes and where code modules are built together as part of the integration build. In the Agile world, continuous builds are, in effect, integration builds, since the objective of continuous build is to ensure all new code builds together successfully with the latest good project code after a programmer promotes code that they have successfully built and tested in their private workspace. This continuous process reduces the effort of merging individual code changes and uncovers build issues sooner. While most integration builds are used to continuously verify that code builds and smoke-tests together, some builds become more formal depending on the goal.
  - If the result of the build has no errors and passes a prescribed level of smoke test and meets a prescribed level of requirements, the integration build may evolve into the "test" build or a "release" build. In this case, a new build will not actually occur, but the integration build becomes the new baseline for test or potential release. This evolving approach is recommended for Agile to avoid the need to initiate a separate build for the test and release level. If the evolved test baseline (a.k.a., build) successfully passes all the systems and acceptance tests, then it evolves into the release build.

7.1.5.2   Build Automation for Continuous Integration

From an Agile perspective, the build should be very fast and well automated. Traditionally, build environments tend to be established with simple in-house scripts cobbled together between occasional manual steps. In a world of agility where there is much more pressure on building due to the increased frequency of builds, the time allowed for manual steps can constrain progress. Build management has come a long way with newer open-source and vendor-automated build tools and servers that can support multiple platforms, languages, and component reuse. They also tend to be easier to administer, have predefined common actions like building, migrating, and auditing, and have integrations with other tools like CM version control systems and test systems. Remember, integration is happening at much higher frequency when applying Agile methods, and software development is more complex than ever. The goal is to have an automated build system that can support complex environments while still being fast.

In an Agile context, it is highly recommended that you establish build automation for the continuous integration process to minimize the amount of time Agile teams spend on manual processes. In this case, build automation should be present in both the programmer's private workspace (a.k.a., private build) and in the integration branch (i.e., integration builds). Continuous builds typically imply small sets of changes, making it easier to identify what went wrong. The goal for any build automation should be simplicity and performance. In order to achieve this, there should be a focus on the infrastructure for continuous integration and build. What infrastructure needs to be in place to integrate continuously?

- *Fast and centralized server* – Since continuous integration implies frequent building, it is important to have a fast and powerful server to handle the load of the continuous builds. The central server approach is recommended so that the continuous integration technology can monitor the CM version control repository so that they can work effectively together.

- *CM version control tool* – It is important to have quality CM version control technology in place. In relation to continuous integration, the CM technology needs to be available on a centralized server and should have a strong branching and merging capability.

- *Continuous integration & build tool* – The continuous build and integration tool is needed to monitor the CM repository in real time and then initiate actions after the check-in or promote (it kicks off the build, smoke-tests, and reports on the results) when it notices changes to the repository. There are various mature and maturing tools in this space.

In addition, while having successful builds is important, the automated testing piece is critical so that the changes pass specific test criteria before being made available. Once these are in place, you can create a continuous integration environment. In all cases, focus on right-sizing the infrastructure to the need of the team to minimize technical debt (avoid spending time and effort on over-building an infrastructure) while maximizing velocity (ensuring the infrastructure can support the speed and load).

There are many build tools and servers that support continuous build. Ensure you are aware of your requirements and environment details. Consider reading chapter 8 "CM Tool as a Strategic Agile Partner" and chapter 9 "Evaluating Tools Suited for Agile" found later in this book.

7.1.6   Continuous Testing with Teeth

Two types of testing – at least – should be done in a continuous integration context: unit testing and smoke testing. Both of these types of testing should be done before moving the software into a more rigorous testing environment.

7.1.6.1   Unit Testing

Unit testing is a programmer task that should be run after changes are made to the code and it builds successfully in a private workspace context. It is a method where the program or function is tested in a modular way to ensure it meets the individual conditions of a requirement or story (or task therein).

Unit testing is also valuable in that it can be used as a unit regression test to ensure future changes do not regress the code. It is very important that the unit test cases are version controlled. Better yet, consider version controlling the unit test case within the same directory as the code it supports. The unit test case can also form the building block for the smoke test, input into integration and regression testing, and input to establishing a full test suite for integration and system testing of the functionality of the product.

7.1.6.2   Smoke Testing

Smoke testing is done after the build completes successfully and prior to migrating it to the test team for more formal testing (functional test, regression test, etc.). The smoke test is designed as a broad test to ensure the built product can execute. It is also used to perform a cursory examination of functionality to ensure the code works and to see if there are any more problems that would prevent it from running in a full test environment. In effect, the smoke test provides immediate and continuous feedback as to the quality of the build package.

If you are not already performing smoke tests after the build, irrespective of the method used, it is highly recommended. It can be a cost-effective way of identifying simple execution and high-level functionality problems prior to engaging expensive testing resources and environments. If the smoke test does not pass, then there is no reason to migrate the build package to the more formal testing done by professional testers. Also, because it should be run at least every day, it makes it much easier to identify when (the date) and where (which code was changed) the code breaks.

The most effective approach to smoke testing is to include this action into an automated continuous integration and build process. Repeatable and automated processes help reduce manual intervention. If you want to include a smoke test into the continuous integration and build process, this type of smoke test may need to be a shorter version of a smoke test that you may run on a nightly basis. The reason for this is that if there are frequent check-ins occurring on the code, this may overload the system, since the smoke test is often the longest running part of the continuous integration and build process. However, the frequency of check-ins that initiate the continuous integration and build process should be evaluated to determine if this is appropriate. If there are frequent check-ins, a simplified version of the full smoke test can be used for each check-in, while the full smoke test could be run on a nightly basis. There is no right or wrong way, as long as you apply smoke tests to your benefit.

If you do not have a smoke test process and want to know where to begin, the key ingredients include: a master test case that includes a series of test cases that exercise the high-level functions of the product release; a smoke test environment; a script that initiates the smoke test after the product has been built successfully and can be included into an automated continuous integration and build process.

7.1.7   Reflections on Continuous Integration and Build

As we conclude the section on adapting to continuous integration and build, consider the following:

- Consider adjusting story or requirement tasks to a bite-size level more appropriate for continuous integration.
- Focus on establishing or adjusting the branching strategy to suit the team's specific needs, including ways to minimize merging.

- Give thought to the benefit of having developers work off the private branch.

- Consider realigning merge and build responsibilities for Agile teams.

- Focus on understanding build levels and consider the importance of private workspaces.

- Consider if appropriate levels of testing (the unit test and smoke test) are being built into the continuous integration and build process.

7.2   Adapting CM Planning

In traditional phased project lifecycle methods, CM planning tends to be a big effort up front (BEUF). The goal is to move away from BEUF CM planning to a more incremental CM planning approach. This approach is not unlike the way Agile has moved from a BEUF approach to the iteration planning approach. Because CM forms the basis for controlling changes, CM planning may be more important than initially realized, particularly given the volume and rate of change when following an Agile method. Also, it may be better to have a thoughtful approach in considering your CM needs (e.g., incremental) rather than an ad hoc approach where you may increase your risk, find yourself missing code, not know who is responsible for a certain CM task, all because you did not take a moment to consider your needs.

The incremental deployment approach of CM focuses on building out CM functions over a period of time based on the value perceived and resources available so they can be more easily accomplished and offered to the product team on a "just-in-time" basis. This ultimately provides a balance between funding, resources, and risk management.

Allow the trained and experienced Agile individuals and their interactions to contribute to the CM structure while still maintaining CM integrity. Even when using traditional methods or when you have to follow an industry standard, the best CM plans I have seen are those that are brief and to the point and follow lean and creative approaches. Also, in an Agile framework, ensure the CM planning approach and any documents therein are allowed to evolve over time so that CM does not get too brittle or rigid and instead continues to adapt to the team's needs.

7.2.1   Balancing Agile Values with Organization Needs

Some Agile professionals may push back on formal CM planning since they will not see that it provides immediate value to their project. While not always aligned with an Agile mindset, Agile professionals need to understand that there is a belief by some companies that either some structure or industry standards are needed to achieve an organizational goal. Keep in mind that Agile methods apply at the product and/or project level while Standards (e.g., ISO, IEEE) and Frameworks (e.g., Cobit, ITIL) are usually implemented at the organizational level and tailored to meet the individual needs of a particular project. This is important to understand, since Agile teams look at what is the optimal value for the project while management is looking at what is of value at the organizational level. Standards and frameworks may not be so easily discarded and often must be integrated.

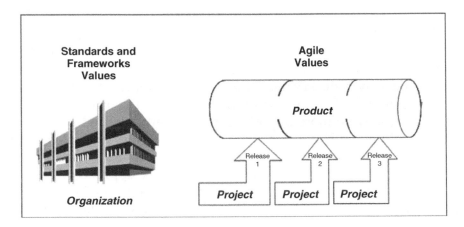

Figure 7-14   Different focuses of standards/frameworks and Agile.

Of course, there can be debate as to the real value of the frameworks and standards depending on the clarity of management goals (i.e., is it to get the certification name tag or does management really understand the value?) and if the framework or standard is being implemented in a reasonable way.

As you are considering the lean aspects of CM planning, also consider the various approaches that can be applied. They include applying an iterative approach, considering reuse options, utilizing an iteration 0, and considering less traditional formats for the CM plan. Below are details of these approaches with hopes to better support you with information when adapting the CM plan for Agile.

7.2.2   Getting Started with Iteration 0

If you are a team working on a new product using Agile methods, early on you will need CM infrastructure and some high-value CM practices such as version control and build management. The CM infrastructure and practices needed can be discussed in a time-boxed iteration 0. Since iteration 0 is no longer uncommon to new product development using Agile, this may be an appropriate place to consider your CM needs via CM planning.

In general, reviewing the areas of CM planning (i.e., roles and responsibilities, overall CM structure, CM processes and tasks around identification, controls, audits, and reports) can help you understand elements of CM, and then the team can prioritize these elements based on perceived value. In effect this forms the basis for CM planning. During iteration 0, some of the higher-value tasks of CM planning may begin.

A focus on CM roles and responsibilities may prove important as the overall Agile roles and responsibilities are being discussed. Remember, as part of CM planning, we have to consider the attributes of moving quickly to meet Agile needs, while at the same time ensure stability of change to meet CM needs. This allows us to consider both the Agile and CM values and perspectives.

The output of iteration 0 from a CM perspective is the identification of those areas of CM that an Agile team considers as "must-have" (a.k.a., of highest value) and those with lesser value. Those that are considered as "must-have" may be started as early as reasonable or may be included in the product backlog and managed with other stories and tasks. Another output of iteration 0 for CM may be the beginning of a CM plan that can be implemented in various formats (to be discussed in subsequent sections).

7.2.3   Evolutionary CM Plan

The evolutionary approach to CM planning involves iteratively identifying your CM needs over time. This is effectively applying an Agile approach to CM planning, much like applying iterative planning to projects based on Agile methods. If you are working on a new product, consider starting iteration 0 including CM planning during this timeframe. In this scenario, CM planning can be part of the CM envisioning effort (see section 6.1 – "CM Envisioning" for more details). The evolutionary or iterative approach to CM planning allows the Agile team to establish CM as needs are uncovered. This approach is best suited for Agile teams without any dependencies on organization or industry standards.

As you consider the typical contents for a CM plan, prioritize the areas of focus. Consider focusing on the areas of CM roles and responsibilities, CM tasks to keep development in control, and simple procedures (e.g., version control and build management) that are based on team interactions as code is changed while ensuring control and integrity.

Using iteration 0 with the evolutionary CM planning approach provides a powerful way to introduce CM value while limiting CM debt. Once iteration 0 is complete, iteratively evaluate the CM needs as part of the retrospective and incrementally establish the CM plan in the appropriate format (discussed in a subsequent section).

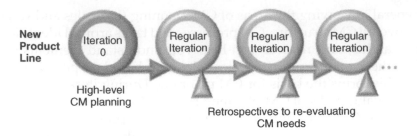

Figure 7-15   Evolutionary CM planning (with iteration 0).

7.2.4   Reusable CM Plan

If the organization would like to have a consistent level of CM or is looking to attain an organization level certification such as CMMI level 3, ISO, etc., a standard organizational level CM Plan may be established. This approach includes content for infrastructure, security, policies, processes, roles, etc. The advantage of having an organization or enterprise-wide CM plan is that it can be reused as the basis for creating product-level CM plans, minimizing effort in writing it again and again.

At the organizational level, you may have a CM plan for the traditional methods following a more big effort up front approach and a CM plan for Agile methods following a more evolutionary approach (as mentioned in the previous section). In both cases, the CM plan templates should be tested and improved, based on feedback from projects using traditional methods and those using Agile methods. This makes the CM planning approach and templates more representative of the methods they support and also a better starting point for teams.

The big advantage of the organizational CM plan approach for an Agile team is that some Agile teams may find themselves in the conundrum of having to satisfy an organization certification while wanting to minimize the effort it takes to create a CM plan. The "re-use" approach can be used whether the product is brand new or legacy. It significantly reduces the effort of constructing a CM plan, allowing the Agile team to focus the recovered time on development work. Then as the team moves forward, the details of the plan will change as the team establishes their own process through interactions with each other and tools they use.

> **Pit Stop**
>
> Some Agile teams find themselves in the conundrum of having to satisfy a standard or framework (CMMI, ISO, IEEE, ITIL, etc.) while wanting to minimize the effort it takes to create a CM plan. While not ideal for an Agile method, the "reuse" approach takes into consideration the balance between following Agile and achieving organizational goals.

Following this "reuse" approach, the CM engineer who represents the product team will acquire the organizational CM plan template that is appropriate for the method being used and create a copy of it to establish a product-level CM plan for the product and team therein. If it is a brand new product or a legacy product that does not have an existing CM plan that is following an Agile method, then once the CM plan template is procured, using a combination of the iteration 0 and the evolutionary CM plan approach referenced above can be a good way to validate and iteratively improve the CM plan for the product.

If it is a legacy product that does have an existing CM plan and must now meet a new certification, then a gap analysis can be conducted and the existing CM plan can be updated in a whole or incremental manner depending on the changes needed to the existing CM plan. A reuse approach is best suited for Agile teams that have dependencies on organization or industry standards or frameworks. This way the CM plan can be pre-structured and reused to meet the needs of both Agile and the organization direction. While not ideal for an Agile approach, it takes into consideration the balance between following Agile and achieving organizational goals.

7.2.5   Inherited CM Plan

When a legacy product team transitions from using traditional methods to Agile methods, you may encounter many existing documents. Within this set of materials, you may also find that numerous inherited documents have not been used for quite some time after their initial creation. It is a good practice, in this case, to remove the unused documents if they serve no purpose or have little or no value. However, you may find that a few inherited documents have value.

The value of an inherited CM plan if actively used is that it will provide you with the details of how CM is being implemented on the legacy product. For those new to the product team, this document can be used as the basis for CM training, so you are combining uses for the CM plan.

If you appreciate the value of the CM plan, then the first step is to review and evaluate the inherited CM plan. If it is unreasonable (e.g., outdated, too heavy, complex, or cryptic), then consider not using it but keeping it handy as reference (to be thrown out once a leaner and better CM plan is established). If you start anew, consider utilizing the evolutionary CM planning approach mentioned above.

If the inherited CM plan is reasonable, then it may form a good baseline for understanding what exists (i.e., the CM process and tools baseline), which in turn provides a basis for understanding where to adapt. As you think about adapting, consider using a prioritization approach where you identify the CM areas that have higher value and where change may need to occur earlier rather than later. Typically, the areas that may require some initial adjustment are realigning CM roles and some of the CM procedures (particularly the build procedure) as they apply to Agile.

7.2.6 Types of CM Planning Formats

When most people think of the deliverable of CM planning, they typically think of a CM plan as an individual document created with one of the common word-processing programs. While this may still be a common format, with the advent of wikis and other collaborative software, there are options that may be better suited for Agile teams. It is important to stop thinking of a document as a physical word-processing artifact in the traditional sense. While a document can be stand-alone, it can also be a virtual document and collaborative document.

Considerations for Format Type

As you review the format types, there are several factors that should be considered by a team. Factors include the:

- Effort: The level of effort to implement and maintain the software that supports the format type may factor into the decision on which format to select. Some format types are prepackaged with software that comes with a user interface and other format types may require a separate installation.

- Ease of use: This is the level of knowledge and effort it takes to use the format type and change an artifact (CM plan, etc.) within the format. These may factor into the decision on which format to select. Some format types are based on software that is already known by most people. Others may require a learning curve. For example, some formats use plain text while others require the ability to format headers, lists, etc. or the ability to use special commands.

- Versioning capabilities: This means the level of version functionality that exists within the format type. Essentially this means that changes are versioned and you can go back to an existing version of a document. For example, having a check-out/check-in feature may be of benefit. This factors in the ability to recover to a past version and ensure that changes are being captured.

- Ability to provide notification of changes: This is the ability to notify users when changes have been made to the artifact. Some format types include this feature while others do not. For example, every time a change is saved or checked in, users who are interested will be notified of the change, especially when they have versions of a document they are working with.

- Distributed capability: This is the level to which the format type incorporates the ability to convey or distribute the artifact across multiple sites. This is particularly valuable when the team is distributed and everyone needs to see the same document at the same time.

- Collaboration capability: This is the level to which the format type provides an environment that supports capabilities for sharing and collaborating. On an Agile team, it is important to have an environment that promotes sharing, updating, and collaborating as one method of continuous interaction amongst team members.

While I consider these key factors, you should prioritize or weigh the importance of each and identify other factors that can help you make a decision for your situation. Another factor to consider which is not format-specific is that the team should agree on what constitutes an approved change to a document. On the one hand, this does not need to be formal change approval, but on the other hand, random changes by many folks can lead to instability of the artifact or worse, when two people disagree with each other, which can lead to change wars resulting in missing details. Also keep in mind that within a team, more than one format can be used.

Pit Stop

Irrespective of the document format chosen, the goal for an Agile team is to establish a CM plan that defines the CM rules of the road for the team while keeping the plan lean, then to add more incrementally as you find additional CM value.

Below are several format types that I have used or seen used by Agile teams. Consider your team situation and format types below. At the end of the format types section, there is a table that presents the format types with a high-level view of their pros and cons. Let us explore these options in more detail.

Physical document created by word-processing program – As mentioned, this is the traditional approach to establishing an online CM plan, using the common word-processing programs. The advantage of creating a document in this format is that it is what many people are used to. Another advantage to this approach is that it can be easily duplicated (reused) from project to project (as needed) and it can be easily marked with a version number.

A disadvantage with this approach is that in order to share an artifact in this format, it requires another tool to host it. There is no real collaboration feature since it is effectively a standalone document. Another disadvantage is that while it can be emailed out to the team, it is not always clear that it is the latest version since you do not know where it originated or where its hosting site is. Often when something is changed, unless you commonly use change tracking, it is hard to tell what has specifically changed from version to version.

Physical document placed on a document hosting/collaboration solution – In order to make a document available, such as an online CM plan for all to see at the same time, a hosting solution is needed that is accessible by everyone on the team. Common hosting solutions include network drives, while more sophisticated solutions are browser-based collaboration platforms or document management solutions. Each of these hosting solutions offer shared workspaces and access control to the document but their pros and cons will vary.

There are several advantages with using this approach. One advantage of a document hosting solution is that they often come with collaborative features where the document is accessible at all times and team members can be notified when changes are made. Some collaboration hosting solutions allow for threaded conversations and the ability to comment on posted documents. Another advantage of a document hosting solution is that they typically come with options to structure the environment so that documents can be placed in context relating to a theme, a practice, a role, and more. Yet another advantage is that document hosting solutions typically come with search functions to help you locate documents on topics. And finally, many document hosting solutions can be set up to allow distributed access, which is very useful for distributed teams.

A key disadvantage is that someone needs to set up and maintain the document hosting solution and keep abreast of the disk space requirements and usage. Another advantage is that there is typically a cost associated with a hosting solution, whether it is for licensing or maintenance, and even if it is freeware, there is a cost for someone to set up and maintain the environment.

Virtual document created by a wiki – The wiki approach effectively wraps the document around the actual hosting solution within a shared online workspace. Wikis provide the team with the ability to collaboratively write documents through the intranet and Internet depending on the distributed nature of the team. A simple form of a wiki is a notepad that emulates a document. A complex form of an Internet wiki is Wikipedia (http://www.wikipedia.org/), which is an online encyclopedia that is written and edited by a virtual team of volunteers from across the world.

There are several advantages with using this approach. One advantage of a wiki as a document is that it provides a collaborative environment where the full team has access to write and edit. This can be an advantage for Agile teams and follows a collective code-sharing approach. Many wikis provide version control functions and the ability to track, compare, and restore previous versions. Another advantage is that Internet wikis allow distributed access, which is very useful for virtual and distributed teams. This allows dispersed teams to collaborate together and see the updates as they get published. Wikis typically provide an edit, review, and publish process to allow the changes to be considered prior to making them live. You can also write the CM plan at a very high level to keep it short and then link to modular wiki pages for CM procedures/training and other CM components, similar to a hub and spoke model. Many of these benefits are beneficial to an Agile team.

A disadvantage to some wikis is that they require the users to learn the syntax of formatting headings, lists, or tables, bolding or italicizing words, etc., similar to the HTML language. However, more recent wikis offer "what you see is what you get" (a.k.a., WYSIWYG) editing. Because a wiki is not a portal approach, it cannot be easily duplicated (reused) by other product teams. Another disadvantage is that because anyone can change a wiki, sections can be accidentally or intentionally deleted. You should consider an approval process for changes to any documents that multiple people rely on. Finally someone needs to set up and maintain the wiki hosting solution and keep abreast of the disk space requirements and usage.

Table 7-1   Document format types and high-level pros and cons.

	Physical Document – Word Processed	Physical Document on Hosting Solution	Virtual Document – Wiki
Implementation Effort	☺ Comes with most computers	☹ Setup hosting solution	😐 Setup of Wiki solution
Effort to Change Document	☺ Easy	☺ Easy	😐 Medium
Versioning	☹ Manual	☺ Automated	☺ Automated
Notification	☹ No	☺ Yes	☺ Yes
Distributed	☹ Manual (email)	😐 Automatic with Internet setup	😐 Automatic with Internet setup
Collaboration	☹ Standalone	😐 Promotes sharing	☺ Promotes sharing & collaboration

7.2.7   Adapting CM Roles and Responsibilities for Agile

The roles and responsibilities needed to manage CM functions to benefit a product team should be discussed within a CM planning context because they need to be decided and settled, especially toward the beginning of a new product venture. They involve responsibilities to establish the CM function via CM planning, to establish a version control and build environment for the developers to conduct their work, to perform the more common CM practices like check-outs and check-ins, problem management, builds, and releases, and when applying industry standard CM audit and reporting.

With that in mind, consider these two key changes when moving CM into an Agile context. They include:

- CM should be considered as a holistic part of the Agile team.
- CM responsibilities are enacted by many on the team and not just one person.

Both of these changes help move the mindset away from the traditional thinking of the CM roles and responsibilities to more of an Agile mindset, where team involvement is key and people share many responsibilities.

7.2.7.1   CM as Holistic Part of the Agile Team

Within an Agile context, an Agile team will benefit more directly from CM when CM and its functions become a recognized part of the Agile team. CM professionals can join the team in one of two capacities.

- The CM professional can dedicate full-time effort to the Agile team, depending on how big the Agile team is and the product that is being supported. In this case, they can take on additional responsibilities as available.

- The CM professional supports several related Agile teams at once. In this case, they may be limited to only CM responsibilities but could occasionally take on additional responsibilities, prioritized by the Agile team.

In each case, the CM professional who becomes part of the Agile team (particularly a more senior one) will perform some of the more common CM responsibilities, to include:

- Initiating the CM planning within an Agile context.
- Establishing the CM infrastructure needed.
- Helping construct the programmer workspace and build environment.
- Managing the problem management system as needed.
- Conducting CM auditing and reporting as appropriate.
- Playing a role in the coordination and implementation of the release.

Some of the additional responsibilities within the Agile team per opportunity and/or necessity include (adjust as appropriate):

- Helping with automation of the build process and other processes to the level needed by an Agile team.
- Helping with architecture and design since the way the code is structured can have a big impact on simplifying distributed development.
- Supporting integration efforts for development and test and amongst other interdependent product lines.

This type of team attitude encourages a shared understanding of CM where many team members will gain better CM knowledge and will participate more willingly. Also, having CM represented on the team, the

CM function will be seen as more of an enabler of change (which it is) to streamline the CM processes and assist the team. Involving a CM professional in the retrospectives allows them to hear the opportunities for improvement in the CM space and have a better understanding of current CM issues, ultimately leading to CM improvements that are more closely aligned with what an Agile team needs.

It is important to understand the change in team culture for teams that apply an Agile framework. There are benefits to collective "team" responsibility focusing less on the specific roles of a team, in that it reduces the bottleneck and silos of information and increases the CM knowledge of how to do tasks.

This may be a cultural shift for some CM professionals insofar as they will have less ownership of their domain and must shift some of their focus to continuous process improvement of CM and the tools therein.

Pit Stop

In adapting CM roles, two areas that will benefit Agile include considering the CM professional as a holistic part of the Agile team and sharing some of the CM responsibilities with the Agile team.

Finally, when you move to an Agile method, you may have to adjust your staffing model, particularly if your organization follows a phased or project-based method. In order to build an empowered team where there is trust and fair reward, everyone should be on the same team on an ongoing basis (product-based) including the CM professional. When you follow a product-based model, this supports Agile in a more integral way since everyone is already on the same team.

7.2.7.2 Adjusting CM Responsibilities

There will be similar responsibilities for the standard CM functions, but the role or who enacts those responsibilities may change when you are following an Agile method. Consider approaching this by identifying the CM roles and their common responsibilities, then stripping away the role tag so that you are left with CM responsibilities. From there, the responsibilities can be: prioritized and reorganized; made more or less formal; and allocated to those roles within the new product context and method being followed. Within an Agile context, some of the CM responsibilities will be played by more than one person because of the team concept that Agile advocates. The following are some common CM responsibilities that can be adjusted in an Agile context:

- **Change control responsibilities** – In a more traditional method, there is a formal change control board (CCB) that manages changes to requirements and those elements that make up the release. In an Agile context, the product owner and team perform a form of change control in the iteration planning session.

- **Build responsibilities** – More traditional build management has CM professionals doing most of the build activity. The focus when adapting for Agile involves sharing the build activities with developers. The more automated, the easier they are for everyone to do. In order to make the build process a development activity while limiting possible errors, it is important for a CM professional along with a development counterpart to craft an automated build process that may include unit testing but also align with the official integration build process that constructs the formal release build. If the official integration build can be automated enough to be trusted, then anyone on the team can initiate it and it can be used effectively in a continuous integration and build process. This ensures that the way the developers build is the same way that the build should occur for formal builds, keeping the overall build process as streamlined as possible and eliminating the more common build and integration problems. This also implies that the various automated build scripts can be collectively owned with oversight by the CM professionals to ensure they continue to follow CM values and ensure the product builds with integrity.

- **Merge responsibilities** – CM may own the merging process and have exclusive control over the integration branches. Even if developers were not allowed to perform merging activities in the past, there may be good reason to allow them to do so now. Irrespective of the method, it is always beneficial to allow developers to own the merging activities since they have the most knowledge of the code being merged. Ownership of this task will need to be shared with oversight so that continuous integration can work effectively without CM professionals always having to step in. For Agile to work most effectively, the reduction or elimination of extra steps or formal approvals should occur. In order to make merging an activity for developers while limiting possible errors, it is important for a CM professional along with a development counterpart to craft an automated merge and integration process so there is no mistaking which code in which branches should merge together. Please note that automated merging capabilities are found in the more modern CM tools.

7.2.8 Reflections on CM Planning for Agile

As we conclude the section on adapting CM planning for Agile teams, note the following:

- If you are a new product line following Agile, consider initiating an iteration 0 with a focus on CM envisioning.
- For CM planning, determine what approach may be applied (big effort up front, evolutionary, reuse, or inherited).
- Consider the various formats for CM planning (document, hosted, wiki, etc.)
- Give thought to reviewing and realigning CM responsibilities for Agile teams.
- Consider making a CM professional part of the Agile team.

7.3 Adapting to Support Refactoring

Refactoring is a software engineering technique of taking legacy product code and incrementally making it more efficient without affecting the customer and the behavior of the product. The key aspect is that these changes should be very small in nature to minimize the risk of breaking the functionality. There are various goals to refactoring. They include simplifying the code structure, making the code run faster, and enabling the code to run with less memory and disk space requirements. Another aspect of this is that it is not just the code within the file that changes, but often there is a restructuring that occurs where the file name itself changes, the location of the file may change within the directory structure, and even the directory name or structure may change.

What is the implication of refactoring to CM and version control when so much can change because of refactoring? First, the CM tool should have a strong and easy-to-use graphical user interface (GUI) capability. This allows the engineers to easily see the code structure of their product so they can readily identify the files and directories they will work with. Second, within the context of the GUI, the CM tool should have an easy to use drag-and-drop functionality so that files can be moved with ease by the programmers with the ability to see their changes immediately. When the file or directory move action occurs, it should also very quickly move the element to its proper place within the version control repository while still maintaining the history of that change. In other words, integrity and performance are important so the programmers can change code with confidence and not wait around too long for this action to occur.

Pit Stop

With the need to refactor comes the need to change not just files in their current location, but the ability to relocate and rename files. The same applies to relocating and renaming directories. When directories are relocated, the contents of the directories need to be tracked. This requires a CM tool with version control capabilities that can handle this sophisticated tracking of changes.

Third, because refactoring implies a lot of very small changes being made on a continuous basis, the CM tool must have excellent change set capabilities, meaning that refactoring changes can be easily identifiable to keep them separate from the requirement and story changes. With these capabilities come the need for a CM system to have strong version tracking and history capabilities, not only for changes within files, but files that will have name changes, directories that have name changes, and files and directories that may be moved. This requires a CM tool to have a much more dynamic way to track changes beyond the traditional move capabilities.

Lastly, consideration should be given to the branch where the refactoring work occurs. If the refactoring work includes small changes and can be easily mixed with stories and defects, then working from the private workspace is reasonable. If the refactoring changes are fairly complex or if there are two or more people working on refactoring, then establishing a task branch may be appropriate to have a place to verify that the changes are working together and can be staged before promoting them to a team integration branch (main branch or project release branch). In all cases, the changes should be built and unit tested prior to any promotion into an integration branch where many people are working.

7.3.1 Reflections on Refactoring

As we conclude the section on adapting to support refactoring, note the following:

- Investigate a CM version control tool that will support the level of code and code structure changes you envision when refactoring (changing files, moving files, renaming files, moving directories, renaming directories, etc.).

- If you are applying refactoring, investigate if the CM version control tool provides strong GUI capabilities to visually see the code structure, helps with managing code structure changes (e.g., by using drag and drop), and assists with editing the code.

- Consider the extent of the refactoring work and the branch where the refactoring changes will be worked on.

7.4 Adapting to Support Pair Programming

As you may know, pair programming is an Agile practice where two programmers work together at the same computer continuously collaborating as they focus on the same requirement, story, or task therein. As one of the programmers sits and tactically codes (a.k.a., the driver), the other strategically reviews the changes (a.k.a., the navigator) to ensure they are meeting the needs of the requirement or story while ensuring coding standards are met, identifying defects in the code, and in many cases identifying careless mistakes. Then the programmer who was the navigator changes places and becomes the driver. This cycle occurs approximately every 30 minutes or so with short breaks in between.

The primary benefits of utilizing this practice are to improve design quality, reduce defects, and provide a learning opportunity while sharing coding information. The risks associated with pair programming include skill and experience disparity, ego management, and logistical challenges. Some programmers find that working so intimately with another programmer is unsettling and relies on the two programmers being able to work together well. As a result, the pair programming practice appears to be one of the lesser used Agile practices according a 2008 Agile study done by Scott Ambler.

What is the implication of pair programming to CM and version control? Typically, the code produced by pair programmers tends to be of better quality, include more meaningful comments, and may be more reusable. Depending on the type of module the pair are building (e.g., a common function such as login), it can reduce effort by other products that need (and can reuse) such a function. Using a CM version control system, if properly commented on, may create more of an opportunity to reuse the code later and reduce programming time since the function can be more easily identifiable.

Pit Stop

In pair programming, it is very important for each pair member to check-in code when they have finished driving and include a comment with the names of the pair. This ensures the rapid change is being controlled, reduces chances of overwriting, and provides for easy recovery.

More importantly, as previously mentioned, pair programming implies that you have two programmers working on the same task, story, or requirement. However, like most operating systems, CM systems recognize each person separately. A CM workspace is created for each programmer. When the pair team checks in code, there can be confusion as to who "owns" the change. The question is: How committed is the Agile team to ensure that whoever is working on the code is using his or her login or CM account? The answer to this question will steer you to a preferred option. What are some pair programming workspace options to reduce confusion? There are several ways of handling this:

- **Co-located dual CM workspaces** – In this scenario, as the name implies, the pair each have their own login and CM workspace. At the end of each programming period, the driver checks in the code into their own private workspace with both names in the comment field upon check-in. This assures that the changes are frequently saved in the CM system. Then when the other programmer becomes a driver, the new driver checks out the code and begins the next cycle of pair programming following the same process (i.e., the driver checks in the code into their own private workspace with both names in the comment field upon check-in). This option is typically more effective when the pair are working on one or a very small number of code modules. Please note that depending on the CM tool being used (and its capability) and the branching process, the following may be considered:
  - The respective pair member could check into a private workspace backed by a private branch that would require a promotion to the pair task branch so that the other pair member can see the change.

Then a sync must occur to the other pair member's private workspace to get the latest from the pair shared branch. While this may sound complicated, it can be relatively easily automated so that it looks like a simple check-out and check-in.

o   The respective private workspaces could be backed directly by a task branch. Then the check-in goes directly to the task branch and the other pair member checks it out into their workspace. This lacks the usability of the private branch, but is more straightforward in the check-out-check-in model.

Navigator

Driver

- **Co-located single CM workspace** – In this scenario, the pair share a common CM workspace. This is not a recommended CM practice since CM emphasizes modularity and Agile emphasizes personal accountability. The goal is to clearly designate this workspace for the pair. A co-located single CM workspace can be done in one of two ways.

o   Use one of the pair's login and CM credentials and share this workspace on an ongoing basis. Ensure that each time a pair member has finished driving (or programming), then check in the code with a comment as to what was done and who was the driver. Do not worry if the code is not complete or buildable. The goal here is to capture the continuous change.

o   Establish a shared CM account. Depending on how the company establishes logins and accounts for users, this option may not be possible. In the case where it is, create a CM account or establish CM credentials in the CM version control system for the paired team. Name the CM account or credentials with both names or pair-team name to more readily identify them. Ensure that each time a pair member has finished driving (or programming), they check-in the code with a comment as to what was done and who was the driver. At the very least, add who was the driver to the comment. Do not worry if the code is not complete or buildable. The goal here is to capture the continuous change.

- **Distributed pair programming** – For those teams that are attempting distributed pair programming where one member of the pair is at one site and the other is at another site, then in addition to the CM version control tool, you will need a screen-sharing program. This approach can work for both near-shore and off-shore situations.
  - In this scenario, each person can take control of the screen depending on who is driving while the navigator can review the programming as it is occurring and provide comments and suggestions as needed. Keep in mind that the response rate is dependent on the network bandwidth between sites.
  - This approach works more effectively when you apply a "dual CM workspace." In this scenario, the pair each have their own login and private workspace. At the end of each programming period, the driver checks in the code into their own CM workspace with both names in the comment field upon check-in. This assures that the changes are frequently saved in the CM system. Then when the other programmer becomes a driver, the new driver checks out the code and begins the next cycle of pair programming following the same process (i.e., the driver checks in the code into their own CM workspace with both names in the comment field upon check-in).

7.4.1   Reflections on Pair Programming

As we conclude the section on adapting to support pair programming, note the following:

- Investigate the company's standards on sharing accounts.
- Investigate the team structure and interest level to see if distributed pair programming is an option.
- Determine the best pair programming workspace option for those performing pair programming.
- Consider if you plan to use a private workspace with a private branch or not. This impacts the check-in process.

7.5   Adapting to Support Test Driven Development (TDD)

Test-driven development (a.k.a., TDD) is an Agile practice where test cases are written in an incremental manner, slightly ahead of the code that is built to satisfy this test increment. The goal is not to write the full test case or code, but to incrementally build the code as you use the test case as a form of design. In this manner, when the programmer begins coding, they code just enough to successfully pass the test. Because the code changes are typically small and incremental in nature in TDD, defects are more easily identified and corrected. This approach also forces the programmer to have a much clearer understanding of the specification of the change being requested when they write the test case. When the programmer improves the code enough to pass the test, the test may be updated to capture another task of the requirements or story and the programming and test cycle continues. The new functionality is not considered complete until the test cases that support the requirements or story are run successfully.

This practice is particularly valuable to Agile because in iteration 1, the product team starts coding and this focuses attention on serious design and testing early on in the project lifecycle. Within an iteration level, unit test cases are created and used as a means to determine if the code meets the needs. Within a release level, system and integration tests are constructed to ensure the new code works with the existing code and determine the health of the release. These days there are numerous unit test frameworks that can help you build and automate the unit testing process.

How can CM help? A key part of TDD is to create test assets – namely unit, system, and integration tests that support the code. The value of CM is that it is used to store and manage change to important product assets, and in this scenario, the various test cases. Below are considerations of version control and the TDD practice:

- It is critical that these test assets are version controlled and managed as the team would manage changes to the code applying the same version control procedures. Remember, the test case evolves over time as does the code to pass the next test, *ergo* the importance of keeping the test case and code in sync.

- Ensure there is clear relationship in the CM repository between the unit test case and the code that is being developed to meet the test case. It is recommended to place the test case in the same directory as the code it supports.

- Consider meaningful naming conventions to indicate a relationship between the test case and the code it supports.

- This supports traceability but from a different direction. In TDD, the traceability works the other way, from code back to the test case, and really as a pair.

- Consider automating the test case process as much as possible so that the programmer writing the code can quickly and easily run the test case and quickly see the results. Also consider automating the system and integration testing process so that when the integration build occurs, the appropriate functional and integration tests are run.

- As you establish automated system and integration tests, ensure you version control these test assets as well. Ensure the tests are kept in a standard location in the CM version control repository so that the automated build finds and runs the tests.

7.5.1   Reflections on Test-Driven Development

As we conclude the section on adapting to support test-driven development, note the following:

- Ensure the test assets are version controlled and in the same directory as the code it supports.
- Consider automating the private build process to automatically execute the test case upon completion of a successful private build.
- Establish a naming convention to relate the test case with the code it supports.

7.6   Adapting to Support Agile Distributed Teams

While some Agile teams are co-located, many others are distributed. In fact, distributed development teams are commonplace. It is important to consider a CM code access solution that best fits a team's particular situation. This is not only relevant to Agile but to any project or product lifecycle method. A way to approach this is to begin by performing a distributed analysis.

7.6.1   Distributed Analysis for Distributed Teams

Distributed analysis focuses on identifying certain characteristics of the product team's situation that help in determining an appropriate code access solution. The characteristics include:

- Identifying the general proximity of the team. Is the team co-located (i.e, together), are some co-located and some near-shore, or are members both co-located and off-shore (and maybe even some near-shore).
- Identifying the number of team members who will participate in development activities from each site. An example of this is that of a small slightly distributed Agile team (e.g., 7 members locally and 2 off-shore) versus a large highly distributed Agile team (e.g., 50 members divided into 5 working teams separated from each other, where 2 teams are local but in different regions and 3 are off-shore and at separate sites). Each has very different characteristics and will most likely require a different code access solution.

- Identifying the complexity of the development technology used. Complexity may be derived from how much RAM the development technology requires to run and how network-intensive it is. Complexity levels can include:
  - Low complexity – development technology that has low RAM requirements, low network dependency or few network transactions, and ASCII-text-based development.
  - High complexity – development technology that has high RAM requirements, high network dependency or constant network transactions, and object-based development.

This input will be valuable when reviewing the various code access approaches that can be used to access code for a product via a CM system. Once you have completed your analysis, use it to determine the best code access technology approach. The product characteristics from the distributed analysis should drive the decision. A driving factor is the proximity and size of the team. The more co-located the team, the more straightforward the solution.

7.6.2 Code Access Approaches

The following figure illustrates how team size can relate to various possible code access approaches in a simple way.

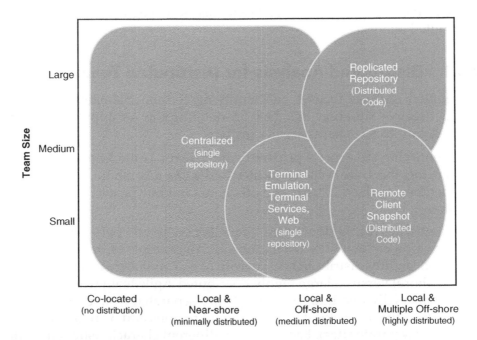

Figure 7-16 Code access approaches based on size and distribution of team.

Of course, a review of your situation should be done in more detail, as well as a review of the details of each code access option. The code access options include:

- Single site for co-located team – This is where you have one CM system with one CM repository for the code. Provided the team is co-located with the infrastructure, this is applicable for any complexity development technologies depending on network performance. The primary approach for this option is:
  - On-premises centralized repository approach – This is where you have a CM repository in one location. The advantages of this approach for local and near-shore situations are that you have lower overhead because you are maintaining one CM system, there is the ability to establish a more streamlined and simple CM process of branching and merging with less merging activity, and the team can directly and efficiently access the code. For folks that are near-shore but still considered "close enough," there may be challenges in that you may suffer from poor performance depending on the level of interaction needed and bandwidth constraints between the local and near-shore folks. Also, when working across a wide area network (WAN), occasionally connectivity, accessibility, and performance issues arise.
  - Cloud infrastructure centralized repository approach – This is where cloud infrastructure is rented, which includes a CM version control tool and provides you with development space. The code is checked out from the cloud and placed within the same cloud local domain. Currently the version control technology on cloud infrastructure in this scenario is still improving. Because you may be working across a wide area network (WAN) to access the cloud infrastructure, there are occasionally connectivity, accessibility, and performance issues that may arise.
- Single Site for distributed team – This is when the code resides only at one site and all off-shore users access the local server and/or clients where the code resides, and through the check-out function, access the code. This is applicable for small to medium size teams that have some distribution of staff (either near-shore and/or off-shore). It may not be scalable to a large team. This is applicable for low to medium complexity development technologies and recommended for low complexity development technologies depending on network performance. This can be implemented in two ways (but not limited to these):
  - Web-enabled CM tool approach – This is when the CM system you are using provides you with a web interface to access the code (a.k.a., check-out) from the CM system to your local workstation or shared server. This method requires low setup effort and may have

high network dependency. The number of personnel at remote sites that may work in this setup is directly proportional to the network bandwidth and performance to the local site. This is only recommended for low complexity development technologies. This may not be ideal for Agile teams due to the continuous nature of the work. Also many web-enabled tools do not come with the full set of features, and neither does the standard local interface.

○ Terminal emulation approach – This is when remote personnel remotely log on to the local system to perform development work. The remote personnel perform check-outs and check-ins on the local server or client similar to what the local personnel do. This allows off-shore personnel to remotely log on directly to a local system where the code resides and is worked on. This method requires low setup effort and has high network (WAN) dependency. The number of personnel at remote sites that may work in this setup is directly proportional to the network bandwidth and performance to the local site, but is typically a low number of personnel. This is only recommended for low to medium complexity development technologies.

○ Terminal Services approach – This is when remote personnel use a local terminal services server or client to host the development technology and product code, which comes directly from the local server. The activity from the local server or client is viewed via the remote client with low network utilization. The remote personnel would perform version control on the local server or client as if it were their own client. This technology minimizes network bandwidth challenges and allows personnel to remotely utilize local systems to access and work on the code on a local system. This method requires medium setup effort and has medium network (WAN) dependency. This may be applicable for a small to medium number of personnel at remote sites working with the local site. This is only recommended for low to medium complexity development technologies.

■ Distributed sites for distributed teams – This is when the code physically resides in two or more locations. This is recommended when you have a larger Agile team (or teams) that have fairly sizable groups in different locations. This scenario is best when members of the team(s) at each off-shore site own their progress of building functionality but must merge continuously or periodically back with the rest of the team. This is applicable for all complexity (low to high) development technologies and recommended for medium to high complexity. This can be implemented in two ways (and not limited to these):

○ Replicated repository – This is where you have one virtual CM system that is made up of one master CM repository for code (at the local site) and one (or more) replicated CM repository for code that is connected via the CM process of branching and merging and updated via incremental and continuous replication processes. The advantage of this approach is that it provides strong performance and accessibility capabilities at each of the local sites. The local sites each access the infrastructure that is co-located near them. This reduces the dependency on a wide area network (WAN) to the times only when the repositories are synchronized. Otherwise, staff from the local site interact with the local code repository. The disadvantages of this approach are that you now have to perform administration and maintenance on two different CM systems and spend extra time and effort on synchronizing the code repositories and the merging effort and conflicts therein.

○ Remote client snapshot – This is when the application code is populated (checked out or retrieved) directly from the local CM repository to the client at the remote site. The initial population of the code baseline to the remote client workspace may take time and varies according to the network performance across sites. However, once a snapshot of the full baseline is on the client workspace, single or multiple check-outs/check-ins of code may be relatively quick (pending any network performance issues). This method requires low setup effort, has low network dependency (unless interacting with the server at the local site for version control or retrieval operations), and has the client working on their own without continuous reliance on the WAN or LAN. This option is effectively like working on a private workspace without a branch so the CM tool does not track any incremental changes in the client workspace. This may be recommended for Agile projects where a small number of people work from remote sites but may not be conducive to continuous integration and build.

It is important to understand that there are numerous ways an Agile development team may share code. An analysis to identify the project characteristics should be used to decide which approach to take. On the one hand, selecting a too simple single site code access technology approach for distributed teams may limit or constraint development due to poor network performance. On the other hand, selecting a too complex distribute site code access technology approach may lead to technology debt with more administrative effort that can overwhelm a small team. Ensure you select the distribute code access technology approach that is right for your development team.

7.6.3　Reflections on Approaching Agile Distributed Teams

As we conclude the section on approaching distributed analysis for distributed teams, note the following:

- Perform a distributed analysis and identify the characteristics of your product development.
- Investigate the various code access solutions, comparing your characteristics to determine the better code access solution for the Agile team.

7.7　Adapting Change Control, Traceability, and Baselines

While change control is not typically thought of as iteration planning, there are some striking similarities. This had me thinking that iteration planning may be the "reformed change control." The first time I participated in an iteration planning meeting, it felt a bit like some of the more lean and change-receptive change control meetings I had participated in. The iteration planning meetings were held every two weeks (in line with the iteration cycle) and so were most of the change control meetings I had participated in. In the iteration planning meetings, the committed folks discussed the existing stories and tasks therein, identified new stories and their tasks, and finally prioritized the story tasks for the iteration. In a change control meeting the team discussed the new changes, determined priorities, and changes were ruled on. Those agreed to are added to the requirements list and worked on. Contrary to the belief that change control is used to constrain change (i.e., gate), many change control meetings I participated in ended up agreeing to most of the changes. Unfortunately change control meetings did so with few changes in schedule or cost.

Pit Stop

Think of iteration planning as the "reformed change control." Iteration planning welcomes change and ensures that the amount of stories fit the time-boxed iteration.

Traditional change control is often clunky but I have seen it work in more of a streamlined manner. Formal change control asks for more formal documentation than Agile teams can bear. Each change is submitted via a change request form (CRF) and logged in a change control log. Iteration planning captures changes in the backlog. Traditional change control often used to be a gate for change, while iteration planning is a funnel for change. In traditional change control, the stakeholders are part of a change control board (CCB) which rules on the change. In iteration planning, there is a team of people discussing the changes, usually with the stakeholders and product manager/owner prioritizing the changes. Both iteration planning and change control are used to manage change, but each goes about it differently, with iteration planning having less formality and ceremony true to the values of Agile. Below is a summary of the similarities and differences.

Table 7-2 Comparison of iteration planning and change control.

Iteration Planning		Change Control Meeting
Per iteration (every 1–4 weeks depending on the length of an iteration)	Cycle	Approximately weekly or every 2 weeks
Changes are discussed with team, stakeholders, and product manager/owner	Attendees	Changes are discussed with stakeholders, PM, and subset of team
Stakeholder(s) via product manager/owner prioritize and rule on next iteration of work	Owner of change disposition	Stakeholder group (customer, project manager, etc.) prioritize and rule on change
Streamlined – changes are discussed at the planning session and are tracked in the backlog	Documentation	Formal – Changes are submitted beforehand in the CRFs and tracked in a change control log
Funnel for change	Change reception	Gate for change, although many changes are accepted

The important thing for CM professionals to understand is that if you have established change control processes along with a CCB, although there are similarities, do not expect the level of formality and ceremony to exist. It is important for Agile professionals to understand that iteration planning is not as unique as you think. It is still about identifying new changes, reviewing them, prioritizing them, then committing the work.

7.7.1 Tracking Requirements or Stories and their Changes

In more traditional methods, there is typically strong emphasis on formally tracking changes. As mentioned, change control uses a change request form (CRF) that is documented and submitted before the change control meeting and includes many details of what the requester is looking for. An analyst typically reviews all CRFs to understand their scope more fully and any impacts to other areas. In the CCB meeting, all changes are discussed and ruled on. In Agile, the changes are discussed and prioritized at the iteration planning meeting and, only further details of those that will make it to the next iteration are discussed, therefore saving time reviewing or discussing lower priority changes.

In many Agile teams that are co-located, stories are tracked using story cards which are sometimes physical index cards. The story cards provide the details of the story or requirements and tasks therein and are used by the Agile team to track the stories. The story cards are kept on a story board (e.g., physical white board, easel, bulletin board) somewhere in the Agile team room for the whole team to see and visit as needed. If this works for the team, then there is no sense in trying to change this process. The focus then is to ensure that the story cards are controlled enough to ensure that they do not get lost.

Using physical story cards in a room can work for co-located teams but when you start moving to more near-shore and certainly off-shore, then strong consideration should be given to tracking stories or requirements online. Many Agile teams use online tools to track the stories for precisely this reason. In general, if stories or requirements are tracked online in a virtual story board and in a backlog or requirements list, then these items can be managed, tracked, and shared across the team. One level of tracking is an online backlog. These documents can be shared during the iteration planning session and if stored on a central project-hosting location, can be visited much like a physical story board can be visited.

Another level of online tracking is using automated Agile planning tools, which capture stories and their details in a virtual story card much like the physical story cards. The advantage of an automated tool is that the numerous stories are used to automatically generate the backlog so you can see at least two views of the stories (in separate story cards or a backlog list) and with the ability to manage, sort, and apply a workflow to the stories more easily. In addition, these Agile planning tools can automatically track your velocity based on the effort estimate of the story (the story points), start and finish dates, and how many tasks are completed to create burn-down or burn-up charts to illustrate progress. Some even come with a version control capability to help manage change to the story cards. The key is to keep the requirements or story process as simple as possible while still being able to manage and track change effectively.

7.7.2 Adjusting the Notion of Baseline

A baseline is described as both the ability to identify a set of work items at a point in time and as the official set of work items on which future work should be based. How formal this concept is when it gets implemented depends on the maturity of the organization, the level of compliance that needs to be followed, and the need of the project to validate relationships to determine the integrity of the product at various stages of development.

The more formal baselines are typically known as functional baselines, allocated baselines, and product baselines, but the names may vary. Both the functional and allocated baselines are typically described in relation to documents that include specific details. For example, a functional baseline specifies the initial request for proposal (RfP) for the work along with system requirements, and an allocated baseline specifies the work products associated with the subsystem functionality and the physical architecture that lead to detailed design and development work.

7.7.2.1   Baseline Considerations for Agile

As you approach the concept of baselines for Agile, you may find that you need to adjust the way baselines are defined and implemented per the iterative nature of Agile. Some issues relating to Agile adjustments include:

- Some detailed level documentation that gets defined in the specifications of certain baselines may be seen as unnecessary and waste in Agile, since some of this knowledge and detail are collected in shared face-to-face discussions with minimal documentation.

- Agile does not follow a phased approach as do traditional methods. Therefore, baselines are not so easily designated nor distinguished by phases and the exit criteria of a phase.

- Agile does not subscribe to BEUF requirements (functional) or a design approach (allocated) but instead uses a much more iterative approach for stories and design; the alignment between the traditional functional and allocated baselines is blurred, since the time between these baselines can be almost nonexistent. Also, the concept of the baseline is much more volatile in Agile than in traditional methods.

7.7.2.2   Baselines for Agile

Because Agile follows an iterative and incremental model of development, the traditional phase approach to baselines may not work. While the level of formality, the name of the baselines, and the implementation approach for baselines in an Agile context can vary, it may be valuable to recognize baselines that do exist in an iterative framework. Below is a suggested approach for baselines using Agile. However, you should ensure that when you choose to recognize and work with baselines, you establish the best approach for your team.

- The first is the backlog baseline. This is a natural baseline that is already established as part of Agile iteration planning activity. However, this baseline is not established in a BEUF way like functional and allocated baselines. Instead this baseline is established and evolves in an iterative manner as stories or requirements are identified and collected into the backlog. This baseline provides you with the value of knowing what is important to work on based on customer value, but be aware that it is subject to welcome change during each iteration planning session.

- The next is an iteration baseline. This baseline combines the design, development, and test elements, since all three occur in an integrated manner in an iteration. This baseline would include the design, code, and test work items that get produced by the end of an iteration. This baseline continuously changes throughout an iteration where a snapshot (static) of the baseline occurs at the end of the iteration as a basis for discussion in the end-of-iteration review.

- The last baseline is the release baseline, which is the result of the work (executables, user documents, etc.) that is delivered to the end customer. Please note that the iteration baseline discussed above actually evolves into the product baseline. However, the iteration baseline continues to change thereafter as the team focus on the next release, while the release baseline will be defined as a static and formally recognized baseline prior to releasing to customers to ensure baseline integrity.

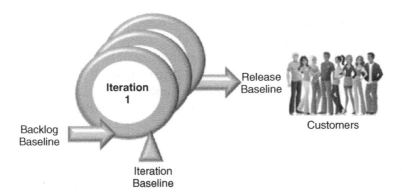

Figure 7-17   Example of baselines for Agile teams.

This is just one variation of applying meaningful baselines for an Agile team. It is incumbent on you to establish the baselines that are right for you by considering the level of desired formality based on the product need and/or organizational need, meaningful names of the baselines, and the implementation approach for baselines, ensuring you keep the whole baseline process lean and with integrity.

7.7.3 Approaching Traceability for Agile

Traceability in software development is defined by the ability to relate items in baselines. This ensures that the work being done in one baseline (the development or iteration baseline) is based on a meaningful discussion and prioritized based on what the customer expects are described in another baseline (the requirements or backlog baseline). In effect, traceability shows the variance from one baseline to another to ensure we are working on the high-priority value-added stories and not focused on extra low priority work.

Typical implementations of traceability come in the form of a traceability matrix, either in a separate manually maintained document or in an automated tool (and sometimes a combination of both) typically as part of a requirements management tool. This matrix is represented by a table that associates baselines (the requirements or stories and where in the code or where in test cases these requirements are covered). The primary advantage to having a traceability matrix in some form is that you can better understand when an item is changed, what of value is ready, and what are the downstream impacts (i.e., it provides you with a basis with which to perform impact assessments). As you consider traceability for Agile, be cautious and think lean.

7.7.3.1 Traceability for the Right Reasons

When considering traceability for an Agile team, you should reflect on the benefits of doing so and the underlying practices. Ensure you are implementing traceability for the right reasons. With this in mind, note the following:

- **Consider Cost** – Discuss the perceived benefit compared to the cost of applying traceability. Establishing and maintaining traceability amongst all baselines may be an expensive proposition. Even between two baselines it is a bit of an effort. If the product you are constructing is mission-critical and has implications for the health and well-being of people, then it is well worth applying traceability to ensure those mission-critical high-value requirements are actually part of the much needed new product release. In all cases, if traceability had occurred in the past or there is a strong organizational direction to apply traceability (e.g., based on meeting

Sarbanes-Oxley or equivalent) for an organization or on a product, it is worth identifying the costs of traceability in whatever form it may take and highlighting the expense to the product owner and/or senior management. Then they can decide the perceived importance of traceability compared to its actual cost.

- **Consider Maturity** – Traceability tends to be a more advanced concept for many organizations. What I often find amusing is that organizations want to perform traceability without having the stories/requirements, development, and testing practices in place in order to do so. For example, if an organization does not yet have their product teams capturing requirements or stories effectively and they do not yet apply test cases consistently, or at all, then there is no sense in attempting traceability until those practices are more effectively applied. Also, if the product team is not yet clear what baselines they have or what pieces along a project lifecycle should be traced together, then there is no sense in implementing traceability.

Pit Stop

Traceability can be a powerful practice to ensure the integrity of a product. However, ensure that you understand the costs associated with this practice and that you have the other practices in place (stories/requirements, development, and testing) to effectively apply traceability.

7.7.3.2 Traceability Considerations for Agile

If you must perform traceability, then some adjustments should be made when working on an Agile project. Some considerations include:

- When initiating traceability for any method, identify the baselines that you wish to trace between. Possibly the first choice is to compare what code was changed in the iteration baseline at the end of an iteration against the stories or tasks therein that were to be prioritized for that iteration as indicated in the backlog baseline.
- It is important to remember that one of the Agile principles refers to minimizing documentation. Consider using the backlog as the basis for traceability (if feasible) and not introduce yet another document.
- It is recommended to wait until the third or fourth iteration before tracing is initiated, particularly when you plan to trace to the requirements or "story" baseline (a.k.a., backlog baseline). This is

because the requirements may not be very stable early on, which could be very disruptive when trying to establish a stable trace path.

- When you perform traceability for the first time, never under any circumstances attempt to trace all baselines together. Pick two baselines that are managed most effectively, and start there.

- If you are applying test-driven development (TDD), then you compare code to the test baseline since the test cases get created prior to the code. However, there may not be a reason to trace between them since they are worked on almost concurrently.

- Since traceability can be an arduous effort to keep the trace items up to date, attempt to automate as much as possible.

- CM version control tools can help you with establishing and maintaining traceability between the code and the executables, assuming you version control both. If you version control test cases as well, then the connection with code and test cases can be established more easily. For some CM tools, this can be automated.

7.7.4 Reflections on Change Control, Traceability, and Baselines for Agile

As we conclude the section on adapting change control, Traceability, and Baselines for Agile teams, note the following:

- Consider how close iteration planning is to change control.
- Investigate what baselines are applicable on your Agile project.
- Determine if you are implementing the stories/requirements, development, and testing practices well enough to make it worth initiating traceability.
- Give thought to how important traceability is to your project. If you have to initiate it, consider streamlining the traceability process.

7.8 Adapting CM Audit

CM audit is an activity focusing on identifying baselines, verifying that each baseline includes what was agreed upon, and that you can explain how and when changes were made to the baselines. The benefits of auditing are twofold. The first is to ensure that what you are building is based on what the customers want (i.e., you are building the right product). The second is to ensure you have the ability to reproduce your baselines, your builds, your packages that go to the customer and have an audit trail of who did what to which file, and when, and for what reason (you are building the product right). This leads to baseline integrity.

Pit Stop

Assuring baseline integrity of a product is a goal of a CM audit. The baseline audit activity ensures that the team is "building the right product" while the process audit activity ensures the team is "building the product right."

7.8.1   Agile Considerations for Audit

As you consider audit for Agile, you should understand the challenges in doing so and some ways to approach it in a lean manner.

7.8.1.1   Trust or Verification

Probably one of the biggest issues with a CM audit (or any audit) in an Agile context is that it gives the appearance of checking up on people. Within the context of Agile, trust and shared responsibility drive the self-empowered team toward more productivity. An audit gives the impression that trust is not assumed. When there is trust, there is less waste focused on verification, audits, and paperwork. To be sure, much of the CM audit is focused on ensuring baseline integrity, but part is associated with a process audit. This implies that we ensure people are following the established CM processes. By focusing more on the trust side and assuming that everyone is attempting to utilize the process (and do the right thing), the process audit can be used to reduce the risk of accidently applying the process incorrectly and focused on improvement of the process (i.e., with less focus on the people and more on the process).

7.8.1.2   What Baselines to Audit Against

As discussed in the traceability section, Agile does not follow a phased approach like traditional methods. Therefore, baselines are not so easily designated nor distinguished by phases and the exit criteria of a phase. Therefore, when attempting to verify what you are building based on a previous baseline, utilize the baselines within an Agile context (e.g., iteration baseline compared to the backlog baseline).

7.8.1.3   Challenges with BEUF Specifications

Often when you verify a baseline based on what was agreed upon, this is reflected in a specification or document. For example, you may assess the development baseline against the design specification. Because BEUF design specifications are not produced in the Agile methods context, this manner of audit may not be possible. Also the notion of comparing what we are building based on a relatively static design document is not aligned with the iterative and evolutionary nature of Agile, where design and development are occurring simultaneously.

7.8.1.4   Audit after the Third Iteration

In the traditional baseline audit where you are auditing the code baseline against the requirements baseline, the requirements baseline is typically fairly stable when you audit the code baseline in the development phase against the requirements baseline. In Agile, the requirements or "story" baseline (a.k.a., backlog baseline) is typically not very stable until around the third or fourth iteration (this will vary from project to project). This is because the customer may not be clear on their needs until they have seen a few iterations of functionality. With this in mind, it is recommended that if you are conducting CM auditing, not to start until you have some stability in the requirements or story baseline.

7.8.2   Approaching Audit for Agile

How important CM audit is to a team depends on what value you perceive it provides and/or whether you have a regulatory requirement that has to be met. In general, most Agile teams will find the traditional CM audit approach as too "heavy", even if they find value in knowing the level of integrity of their baselines. So what are some possible ways to approach CM audits?

7.8.2.1   Automating Code to Build Baselines

One way is to narrow the scope of the baseline audits to what is in the iteration baseline (comparing the built deliverables for the end-of-iteration baseline with the code in the version control system). In this case, you can utilize an automated approach within the build process so that it can automatically produce a bill-of-materials list from the build and store these individual lists in order to compare progress from build to build. Continuing on the automation theme, if you capture what gets checked in or promoted to each branch (change records), then the changes from build to build can be compared to what was checked in or promoted to ensure what we expect in the build is actually there (changes made it to the right branch, all changes were included, etc). From there some CM tools can provide a relationship between the source code and the built executables. It is important to audit this so that there is a reliable way to ensure that what package we release to the customer is based on the source in the version control system. A big advantage of doing this, irrespective of the method, is that if the build begins to break, particularly when there are many changes occurring, the automated bill-of-materials and change records from the build can help narrow down where the breakage is occurring.

7.8.2.2   Move the Process Audit to the Retrospective

A way to approach the "ensure people are following the established CM processes" part of the audit is to move it into the Agile retrospective at the end of each iteration. The mindset change is not to verify if people are following the established CM process, but to promote a process improvement approach by asking the team if the CM processes are effective for their work. Also, given that in Agile the work is fast and rigorous where processes, whether manual or automated, must be lean and willingly followed or the velocity drops off, it may be better to utilize the retrospective as an alternative to a process audit.

7.8.2.3   Move the Baseline Audit to the Review

A way to approach ensuring what we are building is based on what we said we would build (a.k.a., baseline audit) is to move the audit into the Agile review at the end of each iteration. At the review, we examine what we built based on what we said we were going to build in the iteration planning session. This is already part of the review process so it is advantageous to leverage what is already in place. Interestingly enough, this is effectively what occurs in a CM audit, albeit with less formality. This iterative activity actually provides a more frequent assurance (audit) that compares the iteration baseline against the backlog baseline. Because Agile is focused on delivering high value based on what was decided in the iteration planning session and because there is daily focus (in the daily stand-up) on what programmers are working on, most programmers stick to their committed work and stray less into other work areas.

7.8.2.4   Giving Cadence to Industry Standards

In some cases, while the team applies Agile as their software development method, the organization may be applying one of the industry standards (e.g., IEEE) or frameworks (e.g., CMMI) or laws (Sarbanes-Oxley). If this is the case, then CM audits will need to be applied and a record of the audit will need to be produced. If you are faced with having to do audits within an Agile context because of an organizational directive, here are several suggested steps in approaching this:

- Establish your baselines as discussed in section 7.7.2.2 – "Baselines for Agile". This section provides recommendations for baselines but you need to identify the formal baselines that are the natural part of your method.

- Determine the leanest way to initiate audits as discussed in section 7.8.2.3 – "Move the Baseline Audit to the Review". This is one example where the review already assesses what was completed, based on what was planned in the iteration planning session.

- Consider automation as much as possible within the confines of the CM version control tool, continuous integration and build tool, and problem management tool. If these three tools are integrated, they can be used as an automated way to identify the changes from build to build, to know what was checked in or promoted, and to verify the integrity of the build baselines. Some of the resulting record of the audit can be derived in an automated manner from the tools.

Because many industry standards operate at the organizational level and require records as evidence at a project level, there may simply have to be some extra work to satisfy the standards criteria. And ultimately, consider ensuring that whatever audit you do focuses on the improvement of your processes for the benefit of the team and not on the audit itself.

7.8.3   Reflections on CM Audit for Agile

As we conclude the section on adapting CM audit for Agile teams, consider the following:

- Ensure you approach audits from a trust perspective.
- Identify what baselines you may have on your project.
- Consider using audits as a means to identify ways to improve the process and ensure product integrity.
- Consider using the retrospectives and reviews as a way to apply aspects of the process audit.
- Give thought to automating the audit of any items that can be version controlled.

7.9 Adapting Problem Management

Problem management focuses on addressing and managing the problems (incidents, issues, defects) found on a product and projects therein and applying a level of severity to each problem identified. It follows a closed-loop system where as problems are identified, they are captured, reviewed, corrected, and closed. Irrespective of the method used, you would want to apply this practice. For all practical purposes, the problem management process remains the same for teams applying Agile methods. However, there are some modifications that can be made to align better with Agile.

7.9.1 Establishing Problem Management Upfront

The biggest implementation consideration for Agile teams is that problem management should be in place at the very beginning. Remember, Agile has teams working on development functionality and testing right away (i.e., starting in the first iteration). Having a place to capture problems, issues, and defects is vital for ensuring that when they have been identified, they are safely kept for continued focus without losing this important information. Starting with a reasonable problem management process and tool is particularly important if you are a new product line and little infrastructure is yet in place. In this case, starting with a manual process may be reasonable if the team is small.

7.9.2 From Phase to Iteration

In some problem management processes, the phase where the problem was identified is captured. This is specific to the phases found in phase-based methods. Since Agile follows an iterative model, this attribute has to be either removed or adjusted to the iteration in which the problem was uncovered. This detail can help in tracking defect metrics (e.g., closure rates, etc.).

Pit Stop

With a phased-base method, it is not uncommon to report the phase where the defect was found. With Agile methods, this attribute should be adjusted to indicate the iteration where the defect was found.

7.9.3 Problem Management for Pair Programming

Another consideration is that if you are applying pair programming, you will have to determine the best way to adjust the name of the "assigned to" or "owner of" the problem in order to indicate the pair of programmers. In most cases the pair do not work on defects, but sometimes they do when the resolution of the defect is complex and a pair approach can be applied. Also, when pairs have made changes based on the story tasks they have worked on, then it may be best to assign to the pair the responsibility of correcting the defect.

7.9.4 Problem Management Automation

Having an automated problem management tool where problems can be captured and tracked to closure saves time, especially as more problems are captured and tracking becomes too onerous to manage. As the team gets larger and more distributed, an online and automated problem management system allows team members from any location to see the defects immediately, which promotes communication and ensures everyone has the same access to all defects. If this is a need, then an Agile team will have to figure out how to establish this process and tool as they are beginning their development of functionality. You can start by identifying if there is already an established problem management system in place that your team can leverage and create your own instance or attribute to separate your problems from the problems of other product teams. If you are working on an existing product line that already has a problem management tool available, then you can continue to capture defects and other problem-related activities in this tool.

Within an Agile context, there is probably little need to document the problem management process. This is because the problem management process and tool tend to be fairly easy to use (or should be) and because the process is a shared activity where most people on the team have knowledge. However, it may be of value to have a short training session on how to use the problem management tool and the process.

7.9.5 Reflections on Problem Management for Agile

As we conclude the section on adapting problem management for Agile teams, note the following:

- If the product line is brand new, then consider feasible ways to get problem management started, since it will be needed right away.

- Understand that in Agile, you may want to capture the iteration where you found the problem, since phase information does not exist in Agile.
- If there are pair programmers on the team, then consider how you assign ownership of problems to the pair.
- Consider having an automated problem management process which is typically established through a problem management tool.

7.10 Adapting CM Report and Review

CM report and review focuses on preparing CM status and metrics and communicating these CM tasks to the project team and management. It typically follows a repeatable report and review process that collects and communicates CM status on progress, measures, training, resources, achievements, compliance, outstanding issues, and opportunities for improvement. A key type of CM reporting includes CM metrics. This is utilized to highlight trends in the CM process areas (e.g., build success rates, lines of code checked in, etc.).

Even within a traditional phased method, CM review and reporting can be implemented in different ways. Some will produce separate CM reports and have separate CM review meetings to review CM status and discuss CM metrics. Others will incorporate their CM reports and metrics into the project status and metrics reporting. While there is no one correct way of doing this, the emphasis for CM review and reporting in an Agile context is to be as lean and value-added as possible.

In all cases, the goal of the CM professional is to identify opportunities for improvement in the area of CM to the benefit of the team they support and any method they use.

7.10.1 Moving CM Report and Review into the Retrospective

The first approach focuses on identifying the level of status reporting that is done on the Agile team. Some Agile teams have no status reporting, while some have a minimal amount to appease their management and often it is based on their already existing backlog and burn-down charts. What are a few ways to approach CM reporting in an Agile team context?

For an Agile team that has no status reporting, then CM reporting should be moved into the Agile retrospective at the end of each iteration. The effort is focused on contributing CM status and listening to the team's concerns (if any) in the area of CM with the goal of continuous CM process improvement.

For an Agile team that does have some status reporting then consider integrating CM reporting as part of the project reporting already being done. Identify the key CM status areas which you would like to incorporate into the project status report. This continues to keep the reporting lean and focused on value.

If there are CM metrics being captured, the reporting of these metrics should be made available at the end-of-iteration retrospective. This way, as the team is discussing opportunities for improvement, they have metrics data as input.

7.10.2   Adjusting CM Metrics that Help Deliver Value

Within the Agile context, in order to minimize waste and increase value delivered (key Agile metrics focus areas), some metrics need to be in place to ensure the team is keeping it lean. In order to achieve lean metrics, we need to balance the value of metrics for the team against the cost of collecting the metrics. In Agile, the focus should be to deliver the value (a.k.a., the product) more quickly and with high value, so every metric considered should be based on these two factors. A way to approach this is to identify and construct a value-added metric.

Pit Stop

The objective of every metric for Agile teams should be to improve on the delivery of value (the right product) to the customer with emphasis on speed and quality while minimizing waste.

7.10.3   Constructing a Value-Added Metric

A value-added metric is one where the benefit of utilizing the metric data far exceeds the effort of establishing and maintaining the metric. By assessing the benefit versus the effort, a value rating can be assigned to each metric. Those that have high value ratings may be implemented. Once a metric is in place, then monitoring should occur to verify if the metric is actually being used. If it is not, discard the metric. Sometimes a metric is used to manage a problem or improvement. Once it has achieved its purpose then it is no longer needed. This would be another time to discard the metric (after it has outlived its usefulness). In no circumstance should you introduce metrics for no particular reason or continue the metrics if they are no longer being used. It is amazing how many metrics created in an organization are not really being used or are without a clear understanding of their benefit.

As you approach metrics, consider the ways to identify value added metrics. One way is to establish metrics to help solve a problem area in the product team or on a specific project and the second is to identify the Agile value-added metrics that other organizations are using and consider whether they may be beneficial to the current project. The possibility of effectively using metrics to alleviate the pain felt by groups in certain areas, or understanding what is being used effectively by others applying Agile in the company or in a similar industry can be a big motivator for implementing metrics.

7.10.3.1 Metric Building Blocks

Now that we have some context for initiating metrics and doing so for the right reasons, let us examine the key building blocks in establishing value-added metrics. They are:

- Providing clarity on what benefits are gained from using the metric.
- Understanding the level of effort to collect the metrics (both to establish the metric and maintain it).
- Ensuring the Agile team and CM understand the benefit of the metric and how it can be used to improve the product or project. Metrics that are of higher value should be those that help you determine if you are delivering value (i.e., the right product) more quickly and with quality.

Let us explore the key building blocks in more detail by proposing a metric case study called "Time to Build the Product."

7.10.3.2 Considering the Benefit of the Metric

When considering the benefit of the metric, first take a moment to describe it. In the case of "Time to Build the Product," it is a metric that determines the average duration to build the product (i.e., including the steps to initiate, compile, package, and smoke test) from start to finish. Essentially, this is the "what" (what is the metric).

Next, consider the areas where the metric can be used (i.e., the benefits). This can be a consensus-driven discussion where the problem it solves or the opportunities it gains are considered. Essentially, this is the "why" (why we want to establish this metric). Several examples of why the metric can be of benefit and how it can be used to improve an Agile team's effort are:

- To measure expected build time gains (or losses) when introducing build improvements to delivery more quickly to test or for end-of-iteration reviews.

- To identify potential problems when there are large deviations from average build times.

- To set expectations: e.g., if it regularly takes 2 hours to build a product, and management asks for a build in 30 minutes, it is much better to have hard numbers ready to set expectations.

- To understand the difference in build times when introducing new functionality in a product.

- To understand the difference in build times when introducing system change.

As an Agile team (or subset of the team), you should determine a perceived benefit rating of the metric. Consider using 0–100 as the range (where 100 is the most beneficial). Any range is adequate as long as you use the same range to determine the benefit of each metric being considered. For the sake of this case study, the team decides that the benefit rating of the "Time to Build the Product" metric is 75.

Note, you can approach the benefit rating in several ways. Two possible ways include:

- Asking each team member their perceived benefit rating for the metric, then adding the ratings up and dividing by the number of team members who contributed a score.

- Discussing the metric and seeing if you can agree to a single benefit rating in a consensus-driven manner.

Pit Stop

It is important to understand that the perceived benefit of a metric is subjective. If the metric is implemented, the perceived benefit should be revisited over time to ensure the value rating is such that it is worth continuing the collection of data to produce the metric.

7.10.3.3 Determining Effort to Collect the Metric

Now that folks are aware of the benefits and use of the metric, it is time to consider the level of effort needed to collect the metric. This is critical because there are many cases where the effort to collect the metric outweighs the perceived benefit. If this is the case, then it is not worth proceeding forward with the metric. Total effort should include the setup effort and the ongoing collection effort, and any maintenance and upkeep effort. Typically the time used to determine the effort of a build is measured in hours. The tricky part is to establish meaningful measures to determine the benefit of a metric. This can be subjective from person to person. A tip is to consider how many hours in a given year are worth devoting to setting up and maintaining a metric.

Here is an example of considerations in setting up a "Time to Build the Product" metric:

- Capture the effort to identify/document the process of collecting the metric.
- Capture the effort to automate the process so it can automatically run.
  - When the build is initiated, record a time stamp. At the start of each step in the build process (build, compile, package, and smoke test) record a time stamp, and at the end of the build process record another time stamp. The data should be written into a build log.
  - Determine average time for each step in the build process.
  - Send output to a log (average time for each step with total time).
- Capture the effort to test the automated process.
- Capture the effort to reformat (if any) the metric to align with other team or management output.
- Adjust as needed.

This metric assumes that the owner of the metric is establishing an automated approach to collecting the metrics. While this takes more setup effort up front, it reduces the ongoing metrics collection if done manually. It may not always be easy to automate a metrics collection process depending on where the data needs to come from.

Using this case study, the total effort includes the setup time and the ongoing effort to maintain the metric. Consider calculating the effort in hours:

Table 7-3 Measuring metrics effort in hours.

Task	Effort in hours
Setup effort (define, automate, and test the process)	25
Ongoing collection/reformatting effort (monthly)	12 (1 monthly)
Effort per Year	**37**

7.10.3.4 Assessing the Value of the Metric

Now that you have both the perceived benefit rating and the estimated effort in hours, the value of the metric can be assessed. The value rating is calculated using the perceived benefit of the metric, divided by the effort per year in hours. You are looking for those metrics where the "perceived benefit" exceeds the "total effort hours" in a year (i.e., the "value rating" is greater than 1 when the perceived value is divided by hours). Again, you can use any equation you would like as long as you use it consistently for all of your metrics decisions. If you have several metrics you are considering, then this approach allows you to equitably compare the benefits versus the effort of all of the metrics under consideration so that a more informative decision can be made.

In the case of the "Time to Build the Product" metric, if we divide the perceived benefit of 75 by the total effort hours in a year, in this case 37, we get a 2.03 value rating (rounded up). When using this approach, you may often find that the effort is greater than the perceived benefit (i.e., the value rating is less than 1, suggesting caution when considering this as a potential metric).

7.10.3.5   Comparing amongst Potential Metrics

When embarking on metrics, it is important to brainstorm several potential metrics in order to determine their value rating in relation to each other so that you can more objectively understand which metrics more closely align with delivering value to the customer, with emphasis on speed and quality. Here is an example of a CM-related metrics comparison table that uses the value rating as its gauge. It includes the "Time to Build the Product" metric discussed above:

Table 7-4   Metrics comparison based on the value rating.

Potential Metric Name	Perceived Benefit	Effort	Value Rating
Time to Build the Product	75	37	2.03
Build Errors	85	45	1.89
Code Volatility	45	60	0.75
Change Volatility (during change control or iteration planning)	55	45	1.22

In this case, we see four potential metrics. Of the four, the team may only choose to pursue the "Time to Build the Product" and the "Build Errors" metrics, since they have the highest metrics value ratings. There will be times when the value rating is below 1 but the organization still wants to proceed with a metric. In these cases, it is important to communicate the risk of the metric being perceived as not adding value.

7.10.3.6   Monitoring of the Metric

As time goes on, any metric that has been established and is being produced on an ongoing basis, should be revisited periodically. The reasons are two-fold. First, it is important to periodically assess if the metric is actually being used. If it is not being used, then the metric should be discontinued. Second, the value rating of the metric should be re-measured. Is the benefit still perceived to be high as time moves forward? Is the effort more or less than what was initially calculated? In some cases, once a metric is used and drives a positive change in the organization, then the metric has done its job and may no longer need to be generated (or can be generated less frequently).

Also, it is critical to collect the metric data for a few cycles prior to prescribing a target for a metric. It is important to identify the range of data a metric produces over a reasonable time period to understand what "average" is and what the variations are. Once this is done, then a target for improvement may be considered.

7.10.4   Waste and Examples of Value-Added CM Metrics

In an Agile context (or any product or project lifecycle method), metrics should focus on minimizing waste in order to improve flow and deliver value. The goal is to identify areas where flow is being blocked. This reduces velocity or speed and inhibits the team's ability to deliver value in a timely manner. The main culprit to impacting flow and reducing the ability to deliver value is waste. Identifying waste was initially a manufacturing focus and has evolved to the software development area. Below is a table that illustrates the waste types that Taiichi Ohno identified for manufacturing, and similar waste types that Mary Poppendieck adapted for the software development industry.

Table 7-5   Waste types in manufacturing and software development.

Taiichi Ohno, an executive from Toyota, was the creator of the Toyota Product System, which identified seven types of manufacturing waste.		Mary Poppendieck took this a step further where she aligned the manufacturing waste to software development waste.
overproduction	=	extra features
inventory	=	requirements
extra processing steps	=	extra steps
motion	=	finding information
defects	=	defects not found in testing
waiting	=	waiting
transportation	=	handoffs

It is important to understand the types of waste so that it may help you establish value-added metrics focused on reducing it. When waste is identified and removed, flow is increased and value to the customer is seen sooner than later. With that in mind, below are some suggested CM metrics that can be used to identify waste:

- Broken integration builds – This is applicable to both the standard periodic integration builds (e.g., nightly, weekly, etc.) and continuous integration builds that may occur in any integration branch (e.g., project release branch, main branch, shared branch, etc.) where the build "breaks" during the integration build process. This may be caused by defects that "escaped" from the developer's build, which result in time spent to repair broken integration builds and may cause a delay for those waiting to check-in/promote into the integration stream or waiting for the integration build, including developers waiting to sync the latest to their private workspaces or customers wanting to view it at the upcoming end-of-iteration review. Sometimes if the same code keeps breaking the build, it could be because some code modules are too large or complex and may need to be broken up or refactored.

- Building priority – This is where you measure the difference between what was prioritized and expected to change against what was actually changed in the code. This is a result where the team may be focusing on extra features that are not considered high value to the customer (e.g., overproduction).

- Story to defect ratio – This is where for each end-of-iteration build, you measure the story/requirements completed against the defects being repaired to get a ratio of the value actually being delivered. The lower the percentage of story/requirements being delivered, the lower the flow of value and higher the defect waste.

- Velocity to defect ratio – This is where you compare the velocity of the team with the number of defects being introduced. Sometimes, the team gets focused on the velocity without looking at the damage that is being done to maintain or exceed velocity goals. This ensures that speed does not override quality goals. You may need to investigate if the team is being pushed too much. Remember, the goal is to optimize the whole project, not just parts of it.

The reporting of any available metrics should be made available at the end-of-iteration retrospective. This way, as the team is discussing opportunities for improvement, they have metrics input that are focused on reducing waste and improving the flow of value to the customer.

7.10.5   Reflections on Adapting CM Report and Review for Agile

As we conclude the section on adapting CM report and review for Agile teams, consider the following:

- Constructing a value-added metrics approach is a must. The metric must be perceived to solve problems, reduce waste, and improve the flow of value.

- Understand the perceived benefit of the metric compared to the effort it takes to establish and maintain the metric in order to determine the value to the team.

- After a metric is established, monitor the metric to ensure the value remains constant and continues to be used to manage the team direction or business. This also ensures a healthy and dynamic metrics program that continually ensures value.

- As old metrics lose value, they can be dropped and new metrics may be considered to solve new problems, reduce waste, and improve the flow of value.

CHAPTER 8

CM Tool as a Strategic Agile Partner

Contributed by Damon Poole

The phrase "individuals and interactions over process and tools" is the first of four value statements in the Agile Manifesto. This could be interpreted as saying that process and tools do not matter in an Agile world. But shortly thereafter the Manifesto says: "That is, while there is value in the items on the right, we value the items on the left more." Of course the individuals and interactions are the most important ingredient, because it is the people who are doing the creative work, but the process and tools are also important. After all, we don't use punch cards anymore and the whole purpose of the software industry is to increase productivity through automation.

The important point is that the process and tools should serve the individuals, not the other way around. The question is, what makes a tool well suited to the needs of Agile teams? The focus of this chapter is on your Configuration Management (CM) tool and how, when properly leveraged, your CM tool can be a strategic partner in the success of your Agile development process.

The first section provides an overview of what a CM tool does and how it supports your process. The next section discusses the Agile practices that most impact your CM tool. The last section describes specific CM tool features that facilitate Agile development.

8.1 CM Tool Support for Software Development

Software development is a team effort involving many participants and many tools. Successful collaboration requires coordination and synchronization of the work performed by the team, whether they are all located together or distributed across the globe. Most of the tasks involved in developing software involve creating, modifying, or retrieving and building files. The people using the system include developers, doc writers and other folks who contribute content: testers, managers, build-meisters, and release engineers. A CM tool is good at keeping track of all of this. It enables many people to work on many different versions of a software product at many locations at the same time.

Consider how much you and the people you work with rely on your CM system. When you need to make changes to the source code of your software, you go to your CM system to find out where it is and then check it out. When you want to make your changes available to other people, you need to resolve merge conflicts using the CM system and then check them into the CM system. If you want to know what other people are working on, why something was changed, what has changed since the build last worked, or what files changed to implement a particular story, you have to consult with the CM system. The nightly builds, continuous builds, product releases, hot fixes, and service packs are derived from your CM system. In short, your software development process is deeply embedded in your CM system.

A CM tool facilitates and coordinates the work of the users via the following concepts and capabilities.

Configurations

In order to manage CM well, all parties need to have a common understanding of what you are managing. Configurations are the foundation of good CM. A configuration is simply a named, well-defined, and easily reproducible set of content. The term "configuration" is mostly used by CM practitioners. Users typically refer to particular kinds of configurations, such as the mainline (or trunk), user workspaces, teams, components, features, staging areas, milestones, snapshots, and releases. In any case, configurations are what the CM system manages. Depending on the CM tool and the environment in which it is used, these configurations may be represented with files in a directory tree, branches, codelines, streams, labels, snapshots, baselines, components, other similar objects, or a combination of all of these objects.

Repository

In order to manage configurations, there first has to be content for the configuration to refer to. All content and metadata describing the content is stored in the repository. The repository may be centralized or distributed and it may consist of a database or flat files or both, but all data should be mastered at a single location in order to facilitate backups and reproducibility.

Distributed File System

In order to use a CM tool at all, there must be a way to get content in and out of the repository from wherever and to wherever the user specifies. In essence, a CM tool is a distributed and versioned file system. The most common way to get files in and out of the repository is via a workspace.

Workspace (a.k.a. Sandbox)

Workspaces are the most frequently used part of a CM system. A workspace consists of the particular set of files that a user is working on as managed by the CM system. The initial content of a workspace is based on a preexisting configuration, such as the mainline. Some CM systems use physical files and local metadata to represent a workspace, some use a virtual file system, some incorporate private branches, and some mix and match these techniques.

Mainline

The mainline (a.k.a. "trunk") serves one of two purposes, depending on the environment and the CM tool in use. One common pattern is for developers to base their workspaces directly on the mainline and to use the mainline as a developer check-in area. The other common pattern is to use mainline as the final stage of a set of promotion levels. In this case, developers base their workspaces on an initial stage and then promote their changes from stage to stage toward the mainline as those changes meet the promotion criteria for each stage.

Milestones and Iterations

Milestones represent well-defined points along the road to a release. They can be used for many purposes including: measuring progress towards goals, helping to pinpoint problems by serving as a point of comparison, providing stable and well known touch points for quality assurance efforts, and supporting componentized development by allowing teams to move their basis from validated milestone to validated milestone. For Agile development, a variation of milestone is an iteration. A completion of an iteration of work represents a milestone that is created at the end of a regularly scheduled period of time.

Baselines and Snapshots

A baseline can be a single item or a collection of similar items that can be demarked at points in time either formally or informally to measure progress. Examples of formal baselines include allocated, functional, production, etc. that are typically managed with change control processes. Less formal baselines such as code are still managed with version control processes. A static baseline can be well-defined much like a milestone or more informal such as a "snapshot" representing a current configuration of a baseline at any point in time. Baselines are dynamic in that they are subject to change and the change from one milestone or point in time to the next represents a delta that can indicate progress.

Releases

Everything that is delivered to a customer, whether it is internal or external, is a release. A release is an example of a configuration and is usually associated with a formal production baseline. Releases may include new products, new versions of existing products, hot-fixes, service packs, and customer one-offs.

Process (a.k.a. Workflow)

All software is developed according to a process, whether it is documented or not. After all, decisions such as what work to do, how to do it, who will do it, how it will be tested, and how and when work will be integrated together won't just pop out of thin air. Most organizations have two processes: their desired process and their actual process. Often, the desired process is recorded in a process document, wiki, or other form of documentation. Your actual process on the other hand is the process that people actually follow day to day. If you are lucky, your desired process and actual process are the same. Typical parts of the development process that a CM tool is involved with are the flow of work from initial entry within a workspace to the mainline and then to one or more releases or patches. In larger development projects, development is broken up by teams, components, or features and may also include staging areas for integration and QA. Regardless of the approach that is used, the basic idea of these concepts is to group related work together.

Reproducibility

A CM tool records, versions, and manages all configurations. As a result, it can also reproduce any configuration at any time. A CM tool is your safety net. It allows you to move forward confidently because you know you can always quickly and easily backtrack and recover from mistakes. And if you reverted to an earlier version by mistake or realize later that you still need the "bad" version, you can even undo your undo! Reproducibility allows you to know what you currently have deployed at customer sites. If a customer reports a problem with a release, the CM tool allows you to easily create a new configuration based on the release that the customer is using and then produce a new release with just that one problem fixed.

Auditability

"Auditability" is a beneficial side-effect of reproducibility. Auditability is the ability of the CM tool to provide an audit trail of who did what when, with which files or other objects, and for what reason. This is especially useful for regulated industries that have compliance requirements. The level of auditability depends on the CM tool. At the simplest level, each file change is versioned and a record of the user, time stamp, and reason for the change is kept. More sophisticated tools provide this record keeping for all actions performed in the system, including operations that are attempted but do not succeed.

Traceability

A common requirement of a CM tool is to provide a full trace from the initiation of a request to the fulfillment of that request as part of a release to a customer. Traceability allows you to find out why each change was made for a release and if something that was planned for a release is actually in it. In order to provide traceability, the CM system must record relationships between different kinds of objects and events. Typical relationships are those between requirement and work item, work item and files changed, and work item and release. Some CM tools also provide relationships between requirements and tests, tests and source files, and/or source files and executables. The more relationships that the CM tool tracks, the more traceability you will have.

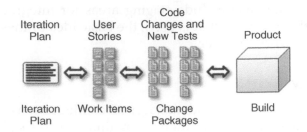

Figure 8-1 Traceability trail for Agile.

Comparison and Merging

In order for people to collaborate effectively, there must be a means of finding differences between configurations and resolving conflicts. Developing a single product for a single customer is hard enough. When there are multiple customers and/or multiple products, there are usually multiple versions of the software to maintain. When you have multiple versions you also have a logistical challenge in making sure that all of the changes get to all of the versions of the software that need them. CM tools are very good at figuring out the difference between any two given configurations and facilitating the process of merging them together. For instance, if you have a broken build, you can find the difference between a previously known good build and what you currently have in order to help track down the problem.

8.2 The Agile Practices that Impact a CM Tool

Agile puts different stresses on a CM tool than traditional development does. The following are the Agile practices that have the most impact on the use of a CM tool and the process supported by that tool. The recurring pattern is that Agile increases the frequency of most CM activities and creates more instances of artifacts stored in the CM tool.

8.2.1 Whole Team

One of the core principals of Agile is that work is accomplished by small (no more than 12 people) teams. Each team is self-sufficient and cross-functional. They have all of the skills they need in order to accomplish their goals without impediments. That does not mean that you cannot have 500 people all working toward the same deliverable, only that it will be comprised of 40–50 distinct teams.

Part of being self-sufficient means that the CM tool and the CM practices you use should be something that your team can use on their own and that most or all of the CM expertise should also reside in the team. The emphasis on teams means that features in your CM tool specifically designed for teams, such as defining teams and the members of each team, will get used more heavily.

8.2.2   Retrospectives

At the end of every iteration, the team gets together to discuss how to keep the team functioning as effectively as possible and to find ways to become even more productive through continuous improvement. The less that the team has to rely on a centralized CM team or those in charge of your infrastructure, the more that they will be able to focus on being the best team that they can be through continuous improvement.

8.2.3   Backlog

In an Agile project, all work is contained in a backlog. The backlog is a list of all work to be performed, including both user stories and defects, ranked from highest to lowest business value. Work is performed from the top of the list to the bottom, one iteration's worth of work at a time.

When all of the work you are going to do is associated with backlog items, you can use work items to define each backlog item. "Work items" are the generic term for any defect, bug, change request, enhancement request, requirement, user story, or other similar item. This works best when the CM tool provides good links between work items, the work done to fulfill those work items, and the build(s) that contain those work items.

8.2.4   Short Iterations

Short iterations are 1–4-week development cycles that each produce a shippable increment of work and are part of a larger overall release plan. Operations that may have previously been done only once every six months or so are now done on a weekly, hourly, or even continuous basis. Not only does that mean many more operations, it also means the creation and management of many more artifacts and versions of those artifacts in the CM tool. For instance, in order to break a release down into short iterations, you will end up with a larger number of smaller tasks. This creates many more work items than a traditional process. Since your CM tool ends up handling many of the operations that need to be done, such as checking files in and linking them to work items and creating and managing iterations (as milestones), short iterations are one of the primary sources of stress that Agile puts on your CM tool.

8.2.5   Iteration Review

At the end of the iteration, the team demonstrates the user stories they committed to doing in that iteration. The audience consists of the customer or customers, which often means the product owner acting as the customer proxy. Ideally, the team should be able to prove to the product owner that they are demonstrating bits that come from the automated build process, that the CM tool confirms that the committed user stories are in that build, and that those user stories have a status indicating that they are done. This creates a new driver for traceability.

8.2.6   One Piece Flow

One piece flow consists of two key principles: There is only ever as much work in progress as the team can reasonably do, and for each work item, all of the steps required to get it shippable are done in rapid succession. The result of this is that all steps required for a work item are done in close proximity to each other, reducing the chance of errors and omissions, and there is very little work that is started but never finished. One piece flow is a necessary part of doing short iterations and keeping the whole team productive. Developers focus on a single short task at a time, which means they will be checking in, merging, and updating their workspaces more frequently. This practice comes from Lean/Kanban, but underlies most Agile methods one way or another. For instance, in test-driven development (TDD), you write a failing test, write just enough code to create a passing test, and repeat.

8.2.7   Continuous Integration (CI)

With CI, all work from all teams is integrated into a single codeline as frequently as possible. Every check-in automatically triggers a build and subsequently a run of the automated test suite. CI encourages more frequent check-ins with smaller amounts of work. CI also means more merging and getting more changes from other people. The CI system is also going to poll for changes more frequently (unless the CM system supports event-based CI) and pull sources on a regular basis. All by itself, this one practice can double or triple the load on the CM system.

8.2.8   Refactoring

Refactoring is the continuous improvement of usability, maintainability, and adaptability of code without changing its behavior. Ideally, changes to the existing code base are made in such a way that it appears that the new functionality was included in the design from the beginning. As a result, each change to your software will involve more changes to more files, which in turn means more check-ins of more files. Refactoring also causes files to be renamed and moved. Teams soon learn that an important way to simplify refactoring is to break source files up into multiple smaller files. All of those check-ins, renames, moves, and file creations are handled by your CM tool. Not only do these operations put more stress on your CM tool by themselves, they also complicate patching, renaming, merging, version ancestry determination, history, comparison, replication, and workspace update operations.

8.2.9   Collective Code Ownership

Collective code ownership is simply the practice of allowing anybody to make any changes to any code at any time as required to implement a user story. This complements the practice of refactoring because refactoring may require changes to modules in many places. With shared code ownership, there is an increased likelihood that multiple people will be working on the same file or files at the same time. This increases the importance of having good facilities for parallel development in your CM tool, such as a good source code merge tool.

8.2.10   Frequent Releases

This is the practice of releasing at the same rate or nearly the same rate that you produce iterations. The benefit of frequent releases is that you get more useful feedback from customers and also have the potential to collect revenues earlier. Although releasing into production at the same rate that you produce iterations is still rare, going through enough of the release process to produce something useful, for instance for customer demos, is fairly common.

8.2.11   Traceability vs. Variance

The assumption in traditional development is that you are going to do lots of upfront planning and then carry out that plan. This creates lots of requirements documents, specification documents, design documents, approvals, status reports, and other documentation. In this context, traceability is important to show variance from the plan in order to take corrective action.

In Agile development, the focus is on keeping the software operational all the way through development. This is expressed in the Agile Manifesto as "Working software over comprehensive documentation" and "Responding to changeover following a plan." Agile still provides for traceability, but the emphasis is on what was actually done in order to implement user stories as the backlog changed, either in response to changing customer needs or in response to information learned during development. In order to take advantage of the traceability that a CM tool can provide in an Agile environment, the features related to traceability must be as transparent and automatic as possible. The emphasis must be on keeping good records of what was done rather than keeping people on plan by restricting what they can do.

8.3   Evaluating Your Situation

Software development practices will always run more smoothly if your tool infrastructure is supporting them rather than requiring people to work around the tools to follow the practices. Sometimes, the infrastructure is so geared to doing things a certain way that it reinforces established practices and makes it difficult for people to move to new practices. The transition to Agile development requires the implementation of many new development practices. The last thing you want is for your infrastructure to get in the way of the transition. A good way to assess the current state of your infrastructure is to evaluate it as though you were starting from scratch and going Agile. How would it stand up to the points raised in this chapter?

8.3.1   Homegrown Tools

By definition, homegrown tools are created and tailored over time to fit one very specific and unique environment: yours. The advantage is that it is a custom fit. The disadvantage is that your needs are changing rapidly with the adoption of Agile practices. Without change, those tools are more likely to keep you tethered to your current process rather than aid you in transitioning to an Agile process. It is unlikely that the bandwidth that you have for maintaining your homegrown tools will allow you to completely overhaul them. You will also need to add tooling to support continuous integration and Agile project management. It is wise to do a "build or buy" analysis to consider the cost of changing and extending your homegrown tools, versus the cost of replacing them with new tools, configuring the new tools, and training your people on the new tools.

8.3.2   Outdated Tools

The majority of the CM tools in use today can trace their lineage in whole or in part back to either SCCS or RCS, introduced in the early 70s and the early 80s respectively. The underlying data models of RCS and SCCS are the same. The only significant difference between these two tools is that RCS uses symbolic names for branches and labels. Essentially, the underlying data model of most of the CM tools available today was invented more than 35 years before the widespread adoption of Agile. If you have old versions of off-the-shelf tools or older tools that are more suited for traditional development, it is worth taking the time to become familiar with the new capabilities that modern CM tools can provide.

8.4 CM Tool Features that Facilitate Agile Development

Since your CM tool plays such a central role in your software development process, it will also play a central role in your transition to Agile development. It can either be an impediment to that transition, or a strategic partner that helps the transition go smoothly. It all depends on whether it has the necessary capabilities and whether or not you leverage those capabilities. Let's take a look at specific features and attributes you need to consider when evaluating the suitability of a CM tool for an Agile environment. This list can be used either to take stock of your current situation or as a list of potential requirements when evaluating new tools.

8.4.1   High Performance

In an Agile environment, waiting is not an option. In order to support the extra load that Agile puts on a CM tool, it is important that the CM tool has performance-oriented capabilities. This includes fast configuration creation, native Internet support, and replication.

8.4.2   Fast Configuration Creation (a.k.a. Branching and Labeling)

To create frequent releases, monthly iteration milestones, and snapshots of known good builds done by your CI tool, configurations need to be able to be created instantaneously, or at most within minutes.

8.4.3   Native Internet Support

Modern software development tools are well equipped to efficiently transfer large amounts of data over the Internet. A good rule of thumb is to use tools which use TCP/IP natively and do not rely on shared network protocols such as SMB, NFS, or other similar protocols designed for local network use.

8.4.4 Replication for Distributed Team Continuous Integration

There are many different forms of replication: read-only replication with writes to the master, caching proxies, fully disconnected operation with branch mastership, and peer-to-peer replication. The main problem solved by replication is that of providing high performance for all sites when there are multiple development sites. Using some form of replication is important for distributed Agile teams to support continuous integration. If it is difficult or slow to integrate the work of teams at multiple sites, it will be difficult to get the benefits of continuous integration.

8.4.5 All Writeable Files

Refactoring and collective code ownership means that developers may need to change any file at any time. Having to know which files they need to check-out prior to refactoring them can seriously crimp their productivity. Older CM tools make all workspace files read-only by default and require an explicit check-out prior to working on any files. More modern CM tools make all workspace files writeable by default, removing the check-out step.

8.4.6 Codelines (a.k.a. Streams, Lines of Development)

A codeline refers to any development effort toward a particular purpose, such as new development, maintenance, a team working together on a sub-project, etc. Similar terms are "development effort," "stream," and "line of development." At the end of the day, the folks who initiate these things (managers, business people, etc.) do not really care how they are implemented – they just want to ask questions like, "How is the 4.0 release coming along?" and "Are all of the fixes from maintenance in the latest release?" Somebody else then translates that into the appropriate queries, which may be in terms of branches, scripts, codelines, or something else.

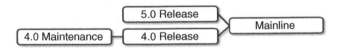

Figure 8-2 Related codelines.

Direct support for codelines removes the need to translate high-level objects into lower-level objects like branches and labels combined with scripts. Instead, you can work directly at a high level. Why should there be any difference between the mental model of codelines and the implementation model?

CM systems that use codelines have a unified user model and implementation model for codelines. Codelines are the basic building block of the architecture. There are no branches or labels, just codelines. Codelines can be used for releases, active development, workspaces, etc. Each codeline except the mainline is defined in terms of a parent codeline and inherits everything from the parent (recursively).

So, if you wanted to do maintenance on the 4.0 release, you would create a new codeline based on 4.0. Through inheritance, it is the same as 4.0. The definition itself is all that is required. In this case, the definition of "4.0 maintenance" is "maintenance of everything in 4.0 plus all of the changes in 4.0."

Since codelines are first-class objects, you can act on them directly. You can assign security attributes, lock them, define other codelines in terms of them, compare them directly, or do queries on them without having to understand how the codelines themselves are composed, etc. Some CM tools allow you to visualize the relationships and dependencies between codelines, which provides you with a visual overview of your entire development process.

In a traditional development lifecycle that spans a 6–18-month timeframe there may be "plenty of time" to emulate codelines with branches, labels, and scripts. But when you are using short iterations, inefficiencies will be magnified by 10 times or more. Codelines mean that developers can concentrate on coding instead of trying to figure out which files from which branches or labels go into which directories in order to build the version of the product that they should be working on. When it is difficult to figure out how to compose the right source files for the product, you will hear the phrase "it works for me" more frequently. The Agile focus on quick feedback and quick turnaround makes it especially important that everybody be on the same page so that problems that are found by the continuous integration build are easily reproducible by any team member.

8.4.7 Change Tracking

Change tracking allows you to link stories and defects to work items, and work items to both the backlog and to the files that were involved in that change. When there is a good link between changes, work items, and your backlog, it is much easier to validate that the work being done is really the work planned for the iteration and that the work planned for the iteration is really getting done.

A common method used for informal linking of work items with the work done for them is to use the work item number in the check-in comment. Some CM tools and add-on products take advantage of this common practice by parsing the check-in comments and then allowing the user to drill down or drill up from work item to check-in or check-in to work item. This information can even be used for reporting, but there are drawbacks. Typing a work item number into a check-in comment is error-prone because it relies on the user to track the work items themselves, remember to put them into the comments, and to type in the right number for the right work item. There are a wide variety of more advanced mechanisms for linking things together. These include integration-based links, merge and patch links, rename links, transactions, change sets, change lists, and change packages.

8.4.7.1   Refactoring: Rename, Merge, and Patch Tracking

Refactoring often requires files to be renamed or moved. Not all CM tools, especially older tools, support the ability to track rename operations. Older tools turn rename and move operations into a copy from the old name or location into the new name or location, followed by a delete of the old name or location. More modern tools either keep track of the link between the old and new name and/or location, or they track the name and location of objects via versioned properties.

Full rename tracking depends heavily on the ability of the CM tool to support merge tracking. Conversely, true merge tracking support depends on the ability of the CM tool to support rename tracking. Some CM tools support rename tracking and merge tracking when used independently, but not when used in conjunction. When a CM tool supports the combined capabilities of rename tracking and merge tracking, then no matter how many files are renamed or moved, the CM system will be able to update workspaces, merge changes, and link changes to work items accurately. If you do a lot of refactoring, incomplete support for renaming and merge tracking can be an impediment.

In an Agile project you will need to merge changes more frequently with less tolerance for error. Once you have resolved a conflict, it is important to then accurately record the resolution so that you don't have to resolve that same conflict again in the future. To support this, many CM tools keep track of all merges via merge links.

Some CM tools also track patches. A patch is a partial merge where you only apply some of the changes that a merge would involve. For instance, there may be three bug fixes that were done during new development, but the customer only wants one of them, preferring not to incur the risk of changes that were done if the other bugs don't affect them.

8.4.7.2   Transactions (a.k.a. Change Lists or Change Sets)

Transactions provide a logical grouping of operations performed on multiple objects. For instance, when you check in 10 files together, a transaction makes it easy to see that it was a single logical operation. Later, when looking at the change to a file, you can also easily find out which other files were changed at the same time.

8.4.7.3 Change Packages

A change package represents all of the work done for a work item, regardless of how many separate check-ins were involved. For instance, a developer may have made a change and then found out later that it didn't make it through QA. The work item gets reopened and then the developer makes another change. The combination of the two changes is the change package. Change packages provide a clear and simple round-trip link from stories in your backlog to the actual work done, and from work done back to stories in the backlog.

Change packages work best when they are simple to use. For example, change packages are easier to use when the CM tool manages the work items that the user is working on, updates the status of the change packages as the user checks in changes, and performs the linking between check-ins and change packages automatically. This way, the user is always looking at descriptions of the changes, such as "create floating toolbar for cut and paste" instead of "CR-A3592."

If you have a workflow which involves multiple codelines, it is important to be able to easily propagate change packages from codeline to codeline. Some CM tools only support the integrity of change packages within a single codeline. That is, it is possible to propagate change packages from codeline to codeline, but the association of the propagated files to change packages is lost. In order to effectively support change packages in a multiple codeline workflow, the CM tool must support the selective propagation of change packages from codeline to codeline where the integrity of each change package is preserved and further propagation of the change package is possible.

Figure 8-3   A simple Agile workflow.

For instance, in an Agile project you may have a workflow where stories start out in the "to do" state and then move on to "coded", "tested", and "done." For this workflow you could use a codeline for each of the code-related states (coded, tested, and done). This would allow you to easily create a build from the tested codeline that included all of the tested stories in order for QA to do exploratory testing on a shippable version of the product. It also allows the product owner to check that the product being demonstrated during the iteration review was built from the "done" codeline, that all stories in that codeline correspond to the current iteration, and that all stories committed to the iteration are in that codeline.

8.4.8   Private Branches

A fairly common pattern in large Agile teams is to do a branch per story. The motivation for this is to be able to work on the story in isolation until it is coded and developer testing is done. One problem with this pattern is that it may encourage delayed integration and thus hide and delay the fixing of problems. A second problem is branch proliferation.

A good compromise is to use private branches. This works best when the CM tool provides a branch type specifically designed for private use. Instead of creating a new branch for each story, you just create a single branch for the current story that you are using. When you finish that story, reuse the branch for your next story.

As a side benefit of using a private branch, the developer can checkpoint their work in progress, revert to an earlier state, and generally use the functionality of the CM tool for their own private use. For instance, a recent trend is for developers to do pre-flight builds (which include automated testing) prior to check-in. With a private branch, you can make sure all of your changes are checked in prior to doing a build and test and then merge your changes with the mainline if it succeeds. If there are failures, you can then make changes from a well-known starting point. This is exactly the same pattern you would follow when using continuous integration: check-in, build, test, and update as necessary.

8.5   Integration with Your Agile Ecosystem

No CM tool is an island; it must coexist with other tools in your Agile ecosystem. To get the most value out of your CM tool, you need good integrations with the rest of your Agile tool set. The three most important Agile tools for your CM tool to integrate with are your continuous integration and build tool, your Agile project management tool, and your test automation tool.

Figure 8-4   Agile ecosystem.

8.5.1   Integration with the Agile Project Management Tool

The most effective use of an Agile project management tool will occur when it is also your main work item tracking tool. This will provide a strong link between backlog, stories, defects, and work items. If you use both an Agile project management tool and a requirements management or defect tracking tool (or all three), then it is important to have tight integrations between them and your Agile project management tool in order to have a unified backlog containing all work.

Whatever your situation, your CM tool needs to integrate with your Agile project management tool in order to link your backlog to the actual work performed. This provides the linkage required in order to manage by stories in your CM tool.

8.5.2   Integration with the Continuous Integration and Build Tool

A build automation tool is responsible for the regular and unattended running of your builds. This includes official builds, nightly builds, on-demand builds, development team builds, and continuous integration builds. Ideally, you have just a single build automation tool which supports workflow and is well adapted for both continuous integration and regularly scheduled or event-triggered builds.

Build automation and CM are connected at the hip. Good CM requires good build automation and good build automation requires good CM. It is important that the integration between them is top-notch.

Continuous Integration (CI) builds can put a serious load on your CM server. To keep this from affecting the performance of your end users, it is recommended that you use a replication solution or other means to re-route CI traffic to a CM server dedicated to CI.

There are two kinds of CI: polling and event-based. Polling requires periodic requests to the CM tool to see if there have been any check-ins since the last poll. In contrast, event-based integrations are driven by the CM tool itself based on check-ins. Additionally, polling can create a delay between when the check-in happens and when the build and test cycle starts. An event-based integration will remove that delay.

8.5.3   Integration with the Test Automation Tool

In an Agile team, there is no separation between development and quality assurance. Just as the best results come from an integrated team, this applies equally to the test assets. The test assets should be kept alongside the source code. Ideally, the test automation IDE used by the QA team is integrated with the CM tool for the same reasons that development IDEs are integrated with the CM tool. At the very least, there should be an automated smoke test which runs after every successful build and it should be kept in the CM tool right alongside the source files.

8.5.4 Configuration vs. Customization

You will always need to do some amount of customization of your CM tool via triggers, APIs, and scripts. New regulations, policies, constraints, and other factors are coming into play on a regular basis. But you should be able to accomplish the bulk of what you need to do either right out of the box or with a minimum of configuration. This is especially true in an Agile environment where the teams are performing retrospectives at every iteration and potentially making process changes at every iteration. If they need to do lots of customization of their tools instead of just re-configuring them, they will not be able to get the full advantage of using Agile.

8.6 Conclusion

A transition to Agile development will test the limits of your adaptability and put many new stresses on your people, process, and tools. Your CM tool is the foundation of your software development process. As such, it has a significant influence on your organization's ability to adapt and change to accommodate ongoing business needs. By reviewing each of the Agile practices that impact your CM tool and evaluating your CM tool from an Agile perspective, you will gain valuable insight into how well suited your CM tool and the process built around it are for Agile development.

Beyond making sure that your CM tool does not get in the way, you can also look to your CM tool to help out in new ways. Your CM tool will be instrumental in supporting whole teams, assisting with linking stories to work done, short iterations, Agile workflow, managing by stories, continuous integration, refactoring, shared code ownership, iteration reviews, and frequent releases. When transitioning to Agile development, your CM tool can be an impediment or strategic partner. The choice is up to you.

Evaluating Tools Suited for Agile

Performing a tool evaluation is an effective way to ensure the technology selected meets the needs of the working processes of the team and the method being followed. In many cases, there is not as much time spent evaluating technology as necessary, even though many of the tools will be highly used in the product lifecycle. Within the Configuration Management (CM) and Agile space, two of these technologies are CM tools and Agile planning tools. As you consider tools suited for Agile, some important steps include scanning the tool marketplace for what exists and what you have internally, identifying the level of evaluation appropriate to the time available, and most importantly, conducting an evaluation based on your need.

9.1   Looking for Tools out there and in here

CM tools have been around for a while and are fairly well established in the industry. CM tool vendors have been investigating user needs in this space for at least a couple of decades, through sales visits, customer advisory boards (CABs), and numerous conferences, seminars, and webinars. While there are still some homegrown tools in use, the majority of the CM tools in use today are either vendor tools or open source freeware tools.

Agile planning tools on the other hand are relatively new to the market and there is a race for vendors to meet the evolving needs of Agile product teams. On one hand it is important to keep track of the evolving progress of the Agile tool vendors and on the other hand organizations may find that they can adapt some previously purchased vendor tools or even some homegrown tools. There are pros and cons with the various approaches.

As you consider evaluating Agile planning tools (or evaluating any tools for that matter), consider the various tool options that may be available to you. These include vendor tools, open source freeware tools, and in-house homegrown tools. Consider and compare factors such as: does the tool have a product roadmap so you know the tool future; is the tool customizable; is it configurable; is the tool installed on the premises or can it be used in the clouds; and what are the costs, including license, support, and staff? As you consider bringing in new tools, it may be beneficial to take a moment and inventory the current set of tools that you have. In some cases, you may be surprised to find tools that you do not know you have.

9.1.1   Using a Vendor Tool Specific for Agile

Many Agile tool vendors have conducted a significant amount of research on the needs that Agile professionals have for the projects following Agile methods. In fact, vendors attempt to anticipate the needs of their customers, and typically have established a tool roadmap on the product direction of a tool, based on the near-term business objectives and requirements from market input that are prioritized, and long-term goals to highlight future market opportunities and technical direction. The roadmap needs to take into account the differentiators that make your product better or more marketable than the competition. It also includes target market segments and a rough return on investment (ROI) based on the cost of developing the product and the potential sales opportunities. It is best to prioritize the features and/or requirements based on the committed customers who have signed the purchase order over the potential customers that may or may not sign. A roadmap has to have buy-in from several inputs from the marketplace (i.e., customers), to sales and marketing, to architecture and development, and senior management. The roadmap must be logical and dynamic since the world around us is dynamic. And finally, the roadmap will have a rough time horizon based on the high-level requirements and market segments being addressed. Having a vendor who focuses on a tool roadmap is a benefit for customers because they understand the tool direction and have a possibility of influencing the direction based on contributed requirements.

> ### Pit Stop
>
> Vendors who have tool/product roadmaps allow the customer to have insight into the future direction of the tool and allow the customer to have possible influence over the tool direction.

Vendors typically design and build tools for the general market, meaning that the version you get is the same release all of the companies receive. The advantages are that you know what customers have by the release number and supporting the release becomes easier. The disadvantage to this approach is that as a customer you get what the vendor has even if it does not exactly fit your needs. Vendors have worked around this is by adding features within the tool so it is configurable, meaning that while the program is fixed, there are some features that can be adjusted to better meet the customer need. However, many customers do not take advantage of the configurable aspects of a vendor tool and typically install it with the standard configuration.

Probably the biggest disadvantage of going with a vendor tool is the cost. Since we are living in a world of open source and freeware tools, cost may be a significant factor in the way companies approach tool selection. When purchasing tools from a vendor, you have to consider cost of the license, cost of maintenance, and cost of staff to support the tool installation. Cost of the license can vary depending on the license approach. Some common license approaches are: licenses per seat, meaning you assign a license to a specific person; floating licenses, meaning that licenses are shared across a group and are used by a person, then made available to others when not in use; and license per server, which serves a fixed or unlimited number of people working (physically or virtually) on that server. However, with all of this being said, sometimes the total cost of ownership for open source and/or freeware tools may be almost as high as the vendor cost, depending on how much extra work you need to do to get it to the level that you would like. Open source and freeware tools may lack in functionality and support compared to the vendor tools.

Some vendors actually use Agile methods to develop the products they are selling to the marketplace. If you believe in the Agile approach, having a vendor who actually uses Agile methods may be an influencing factor into selecting an Agile tool.

9.1.2   Using a Freeware Tool Specific for Agile

There are open source and freeware tools out on the market for both CM and Agile. The immediate advantages are that you can typically begin using them right away. This can be a benefit when you are starting a new company and have little start-up capital, assuming that the tool fits most of your needs. Some freeware tools actually have fairly robust functionality. However, an investigation of functionality should be conducted within an evaluation process.

Another advantage with using freeware tools is that there is no license cost associated with using the tool and no support costs either. However, there will be the cost of someone on the team running and supporting the tool, so it may be hard to determine whether a vendor or freeware approach is cheaper. If it is a simpler and easier tool to use with few users, then freeware is cheaper, but if the freeware tool is more complex and used by many, then costs may be higher than initially thought.

Some neutral points about freeware tools are that if the tool is based on open source software, you can often download the code and customize or re-program the tool to better fit your needs. While this may seem like an advantage, it does require that you have staff who can spend the time to perform this work and then maintain the tool in the long run, particularly if it will be used by more than a few team members. Some freeware tools have configurable features but this is typically limited.

There are disadvantages when using freeware tools. Typically there is no roadmap to advise you of its direction. If you are expecting the freeware tool to have incremental releases with additional functionality added over time, you may be disappointed. However, for many people, the immediate functionality and use it provides will be adequate. Some freeware tools will have a regular release or update schedule, while some have not been updated in quite some time. In some cases, freeware tools come with a minimal level of support limited to information on a website. In addition, the more widely used freeware tools tend to have active user groups where questions, advice, and comments can be posed or queried. The implication is that you may have to assign staff to be available to maintain the freeware installation base, whether on a server or multiple desktops, and who can help your group with training and support, since there is typically little technical support available.

Pit Stop

While a tool may be termed "freeware," it does not mean free of all costs and effort. While there is no license cost, there is still a

cost and effort to set it up and support it. Also, most freeware tools
are not as functionally robust as vendor tools, so trade-offs should be
considered. In all cases, consider an evaluation process when deciding
on freeware tools and/or vendor tools.

A common concern about freeware tools is that there is less of a focus
on security being built into the tool. However, when it is a tool that has
been used by many folks, this is often not the case: security issues are
often worked out earlier in a freeware tool's lifecycle, since many people
are immediately using them, *ergo* the flaws are discovered earlier rather
than later. Another concern is that there may not be anyone legally liable if
the tool causes significant problems within an organization. But of course,
vendor tools tend to be covered from legal liability too with the way the
contracts are written.

9.1.3 Using a Homegrown Tool for Agile

At first glance, a homegrown tool may appear to the best choice for
a team. Homegrown tools are typically developed from a specific set
of requirements for a working team. Since the company owns the tool,
they own the source code so there is the ability to customize for further
needs. The tool may be readily available and typically free of license and
maintenance costs.

However, as you look more closely, some disadvantages arise. The
first disadvantage of a homegrown tool is that it may not be readily
portable, extendable, and scalable. Typically, no effort is made to identify
a packaging and installation process. Also, some homegrown tools may
not be as customizable as you think, since in some cases, the people who
wrote the tool may no longer be around and the code may not be very well
documented. And similar to freeware tools, you may have to assign staff
to be available to maintain the installation, whether on a server or multiple
desktops, and to help groups with training and technical support.

Another disadvantage when using homegrown tools is that there may
be no strategy or roadmap to advise you of its direction. In fact, most
have been cobbled together in an ad hoc manner. If you are expecting the
homegrown tool to have incremental releases over time with additional
functionality being added, you will be disappointed. Often there is little or
no budget assigned to the homegrown tool. However, for many people, the
immediate functionality and use it provides is adequate. Homegrown tools
usually come with ad hoc and limited user documents, but this should be
investigated.

As part of the inventorying task, it is beneficial to take a moment and identify the homegrown tools that are being used, what functional area they cover, and how many users use the tool. While there are a lot of disadvantages with going the homegrown route, your company may have robust and well-used homegrown tools that have genuine support, installation processes, and user help or training.

9.1.4 Tool Classification Comparison

Now that we have explored these various tool classifications in detail, it is worth comparing them, based on the tool direction, how configurable they are, and costs. Below is a view of the three choices with advantages (a happy face), neutral (a bland face), and disadvantages (a sad face). Feel free to change the face choice, but consider applying a similar model when assessing these tool options.

As you consider tool choices, keep in mind that each of these choices may have both an on-premises installation and an in-the-clouds infrastructure option available. These can impact the advantages and disadvantages and more specifically impact the staff support that is needed.

Table 9-1 Snapshot of advantages and disadvantages of various tool classifications.

	Vendor Tool	Freeware Tool	Existing Homegrown Tool
Tool Vision/Roadmap	🙂	😐	😐
Configurable	🙂	😐	🙁
License Cost	🙁	🙂	🙂
Support Cost	😐	🙂	🙂
Staff Cost	😐	🙁	🙁

9.2 Levels of Technology Evaluation

As you approach an evaluation of a technology, it is important to understand that there are levels of tool (i.e., technology) evaluations and each comes with an associated level of risk. Particularly in the case of Agile, there can often be a need to simply pick a tool and move on, more for the sake of speed then for any real demand from the organization or customer. When tools are picked quickly comes increased risk of selecting the incorrect technology. Identifying and communicating this general risk can help you raise the priority given to the importance of a technology evaluation. It can also lead to the level of evaluation being aligned appropriately with the level of risk a product team is willing to assume and accept.

There are several levels of a technology evaluation that may be performed, each with a different level of associated risk. They include the "research evaluation," the "demonstration evaluation," and the "in-house/full evaluation."

Pit Stop

Each level of tool evaluation comes with an associated level of risk. A research evaluation has the highest risk of incorrectly identifying the right tool, the demonstration evaluation reduces the risk, while the in-house/full evaluation has the least risk of incorrectly identifying the right tool.

9.2.1   Research Evaluation

This constitutes an evaluation based on reviewing existing documents (e.g., articles, research, etc), published in technology trade magazines, journals, and evaluation documents that discuss and evaluate tools. It may also include reviewing input in discussion forums from folks with actual working experience. This will give you insight into what you might look for in a specified technology. Specifically, at this level of evaluation, you need to ensure the technology meets the basic entrance criteria for the infrastructure. Entrance criteria will include and not be limited to development platform(s) you will be working in, basic capabilities, and cost factors. After a review of these documents, a decision for selecting the technology can be made. If you perform this level of technology evaluation, you are placing yourself in the highest risk of incorrectly selecting the best tool to fit your needs, since little time is used and no demonstration and hands-on experience is occurring.

9.2.2   Demonstration Evaluation

This level of evaluation would include reviewing the output of the research evaluation and focusing on the top two or three tools in a time-boxed manner. Then it includes defining clear technology requirements for the product's needs. This would involve forming a technology evaluation team, gathering technology requirements, weighting the requirements by importance, getting a demonstration of each requirement from vendors (and asking how their technology meets the requirements), and scoring each requirement. After the demos and scoring of the technology, a selection may be made. Performing this level of technology evaluation reduces the risk of incorrectly selecting the best tool to fit your needs, since you have a good idea of your technology requirements and you have seen demonstrations of vendor products, and hopefully have determined at a high-level which technology best meets your needs.

9.2.3   Pilot/Full Evaluation

This level of evaluation would include the research and demonstration evaluation output. The top one or two products (or as many as desired) from the demonstration evaluation would be brought in-house for one to two months to exercise and test the vendor technology against the requirements specified, and preferably in a project scenario. With CM technologies, it is important to exercise the tools by importing the code into the CM repository and exercising the various CM functionalities. For Agile planning tools, there are options of either hosting the tool on premises or utilizing the tool in the cloud infrastructure hosted by the vendor.

At this level of evaluation, a request for proposal (RfP) should be considered for each potential vendor as input and reviewed as part of the evaluation. The RfP should ask about the options for hosting the technology, how the vendor communicates and delivers releases and patches, how they solicit customer requirements, and how they price their product (amongst other things).

Beyond this, you would want to establish a pilot infrastructure and select a product in which you would actually exercise the tool. This environment should be similar to the working product infrastructure (same platform, sample application code, development tools, etc.). Tasks may include installing the technology and identifying a product that will pilot the technology. This may entail establishing a working process that goes with it. Then you should exercise and test the technology to determine if it meets the requirements that were defined. This type of evaluation has the lowest level of risk of selecting the incorrect technology.

9.2.4   Considerations on Levels

The level of technology evaluation that is chosen and conducted may vary according to the available schedule, effort, resources, and level of technical expertise within the company. If an organization only wants to commit the minimal amount of time to evaluate a technology (research evaluation), then the product owner, project manager, and/or technology users or experts should communicate the risk that is associated with this level of technology evaluation. This is why it is important to understand the risks associated with each level. Overall, a pilot/full evaluation is ideal since it minimizes the most risk and validates that the technology can actually met the requirements. The minimal evaluation level for any technology that will be highly used in the product lifecycle is in my opinion the demonstration evaluation, since it can impact the team's day-to-day activities. It is important to at least know your technology requirements and view the vendor products to compare against your requirements.

9.3 Perform a Technology Evaluation

Some people find the process of evaluating technologies that impact their group fairly daunting. Others do not take it seriously enough. Selecting the correct technology can benefit both the effectiveness and efficiency of the working processes. From an Agile perspective, the focus of a technology evaluation should not be on the tool, but first on the people and interactions. The interactions should drive the need and in the case of a technology evaluation, the need can be reinterpreted as the requirements.

With that in mind, the goal of selecting a tool is to limit infrastructure debt by providing just enough capability for the work at hand but not so much that it constrains or overburdens the team. Some high-level areas to consider are:

- Level of process and standards support – The tool should allow you to work according to the process and standards you support.
- Level of automation support – The tool should allow you to easily automate the process to reduce manual steps and potential errors.
- Cross-platform support – The tool should have the ability to run or be used on multiple platforms.
- Ease of integration – Integration of the CM or Agile technology with other tools should be as easy as possible.
- Ease of administration – The tools should be easy to administer and configure as necessary.
- Standards support – The tool should provide the ability to support naming conventions and organizational standards.

- Ability to support various methods – How capable the tool is to support various methods. Agile is a great example where there is a need for continuous build and integration capabilities.
- Knowledge of the area of focus (in this case CM and Agile) – This is helpful, together with understanding your interactions and working processes.
- And of course, knowledge of the functionality that is needed.

9.3.1 Investigating a CM Tool for Your Needs

What exactly is a CM tool? There is no one clear definition on what a CM tool does or exactly the functions it should provide but it goes well beyond simple version control. CM at its very essence covers identification, control, auditing, and reporting. Many would expand control to include version control, change control, build management, and release engineering. It is important to take a step back from the conventional view of what a CM tool offers and what capabilities you may think a CM tool provides. As development becomes more complex, there are demands for more capabilities to handle the complexity. This is very true with CM. While it may have started as a simple version control tool, the better CM tools are now far more complex and rich in their capabilities to handle the complexities of software development.

Selecting an incorrect CM tool can make the CM tool administrator, build engineer, release engineer, and developer's lives unhappy. Ovum, a premier objective technology evaluation company, writes, "Selecting a Software Configuration Management product is complicated, involving organizational and business factors as well as technical and cultural considerations. What is 'best' depends on what specific needs exist."

The upcoming sections will attempt to identify the various CM capabilities within a rough framework and is not meant to be comprehensive. Even if you do not agree with this division or you think that some of these areas are misplaced, it is important to have a clear understanding of these capabilities.

9.3.1.1 Version Control

These tools offer the capability to store elements and manage incremental changes to elements (versioning), most commonly source code, but often executables and documentation. In addition, there is an assumption that a reporting ability exists that can list the elements within a version control repository specific to a release. This helps in the ability to audit baselines of code. In general, the version control functionality is always considered a part of a CM tool. More details include:

- Tools in this category typically fall into the development phase but can live throughout the full project lifecycle if documents and other artifacts are being managed or when following an Agile method.

- More modern version control tools offer workspace management, and branching and merging capabilities. The latter support continuous integration, which is beneficial to Agile teams.

- Some people consider document management tools as a type of version control tool, since they offer version control functionality and a means for assigning attributes to items.

9.3.1.2 Build Management

These tools offer the capability to identify a code baseline and then build (generate) executables. More advanced tools in this space offer bill-of-materials reports, and dependency and traceability checking that help with integrity and auditing. Many established CM tools include build functionality, while some see tools in this space as separate from CM tools. More details include:

- Tools in this category typically fall into the development phase of the project lifecycle.
- This category may be divided further into build management and continuous build.
  - Build management has a broad focus on providing an automated approach to the full build process (labeling code, setting up build space, executing build, logging build results, and sometimes even some smoke tests).
  - Continuous build has a narrower focus and more specifically on an automated approach to build every time someone checks in code, to ensure that everything builds together, therefore reducing large merge conflicts.

9.3.1.3 Change Control/Problem Management

These are tools that help you document, manage, and track changes. These tools offer the capability to document a change and then establish a workflow by which the change can be tracked along a change lifecycle. In addition, there is an assumption that there is the ability to identify and report on the status of changes being tracked. Some people see tools in this space as separate from CM tools but they are very closely aligned. More details include:

- Tools in this category typically live throughout the project lifecycle where changes that impact the project baselines are being managed.
- Requirements management, change control, problem management, and defect tracking tools may be included in this category, since each provides similar capabilities.

9.3.1.4   Release Engineering

These tools offer the capability to migrate and install deliverables onto a production system. Many people see tools in this space as separate from CM tools but they are very closely aligned. Other details include:

- Tools in this category typically live in the release phase, but may get initiated in the development and test phase or in an iteration.

9.3.1.5   The CM Tool (or Tools) for You

As you exercise the evaluation process, you may find that one CM tool meets all of your requirements. However, you may also find that your requirements are not met by one tool. This may imply that you need two tools (or more) to meet all of your CM needs. This is not unreasonable, in part because there is yet to be a CM tool that meets all of the practices and processes of CM.

9.3.2   Investigating Agile Tools

Right up front, it should be noted that Agile does not advocate tools. As the Agile value says: "People and interactions over process and tools." With that being said, there are a growing number of Agile tools in the market built by proprietary vendors or established within the open source arena. Agile tools are focused primarily on Agile project management and collaboration tools. There are Agile-oriented tools such as continuous integration and build tools, CM tools, and automated testing tools that are focusing their functionality on supporting Agile.

From an Agile perspective, some prefer to initially work with minimal Agile tools, using index cards, spreadsheets, wikis, and whiteboards. Over time, through experience, some find it beneficial to select Agile or Agile-oriented tools because of the automation they provide that can improve productivity and visibility in the working processes. Some functionality that is looked for in Agile project management and collaboration tools includes the ability to:

- support release and iteration planning (based on stories and tasks).
- establish and manage a master product backlog that can be subdivided into release backlogs.
- support the use of index cards for stories in a visual and collaborative manner.
- help with the ability to estimate stories and tasks.
- support task management per iteration from stories.
- establish burndown and velocity charts in an automated manner.
- establish shared collaboration space with web conferencing for continuous discussion.
- allow for integrations with CM, test, defect tracking tools, and development tools including IDEs.
- support the retrospective process and merge the improvement tasks back into the backlog and release or iteration planning.

This set of functionality amongst others can help the Agile team gain a better understanding of the progress and big picture of their effort. In effect, the functionality of an Agile project management tool provides both accurate and real-time data to enable effective leadership on the project, help manage risk, and help understand the progress being made.

Some Agile project management tool vendors are providing options for implementing and deploying their tool. You now have a choice of deploying the tool locally (by physically installing it) on premises or utilizing the vendor's web-based cloud infrastructure (software as a service or application service provider model). The former approach ensures that you have total control over the technology and data, while the latter helps you ramp up quickly and have the ability to scale as needed.

9.3.3 Evaluation Process

As you consider the various tools for Agile (Agile project management, collaboration, CM, test) on the market, having a defined evaluation procedure to work through can be of great benefit. The goal of the evaluation process is to objectively evaluate the tools in the marketplace, narrow the field of potential tools (from external vendors, vendor tools that you already own, and homegrown tools), and select the tool that best meets your needs.

Performing a technology evaluation will require some planning, with the caveat that this should be a time-boxed activity. You may also consider it an iteration planning activity, since the time it takes to conduct an evaluation should be short but it may take several iterations depending on the level of evaluation you are conducting.

Pit Stop

Consider a technology evaluation as a small project. It should be time-boxed, depending on the level of evaluation you are conducting, and may be phase-based or iterative.

While it is useful to prepare a small plan or backlog for the evaluation process, it is important to (at least) list the tasks that will be needed to complete a successful and meaningful technology evaluation. The plan can be used to identify who is working on what task (to avoid confusion) and it may also be used to track progress of tasks. This may allow the leader of the evaluation to proactively remove roadblocks in order to more efficiently get tasks completed. The following are high-level steps in helping you perform an objective technology evaluation.

9.3.3.1   Establishing Evaluation Team

Establishing an evaluation team with members that have a stake in the use of the tool will increase the chance of identifying the best tool for the work. As you consider members of the team, the best candidates are those that have a stake in the outcome, the time to work through an evaluation, and the inclination to do so. As you assemble the team, consider establishing rules of engagement so that the team acts objectively and within a set of guidelines. The objective of these rules is to avoid bias and derailment of the process, understand vendor tactics, and more. Examples of rules can be that only one person speaks at a time, that once a step is passed it will need a team quorum to move back again, that there are no responses to a vendor inquiry until the full team has considered it, etc.

Typically, the personnel involved in a technology evaluation are those who play the following roles. Note: The title of each role may be different or undefined within various organizations and companies.

- **Evaluation Coordinator** – Responsible for developing the evaluation plan/backlog and tracks progress through the evaluation process. Manages the evaluation requirements list and ensures that the key participants are invited to the evaluation sessions.

- **Evaluation Team** – Stakeholders who will use the technology. They must determine the requirements for the product team. Members may include (but not be limited to):
  - *Product Owner/Manager* – This person(s) participates in identifying requirements for the technology from a product lifecycle needs perspective and should ultimately be responsible for purchasing the technology.
  - *Project Management* – Understands how the tools should be used on a project and helps identify the requirements from a project lifecycle needs perspective.
  - *Sub-set of Product Team* – About two to three members of the product team who will have primary interaction with the technology under consideration.
  - *Subject Matter Expert* – An expert who has work and tool experience in the field in which the tool is being selected.
    - *Agile Coach* – Participates in identifying the requirements for Agile-related tools from an Agile needs perspective.
    - *CM Professional* – Participates in identifying the requirements for CM-related tools from an CM needs perspective.

9.3.3.2 Determining Evaluation Level

The product manager/owner should review the different levels of an evaluation and determine the level suitable for the product line. Will it be the research evaluation, demonstration evaluation (a.k.a., demo), or pilot/full evaluation? Keep in mind that the research-based and demo evaluation brings a level of risk that must either be accepted or mitigated in some manner. The output from this task is a decision on which level of evaluation to perform. Other product team members may help the product owner determine the level but it is ultimately the product owner's decision.

9.3.3.3 Conducting a Research Evaluation

Irrespective of which level of evaluation you select, you should always consider starting with research evaluation. Review evaluations published in technology trade magazines, journals, and the Internet. This will give you insight into what you might look for in a tool, such as high-level requirements based on the functionality and features the tool provides, what is the latest direction of tools in a field, and what vendor and/or open source freeware exists. Specifically, at this level of evaluation ensure the technology meets the basic entrance criteria for the infrastructure. Entrance criteria will include and are not limited to development platform(s) you will be working on, cost factors and constraint, and whether you want to host the tools locally on premises or in the clouds by a service provider. Once the entrance criteria and high-level requirements are identified, compare them to the list of new vendor tools (on premises and in the clouds), open source freeware tools, already existing in-house vendor tools, and homegrown tools that have been identified.

If this is just a research evaluation, attempt to find a tool that meets your needs. Identify any risks that may be outstanding to either accept or mitigate as you move forward. Document the reason(s) for selecting the tool, include the risks you have identified, include the costs as you understand them, and summarize the results. This will help you later to understand why you (or others who are also interested in a similar tool) have selected this tool. Move forward in acquiring the tool.

If you are planning to move to the demo evaluation, select the top two to four tools from the research evaluation. This will be input to the technology evaluation team.

9.3.3.4   Conducting a Demo Evaluation

The next step is to gather requirements that are desired in a technology. A brainstorming session with the evaluation team is recommended to collect the requirements. Create an evaluation requirements list (e.g., on a spreadsheet) to record the requirements. Define the requirements that are desired. Requirements will consist of:

- functional requirements of the tool.
- implementation and integration requirements (expertise required for implementation, ease of implementation; other tools integrated with this product, etc.).
- support requirements provided by vendors (available 7×24, website information, 1–800 (toll free) number, etc.).
- cost requirements (price of tool, cost of maintenance, cost of infrastructure setup, etc.).

There may be other requirement types as well. The requirements should be weighted so that the more important requirements get more weight when being scored (the rated "raw score" of each requirement will be multiplied by its weight).

Concurrently with gathering and weighting the requirements, contact the tool vendors, freeware specialists, in-house vendor specialists, and homegrown tool specialists (depending on the tools that have made it this far), to schedule and conduct the demos of the top two to four tools identified in the research evaluation. Ensure a thorough demonstration is done for each prospective tool. During the demos, ask questions relating specifically to your requirements. Each individual who is part of the evaluation team must score (according to their perception) the capability of the tool in relation to the requirement in the evaluation requirements list.

After the demos, all evaluation team members who participated in the requirements scoring should meet to prepare an overall score of each tool. Two possible techniques to derive an average score for each requirement are:

- for each requirement, add each evaluation team member's score and divide by the total number of evaluation team members who contributed to the scoring, then place this score into the appropriate requirements field.
- attempt to derive a general agreement on the requirement score by discussing it as a team. The goal of this session is to narrow down the tool choices to the top one or two.

If (at this stage) one of the tools is a clear winner (i.e., meets all of your needs), you may finish the evaluation process by documenting the reason(s) for selecting the tool, include the risks you have identified, include the costs as you understand them, and summarize the results. This will help you with the acquisition process and in the future help you understand why you (or others who are also interested in a similar tool) have selected this tool. Move forward in acquiring the tool. If there is not a clear winner or if you want to ensure that you evaluate the tool choices in more detail to minimize risk, proceed with the pilot/full evaluation.

9.3.3.5 Conducting a Pilot/Full Evaluation

As stated, the primary reason to conduct a pilot/full evaluation is to reduce the risk of selecting the less effective tool. If there are two or more tools that have similar scores after the requirements scoring from the demo evaluation and you have not been able to decide on which tool, then piloting the tools is in order. Even if you think you have selected a tool, piloting it is a reasonable thing to do to ensure you are correct in your assessment. While piloting the tool will constitute additional time and effort to complete the evaluation process, it will enable a more thorough inspection and understanding of the technology.

This task requires a technology administrator to either implement the tool(s) on premises or implement it in the cloud infrastructure. In each case, many vendors allow for a free trial period to pilot the tool (both CM and Agile tools) in-house prior to purchasing it. Also the cloud infrastructure service providers (for Agile PM tools) allow for either a free trial period or free usage indefinitely for a small team. In all cases, some level of configuration should occur to ensure it aligns with your expected usage.

In the meantime, consider submitting a request for proposal (RfP) to provide you with more information on the tool, the costs, and its vendor or service provider. See details on this in the next section. The RfP can help you score certain requirements on the evaluation requirements list, such as cost and support, more accurately.

During this time, your goal is to establish a pilot infrastructure and craft use cases or stories that are similar to (or the same as) the actual working processes that the team currently follows. Once the pilot infrastructure is established, you should be exercising and testing the tool per the requirements to determine if the tool(s) meets the requirements as defined in the requirements list. Score the capability of the tool in relation to the requirements. Multiply each requirement by the weight of the requirement to derive the weighted score. Add all scores to determine which tool has the highest score at the end of the evaluation. If you have completed the scoring objectively, then the highest scoring tool is the one that should be selected.

Once a tool is deemed the "winner", document the reason(s) for selecting the tool, include the risks you have identified, include the costs as you understand them, and summarize the results. This will help you with the acquisition process and in the future help you understand why you (or others who are also interested in a similar tool) have selected this tool. If all things are in order, move forward in acquiring the tool.

9.3.3.6   Considering a Request for Proposal (RfP)

Concurrently with piloting the tool, consider calling for a request for proposal (RfP) for the tool from each possible vendor. This will provide more input into making an informed decision as to which tool should be selected. An RfP is typically a document that requests more information about the vendor, its business, and its working processes.

Pit Stop

The RfP should be part of the standard evaluation process within the company. This increases the information known about the vendor or service provider and minimizes the risk on the unknowns so that they can be mitigated as appropriate.

Here are the core parts of an RfP. In general, try to keep the questions open-ended and if there are two vendors competing for your business, provide them with the same RfP in order to "compare apples to apples".

- A introductory section with the date, expected date of RfP completion, the evaluator contact within the company, the responding vendor representative, and the tool being considered with its version or release number/name.

- A section on training, with what training will be provided, ways to get training either in-person or online, fees for training, and tool man pages and help text.

- A section on the type of support the vendor will provide, including response time or service levels for problems and support fees.

- A section on how long the company has been in business, their financials, and other companies where they have sold their technology.

- A section that indicates references from other companies, including customer satisfaction levels and if there are any lawsuits completed or pending.

- A section on the upgrade policy and how the vendor plans to communicate to the customers about upgrades, changes, or maintenance of their tool. In addition, how the vendor versions the deliverables, to understand if the changes are major, minor, or patch level changes.

- A section on security and confidentiality of data being provided. Also, if you are using cloud infrastructure – where a vendor is hosting the tool on the Internet, specifics on how they will keep data separate and safe from other company data.

- A section on the proposed cost of the tool. This may be based on per user, per a number of users (e.g., up to 10), per server, or another calculation. Find out if licenses are assigned to specific individuals or floating. A floating structure is better in that once someone has finished using a license, it automatically becomes available for someone else. Also included in costs should be maintenance and other technical components (specific hardware, network, software, etc.) that are needed to ensure the tool under consideration can run. Consider having the cost section on a separate page from the rest of the RfP.

- A section for exhibits and addendums.

The RfP should be part of the standard evaluation and purchasing process within the company, but in case it is not, it is worth asking questions on these issues. This helps increase the information known about the vendor or service provider and minimize risk on the unknowns so that they can be mitigated as appropriate. As part of the RfP process, there are additional considerations: what happens if the vendor does not reply to the RfP or when they do respond, the information is inadequate? Also, what if a vendor needs more time? A set rule for these may be in order so that each vendor is being treated objectively and fairly.

9.3.3.7 Acquisition Process – Owning or Renting

Once a tool is selected, it is important to establish and follow an acquisition process. An acquisition process has several steps. The early steps focus on the contract negotiations, legal matters, and purchasing, while the later steps focus on implementing the tool and getting users up and running.

Most organizations have an established purchasing team that helps with contract negotiations, legal matters, and agreements. If so, use this team. Cost factors from the evaluation and RfP should be input to contract negotiations. Since tools can be purchased or rented, there are different approaches used for each.

For purchasing tools, cost factors focus around the cost per license, which can vary depending on whether it is a fixed per seat license, a floating license, or a server license (amongst other possible licensing terms). In addition, there are costs associated with maintenance of the licenses, professional services, training, etc.

For renting tools in the clouds, cost factors focus on the number of users expected to use the cloud service provider, the length of expected use, whether full payment for the length of use is upfront or in increments, and termination fees. In addition, there may be costs associated with training. It is also important to discuss what happens if the service provider goes out of business and how readily you can secure your data and get it hosted by another vendor.

CHAPTER 10

Using CM Standards and Frameworks to Support Agile

Contributed by Bob Aiello

Configuration Management (CM) best practices are an essential part of any development effort. This chapter is geared toward those who are using or want to use Agile methods, but must also follow specific organizational guidelines regarding CM. In this chapter, I'll explain why industry standards and frameworks are important in an Agile development effort and how these tools can help you do your job better. Clearly, it is not helpful to have a project use verbose and time-consuming documentation – that would certainly be the antithesis of good Agile principles. However, there is a solid rationale for using standards and frameworks which will be explained further.

It is important to highlight the fact that Agile methods apply at the product and/or project level while standards (e.g., ISO, IEEE) and frameworks (e.g., Cobit, ITIL) are sometimes implemented at the organizational level, although often tailored to meet the individual needs of a particular project. Compliance efforts (e.g., SOX) must be done at the organizational level as well. This is a key concept to understand. Agile teams will look at things from an "of what value is it to the project" perspective. Therefore, standards may be discarded initially as not being valuable. However, most organizations find value in these standards so they cannot be ignored unilaterally. This chapter hopes to provide you with a pragmatic understanding of standards and frameworks and how you can better integrate them for Agile teams in a leaner way.

10.1   Importance of CM

While some development practices may be optional, good CM is an absolute requirement for success, but it is not always easy to figure out what you need to do in order to implement good CM. The good news is that you usually do not have to do everything at once in order to achieve success. In fact, sometimes it is best to iteratively build in the right CM practices as your project develops and, of course, becomes more and more complex. Technology professionals face an ever increasing set of challenges and obstacles that must be addressed in the right way in order to ensure success. So, it certainly follows that it can be tricky to figure out which CM practices should be implemented and in what specific order. I always find myself going back to review the business needs, current practices and the relevant standards and frameworks when I want to prioritize and put together a cohesive and effective approach to CM. If the organization is already utilizing some CM practices, then it is important to review any problems or challenges that they are having. Development teams that thrive on agility and can still show that they are following a disciplined methodology are in a strong position to achieve. So just how can standards and frameworks help you do this and when are they really necessary?

10.2   Compliance and IT Governance Requirements

Many financial services, pharmaceuticals, defense contractors, and other firms have strict requirements for compliance with government regulations. I have worked in many such organizations that wanted to employ Agile practices but still needed to comply with government regulations. Initially, this appears to be a challenge, since one seems to emphasize trust (Agile), while the other seems to emphasize "checking up" and confirming that the documentation is complete. However, in most cases, the standards and frameworks focus on minimizing risk to the organization, increasing uniformity throughout the organization and improving quality. Interestingly, Agile methods also focus on minimizing risk to the product and improving quality.

As mentioned, standards and frameworks focus on quality at an organizational level, while Agile focuses on quality at the product and project level. So it is not only possible to implement both, but actually very practical and efficient. I usually begin by explaining how following standards and frameworks will help your team be more productive. Yet, for an increasing number of companies, Compliance is no longer optional and that means that your IT controls must be based upon industry standards and frameworks.

For example, most banks (and other financial services firms) have strict requirements for effective CM. This is often related to the firm's compliance with section 404 of the Sarbanes-Oxley (SOX) Act of 2002. Defense contractors, as well as pharmaceuticals and medical systems developers, also frequently have extensive requirements for employing CM best practices. Government agencies often have their CM practices audited by the Government Accounting Office (GAO) while the Office of the Comptroller of the Currency (OCC) will audit the IT controls established at banks and other financial institutions. I know about these various requirements because I have received the phone calls and emails from the people who have failed an audit and must immediately establish IT controls, including effective configuration audits of their financial systems already in production. Scrambling to remedy an audit violation is certainly not my idea of an optimal way to implement your CM best practices. Too often, these technology managers had no idea that having their best developers (often highly paid consultants) build and promote code directly into production (without the benefit of a separate release team) would be viewed by auditors as a clear violation of commonly accepted IT controls. Meeting your compliance requirements is certainly "square one" in today's challenging business environment. We'll discuss exactly how to do this and how this relates to using standards and frameworks, but there's more to this than just meeting the legal requirements related to SOX.

10.3   Communicating Your Approach to Senior Management

One of the big challenges of scaling agility is communicating your approach to senior management. Using industry standards and frameworks can help by showing your management that your development effort is based upon a disciplined and well-designed approach. This can help you overcome the resistance to change that so often occurs when large organizations struggle with the adoption of Agile practices. I have worked on projects that had contractual obligations to use the CMMI or IEEE or ISO standards for software development. The developers writing the Java code wanted to produce improved products that better met customer needs by employing an Agile approach. We discussed using best practices learned from Scrum and XP with a focus on creating iterative development. The challenge that we always faced was how to communicate that our approach was sound to senior managers who wanted to hear that we would pass a CMMI assessment at Level 2/3 (as was required by the contract). My role frequently was to work with the developers, QA and technology managers to create a fast and efficient build and deploy process that allowed us to complete a release within a one-hour window. This approach greatly facilitated Agile/iterative development. I made it a practice to demonstrate exactly how our approach complied with the required sections of the IEEE 828 CM planning Standard and would easily pass a SOX-related audit. This meant that we were able to enjoy the autonomy of self-directed teams (employing agility) while meeting all compliance-related requirements. However, we had to demonstrate how our Agile practices simultaneously also met the essential requirements described in many non-Agile processes. There are at least two ways to do this. The first is to harmonize existing industry standards and frameworks with your Agile method. Harmonizing standards (and tailoring them down to the right size) is an excellent way to "right-size" the standard implementation within the development process. The second approach is to investigate existing standards that directly cater and relate to Agile development. For example, the IEEE 1648 standard focuses on the recommended practice for the customer-supplier relationship in Agile software development methods.

The IEEE Standards are intended to provide a comprehensive and well-considered approach to developing software and systems. It would certainly be impressive to tell your senior management that your Agile approach is based upon industry standards that would easily pass a compliance audit. It is also worth noting that IEEE Standards are always compared to each other (see the section on harmonizing) and this makes it much easier to use them on a practical basis to support all aspects of the application lifecycle. This means that you can easily show how your Agile approach also meets the requirements for non-Agile standards categories (e.g., testing and quality assurance).

Standards and frameworks are essentially a collection of best practices that have been vetted before a team of industry experts. Considerable thought goes into the publication of any standard or industry framework and you can benefit significantly from reviewing these materials and learning from the experts. Standards are vetted before a standards board (e.g., IEEE or ISO) which generally requires a vote (75% in favor) in order for the standard to be accepted and published. The only problem is that sometimes standards boards will trim a paragraph or two just to gain consensus and get enough votes for the required quorum. However, once passed, the standards carry considerable authority and are often explicitly mentioned in contractual obligations. If you are following the

IEEE Standard for Testing or CM planning then you are able to provide very solid proof that your processes are based upon well-respected industry practices.

Frameworks such as ISACA's Cobit or the IT Service Management Forum's (itSMF) ITIL carry the full backing of their own sponsoring organizations, which tend to have a little more autonomy since they may not require the same rigorous voting procedures as the standards boards. Some frameworks are highly respected for general use, while others are primarily used in very specific situations. This is where it is very important to ensure your organization is following organizational level standards for the right reason. Some industries may simply require that you adopt industry standards and frameworks, but in other cases your organization's adoption of standards may be entirely voluntary and intended to improve quality and productivity. In all cases you need to ensure that your company understands the cost versus benefit of using standards and frameworks and you should approach these efforts in as lean a manner as possible.

Agile processes can benefit considerably from adopting some of these best practices in those particular situations where these standards provide synergy with an Agile approach (which already includes the excellent practices that give agility its unique flavor). For example, CM in an Agile environment may still benefit from the best practices explained in the ISACA Change and Configuration Management controls described in Cobit. We will discuss some of the Cobit control practices and exactly how they can help you implement change and CM.

10.4   Which Standards Should Be Considered?

If your organization is required to meet industry regulations for IT controls then your CM function, even in an Agile environment, must meet all auditing and compliance requirements. The IEEE 828 Standard on CM planning is certainly an excellent place to start. Having served on the IEEE 828 working group, I have always emphasized the importance of using the IEEE 828 CM planning Standard in an Agile environment for the product lifecycle so that each project can take advantage of the CM plan without the additional effort of recreating another CM plan. It is my view that CM is one of the areas that can benefit most from using standards – especially in an Agile environment. Other well-regarded standards include the IEEE 12207 Systems and Software Engineering – Software Life Cycle Processes, which is a broad, all-encompassing approach to defining all of the possible lifecycle processes which may be needed during the software development process. Some of these processes are decidedly not Agile in nature, but others, including testing processes, would complement test-driven development (TDD) or more importantly unit testing (IEEE 1008 – Software Unit Testing). There are some cases where a minimum amount of documentation is necessary, and in these situations the lean approach is often a pragmatic way to ascertain how much is "just enough" to avoid costly mistakes and defects in the code.

CM planning includes the roles and responsibilities of everyone involved, activities required, schedule, physical, and human resources, as well as a plan for updating and maintaining the CM plan. If you must do configuration audits, this would mean that you have defined a specific way to identify all your configuration items and that you have a well-defined procedure for conducting a configuration audit to ensure that the correct versions of the code are in the production environment. While this may appear to be initially "heavy", keep in mind that most continuous integration servers (if you are applying this Agile practice) provide the baseline and traceability of showing exactly which version of the system is successfully built. This is usually a lot easier if the application is designed for traceability by providing a specific function that will display the version of the configuration item. The simplest example of this is the "About" box in your favorite Windows GUI.

Let us delve a little deeper into the required CM functions that are described in well-accepted industry standards. My personal experience is that it is not necessary, or even possible, to document everything upfront in a CM plan and certainly in an Agile project you would not want to do so in order to prevent the big effort up front (BEUF) mentality. For example, you might have no idea of how you are going to deploy your application and will not find out until much later in the development process. I have seen teams change key aspects of their technology halfway through the project, because of unforeseen challenges with the tools and approaches chosen or perhaps necessitated by the demands of late-breaking customer requirements. So the good news is that you can easily start by documenting what you do know early on and then iteratively update your CM on an ongoing basis. For example, you should decide which version control tool you are going to use along with a general approach to parallel development, including your own conventions for branching and merging your code. Naming conventions are essential and should be decided and documented upfront in a quality CM plan. I often produce a general (organization level) CM plan that applies to all projects, followed by a customizable (project level) CM plan that is in alignment with the general CM plan for issues that can be done differently by each group. This reuse approach also helps groups adopt CM planning in an iterative way. It is usually best to define your goals and approach CM planning in a lean and pragmatic way.

10.5   Configuration Management Functions that are most Essential

Every software product contains a series of components, which may be binaries, scripts or other artifacts. In CM terminology these objects are called configuration items (CIs), not to be confused with continuous integration (CI). Each and every CI must have a unique version identifier called a "version ID." A "release" is a packaged set of CIs that work together and can be delivered as a finished product. It is very important to know the exact version of every CI delivered in a release – as well as the version ID of the package itself. This is to avoid regression in later releases, as well as ensuring that the team has the ability to reproduce the release, if needed. Continuous integration is an excellent best practice, but you still have to know the version ID of the product that went out the door. This is the most basic compliance requirement and is one of the reasons why many CM efforts should (and often must) adhere to the best practices described in the IEEE 828 CM planning Standard. This does not necessarily mean that you have to formally "comply" with all of the requirements of the standard, but you may still have to implement the functions as described in the standard in order to pass your next internal audit.

10.5.1   Continuous Integration without the Required Version ID

I have seen projects set up to use continuous integration that included the ability to instantly build the application right after a developer had committed changes to the source code repository. The CI server was robust in many ways. You immediately knew if the build was broken and who had made the most recent changes. The only problem was that the packages produced by the CI server did not have any easy way to display a version ID upon request. It was also difficult and error-prone to grab the release packages from the CI server, because no one had really thought through how the release would be controlled (change control) on its journey from QA to production. Identifying the CI is certainly one of the features that should be given a high priority, but there are other problems and events that can occur as well.

How to Stop the World Economy

In one of my former positions, it was my job to build and package one of the most critical applications used by traders on a major stock exchange located in New York City. Mission-critical systems that affect hundreds of thousands of people often have regulatory requirements that must be met. Certainly, CM on a system that impacts the world economy is an example of just such a mission-critical system. I was told that if a mistake occurred someone from the exchange would likely have to testify before the US Congress to explain exactly what had occurred.

One day, I was told that I had made a mistake (promoting the wrong code) that had literally caused the Stock Exchange computers to go into a race condition and then crash – effectively stopping the world economy for one hour. The senior manager who had explained this to me, asked me to review my procedures and controls and to make certain that I never made this mistake again. To say the least, I was shocked and dismayed to think that carelessness on my part might have caused such a significant outage (and in the end, I was relieved that my CM practices vindicated me and my team). This event dramatically illustrated the value of having excellent CM procedures in place. Even when a significant problem occurred – we could quickly triage, analyze forensics, and recover.

It's a good thing that I had a created a map ... My personally developed CM audit procedures always include creating what I call a "release map." Every one of the configuration items (CIs) had a unique identifier built into the code itself that could be retrieved easily – even while it was running. In the middle of that fateful trading day, I went on to one of the production machines (with one of the Unix administrators, in charge of production operations, at my side) and we regenerated the release map based upon the current code running in production. We compared this to the release map that I had packaged with the release at the time of deployment. That's when we found that we currently had the wrong scripts running in production! We subsequently found the reason that my code was being overwritten and fixed the problem so that it could not happen again. Our management saw that we had effective IT control in place and we could do a CM audit – even while production was live. This story had a happy ending in that we demonstrated that our good CM practices were indeed able to help maintain and support a critical system (plus, we all got our bonuses).

Whether your project is Agile or non-Agile, you absolutely must be able to ascertain the exact version of your code running in production at any time. You also need to be able to create a new development sandbox with the exact versions of the source code used, for a specific release, in order to be able to quickly create a bug fix – without any chance of your code regressing due to the wrong version of a header file or Java class. These are all basic requirements of good IT controls as described in industry standards and frameworks. More than any other IT specialty, CM needs to maintain disciplined and repeatable processes in both Agile and non-Agile development environments.

The IEEE 828 Standard also requires that you have documented procedures to establish a baseline. This simply means that you know the exact versions of all of the configuration items that went into a specific release of the code. As the standard explains:

Appropriate baselines shall be defined at control points within the project life cycle in terms of the following:

a) The event that creates the baseline;

b) The items that are to be controlled in the baseline;

c) The procedures used to establish and change the baseline;

d) The authority required to approve changes to the approved baselined documents.

It's essential to implement these practices with agility in mind. One way to do this is to define the procedural requirements at an organizational level, but customize them at the project level to "right-size" your organizational processes. Remember, the lean approach is always best in these circumstances. It is also always best to automate as many of these functions as possible, including continuous integration and version control tools that have been designed and implemented to automatically embed version IDs into all of the configuration items (CIs) created during the build and deploy process.

10.6 How do Frameworks such as Cobit, ITIL, CMMI, and RUP support Agile?

You may find that your company requires you to work within the guidelines of specific standards and frameworks that are required throughout the entire organization. Many of these have practices that are similar to Agile, but also may have specific requirements that you must meet. The good news is that it is not hard to be Agile and still adhere to these requirements.

10.6.1   ISACA Cobit

The ISACA (www.isaca.com) Cobit Framework consists of 34 IT processes that provide a comprehensive framework most often associated with establishing all of the IT controls required for SOX compliance.

If your company is required to implement SOX-related controls, then you may not have any choice but to get these practices in place right away. But, in practice, many companies also take an iterative approach based upon risk. Two of these controls focus on CM. The first is *AI6 – Manage Changes* and occurs during acquire and implement. This control requires that you manage change requests, assess the impact of changes and prioritize changes based upon business needs. Information regarding any and all changes, such as who gave an authorization, must be accurately tracked.

The second CM-related control is *DS9 – Manage the Configuration* and requires that changes be planned and baselines determined, along with the detection of unauthorized changes. There should also be a repository to store configuration-related information which is regularly verified and audited.

The Cobit framework provides a lot of practical information on exactly how to implement a comprehensive SOX-compliant IT structure control to better support CM.

10.6.2   itSMF ITIL Framework

The ITIL framework provides a comprehensive approach to IT service management, including asset management as part of CM. ITIL, which is heavily focused on CM, specifies many excellent best practices. For example, ITIL practitioners advocate the use of a CM database (CMDB) to control and report interface dependencies between configuration items. Many CMDBs are specialized and may focus narrowly on a specific environmental configuration (e.g., firewall rules and their impact on the application in QA versus production). Other CMDBs report on the version IDs of all configuration items in a specific environment (e.g., production) on a dynamic basis. This makes it much easier to detect and deal with unauthorized changes.

Information from various CMDBs may be consolidated into a global Configuration Management System (CMS). ITIL also expects that all CIs will be controlled and treated as assets (e.g., mice attached to a PC). Overall, ITIL is heavily process-centric and I am not suggesting that the overall ITIL framework is particularly Agile in practice. However, the use of specialized CMDBs does facilitate rapid application deployment and can be an excellent complement to continuous integration. Nonetheless, ITIL suggests many excellent best practices and has dramatically improved IT service management.

10.6.3 CMMI and Agile

I have grown up studying the Key Process Areas (KPAs) of the original Capability Maturity Model (CMM), which might just be one of the most un-Agile frameworks that has ever been developed. The CMMI (CMM – integrated) includes many improvements; however, becoming more Agile is not one of the traits that I would associate with this framework. It's been my experience that, in some industries (e.g., financial services), Agile was basically a reaction to the verbose nature of the CMMI. Even with all of this, the CMMI remains a widely used framework to assess the process maturity of development teams. I have worked on projects where CMMI compliance at Level 2 (or in some cases Level 3) was a contractual obligation. I have also seen efforts to harmonize the process areas of the CMMI with the Agile practices in Scrum or other Agile methods. If you want to work for a defense contractor or a government agency, then there is a high likelihood that you will be required to demonstrate that your development processes meet and/or exceed the requirements described in the CMMI.

10.6.4 Rational Unified Process (RUP) and Agile Unified Process (AUP)

The Rational Unified Process (RUP), currently owned by IBM through their Rational Software Division, is a software development framework that has a strong focus on iterative development. I have also seen government agencies require their contractors to use some form of RUP as a contractual obligation. There is a tremendous amount of wisdom in RUP, although an exhaustive amount of documentation is expected in the form of completing template "artifacts" as part of this risk-based, highly customizable framework. The Agile Unified Process (based on a leaner RUP) describes Agile methods and concepts that can be employed within an iterative framework. Most RUP enthusiasts will tell you that you should always ask yourself the question: "What bad thing will happen if I do not include this artifact?"

10.7   Achieving Synergy through Harmonization and Tailoring

Harmonization means that you compare standards with each other and map the specific functions that are identical or similar to each other. I have worked on mapping IEEE, ISO and EIA standards with each other, along with the CM functions described in frameworks such as Cobit and ITIL. Harmonizing strives to identify the commonality between specific functions in each standard (or framework) along with identifying any gaps or functional areas that should be enhanced or at least described more clearly. When you see the same function described clearly in several places, then that is actually a check on the function's internal validity. To say this another way, seeing that baselines are described in each standard underscores its importance and value as a best practice.

Tailoring means that you trim down a standard because some of the steps described may not be necessary for your particular project. You should employ a lean approach to standards adoption. Anything extra is waste and should be trimmed from the standard. For example, most standards discuss subcontractor maintenance, but your project may treat subcontractors the same as employees and there is no added value to creating additional ceremony by adopting the sections related to subcontractor maintenance. These modifications have to be decided on a case-by-case basis. Nonetheless, the principle of taking a lean approach should be consistently applied throughout the course of the project.

10.7.1   Change Control on Your Standards Tailoring

You absolutely must keep a clear record of what functions you have trimmed out and exactly why you made that choice. Later on in the project you may decide to bring in your market data via a shared service and now you are back to needing that subcontractor maintenance function that previously you had decided on dropping. It's also possible that your contractual obligations require that you "comply" with the standard, instead of just using it as a source of wisdom and best practices, as I have been describing. If your project is in a defense industry, then you may have to look more closely at the requirements that allow you to claim that your CM practices meet the requirements specified in the IEEE standards. It's important to note that most standards indicate practices that are mandatory by using the verb "shall" and delineate the optional (suggested) practices with the verb "should". Either way, you will need to keep track of which functions you chose to tailor from your use of the standard – this is known as "tailoring down".

10.7.2 Overcoming Resistance to Change

This is a topic that I frequently address in organizations that need guidance. You may have advocates who believe that agility is the best way to approach software development – still others may feel that the waterfall approach is necessary – especially if that is what they are accustomed to using. Trying to get a developer or development manager to change the way that they are working is certainly no small task. Gaining consensus among a group of very smart (and usually opinionated) technology professionals can be an exciting task indeed. Once again, I have found that sharing best practices gleaned from industry standards and frameworks can help make this job a little easier. When sharing best practices, I always focus first on the problems to be solved and the goals to be achieved. Then I usually ask, "Please tell me exactly how you are different from every other company in the world that does this task?" For example, if you are working for a bank, it is certainly reasonable to have to comply with the same regulations as required by other banks. The standards and frameworks are detailed descriptions of best practices used by other firms that are my own secret weapon to overcoming resistance to change – especially in large organizations.

10.8 Conclusion

The effective use of industry-accepted CM-related standards and frameworks may be the most important critical success factor in your efforts to successfully adopt Agile methods. Although it is important to ensure your organization is following all industry regulations, the implementation should be done in as lean a manner as possible. You need to focus on adopting Agile practices in the best way possible for your project and then harmonize the organizational required standards with this project level method. The pragmatic and effective use of standards and frameworks can make your current practices even better and result in greater success for you and all of your efforts!

Bibliography

"**2007 Study of Myers-Briggs Types Relative to CM Professionals**", by Mario Moreira, *CM Journal*, September 2007 – http://www.cmcross roads.com/content/view/9087/266/

"**Study of Myers-Briggs Types Relative to CM Professionals**", by Mario Moreira, *CM Journal*, August 2003 – http://www.cmcrossroads. com/content/view/6904/266/

"**Configuration Management, Coming of Age in the Year 2000**", by Clive Burrows, *CrossTalk*, March 1999.

"**Culture in Nonhuman Primates?**", by W. C. McGrew, 1998, *Annual Review of Anthropology* 27: 323.

"**The Product Owner in the Agile Enterprise**", by Dean Leffingwell, *Agile Journal*, February 2009.

"**Team-Based Software Development Extreme Programming Pocket Guide**" – O'Reilly – http://oreilly.com/catalog/extprogpg/chapter/ch05.pdf

Extreme Programming Explained: Embrace Change (2nd Edition) by Kent Beck and Cynthia Andres, 2004, Addison-Wesley Professional.

"**DSDM Role definitions**" – http://www24.brinkster.com/technossomy/DSDM/DSDMrole.htm

Balancing Agility and Discipline: A Guide for the Perplexed by Barry Boehm and Richard Turner, 2003, Addison-Wesley Professional.

"**The New Methodology**", by Martin Fowler (see: http://www.martin fowler.com/articles/newMethodology.html).

"**Iterative and Incremental Development: A Brief History**", by Craig Larman and Victor Basili, published in the *IEEE Computer Society*, June 2003.

"History: The Agile Manifesto", by Jim Highsmith, for the *Agile Alliance*, 2001.

"Extreme Programming: a gentle introduction" at http://www.extreme programming.org/, by Don Wells, Feb 2006.

"Principles of Lean Thinking", by Mary Poppendieck, 2002 – http://www.poppendieck.com/papers/LeanThinking.pdf

"Group Coherence for Project Teams – Collaborative Interaction", by Joanna Zweig and Cesar Idrovo, February 2009.

"Claims and Identify: On-Premise and Cloud Solutions", by Vittorio Bertocci, *The Architecture Journal*, July 2008, http://msdn.microsoft.com/en-us/library/cc836390.aspx

"Refactoring Homepage"–http://www.refactoring.com/, maintained by Martin Fowler, hosted by ThoughtWorks.

"Multistage Continuous Integration", by Damon Poole, http://damon poole.blogspot.com/2007/12/multi-stage-continuous-integration.html

"Agile Model Driven Development (AMDD): The Key to Scaling Agile Software Development", by Scott Ambler, http://www.agilemodeling.com/essays/amdd.htm

http://dictionary.reference.com/browse/continuous - definition for "continuous"

"Infrastructure Architecture", by Daniel Jumelet, March 2007.

http://agilemanifesto.org/ - Agile Manifesto

"Voluntary Technical Debt", by James Shore, Sept 2006.

"Infrastructure Refactoring", by Mario Moreira, published in the *Agile Journal*, Oct 08 (www.agilejournal.com).

"Infrastructure Envisioning", by Mario Moreira, published in the *Agile Journal*, Dec 08 (www.agilejournal.com).

"Comparing the Relative Value of CM Practices", by Mario E. Moreira, published in the *CM Journal*, May 04 (www.cmcrossroads.com).

"Agile Practice and Principles Survey: July 2008", by Scott W. Ambler, published via Ambysoft at http://www.ambysoft.com/surveys/

"Poll – Colocation, The Benefits", by Damon Poole, published via http://damonpoole.blogspot.com

"Has Agile Peaked? Let's look at the numbers", by Scott W. Ambler, May 2008, published in Dr Dobb's Portal: The World of Software Development – http://www.ddj.com/architect/207600615

"The Agile Difference for SCM", by Brad Appleton, Robert Cowham, and Steve Berczuk, published in the *CM Journal*, Oct 04 (www.cmcrossroads.com).

"Information security freeware has its benefits", by Ed Skoudis, published in the Search Security.com website, Dec 06, adjunct to the *Information Security Magazine*.

Section 5.3 "Define a Global SCM/Development Strategy" in Chapter 4 (Establish an SCM Infrastructure for an Application), pp. 90–95 of the *Software Configuration Management Implementation Roadmap* by Mario E. Moreira, John Wiley & Sons, Ltd Publishing, 2004.

Section 7.5 "Establish the Global SCM/Development Infrastructure" in Chapter 4 (Establish an SCM Infrastructure for an Application), pp. 128–130 of the *Software Configuration Management Implementation Roadmap* by Mario E. Moreira, John Wiley & Sons, Ltd Publishing, 2004.

"**Managing Distributed Software Development**", by Randy Guck, *StickyMinds*, http://www.stickyminds.com/sitewide.asp?Function=edetail&ObjectType=ART&ObjectId=6002.

"**Wikis for Supporting Distributed Collaborative Writing**", by Carolyn Wei, Brandon Maust, Jennifer Barrick, Elisabeth Cuddihy, Jan H. Spyridakis, http://www.stc.org/ConfProceed/2005/PDFs/0045.pdf from conference proceedings of stc., 2005.

"**The CMP – An Alternate Approach**", by Ben Weatherall, *CM Journal*, December 2008 ed.

"**Defining Agile SCM: Past, Present, & Future**", by Brad Appleton, Robert Cowham, and Steve Berczuk, *CM Journal* (www.cmcrossroads.com), October 2008.

"**Consider Role Based Configuration Management**", by Ben Weatherall, CM Journal (www.cmcrossroads.com), July 2007.

"**Streamed Lines: Branching Patterns for Parallel Software Development**", by by Brad Appleton, Stephen Berczuk, Ralph Cabrera, and Robert Orenstein, 1998, http://www.cmcrossroads.com/bradapp/acme/branching/patterns.html

"**Characteristics of the Agile SCM Solution**", by Brad Appleton, Robert Cowham, and Steve Berczuk, *CM Journal* (www.cmcrossroads.com), July, 2006.

"**Refactoring: Improving the Design of Existing Code**", by Martin Fowler, Kent Beck, John Brant, William Opdyke, and Don Roberts, via Addison-Wesley, July 1999.

"**Strengthening the Case for Pair Programming**", by Laurie Williams, Robert R Kessler, Ward Cunningham, Ron Jeffries, *IEEE Software*, July/August 2000.

"**From Peer Review to Pair Programming**", by Mario Moreira, *CM Journal*, August 2006.

"**Private Workspaces: Where development meets CM process**", by Brad Appleton, Robert Cowham, and Steve Berczuk, *CM Journal*, March 2006. (www.cmcrossroads.com).

Software Configuration Management Patterns: Effective Teamwork, Practical Integration by Stephen P. Berczuk with Brad Appleton, Addison Wesley 2003.

Software Release Methodology by Michael E. Bays, Prentice Hall PTR1999.

"Building a Meaningful Metrics Mousetrap", by Mario Moreira, *CM Journal*, April 2007.

"Principles of Lean Thinking", by Mary Poppendieck, 2002 - http://www.poppendieck.com/papers/LeanThinking.pdf

Toyota Production System: Beyond Large-Scale Production by Taiichi Ohno, 1988, Productivity Press.

Section "4.2.1 Evaluate and Select an SCM Technology" (pp. 66–67) within Chapter 4 "Establish an SCM Infrastructure for an Application" of the book *Software Configuration Management Implementation Roadmap* by Mario E. Moreira, Wiley, Ltd Publishing 2004.

Ovum Evaluates: Configuration Management (OVUM Ltd.), April 2005 (www.ovum.com).

Crosstalk: The Journal of Defense Software Engineering - Software Technology Support Center - http://www.stsc.hill.af.mil/crosstalk/2005/08/index.html

SD Times: The Industry Newspaper for Software Development Managers – (www.sdtimes.com).

Index

Printed and bound by CPI Group (UK) Ltd, Croydon, CR0 4YY

09/10/2024

14571436-0001